Facebook® Marketing

FOR

DUMMIES®

3RD EDITION

Facebook® Marketing

FOR

DUMMIES®

3RD EDITION

by John Haydon, Paul Dunay, and
Richard Krueger

WILEY

John Wiley & Sons, Inc.

Facebook® Marketing For Dummies,® 3rd Edition

Published by
John Wiley & Sons, Inc.
111 River Street
Hoboken, NJ 07030-5774
www.wiley.com

WILEY

About the Authors

John Haydon is the founder of Inbound Zombie, an Internet marketing consultancy in Cambridge, Massachusetts, that serves small- and medium-sized nonprofits in the United States and Canada. John is also cofounder of 501 Mission Place, an online community for nonprofit executives and leaders. He is an instructor at MarketingProfs.com, conducts educational webinars at CharityHowTo.com, and is a regular contributor to five different blogs, including the Huffington Post. You can read his blogs at www.johnhaydon.com and www.nonprofitfacebookguy.com.

He has presented at BlogWorld Expo, Nonprofit Technology Conference, 140 Characters Conference, and many regional conferences.

Paul Dunay is an award-winning marketer with more than 20 years of success in generating demand and creating buzz for leading technology, consumer products, and financial and professional services organizations.

Paul is Global Managing Director of Services and Social Marketing for Avaya, a global leader in enterprise communications. His unique approach to integrated marketing has led to recognition as a *BtoB* magazine Top 25 B2B Marketer of the Year for 2009 and 2010 and winner of the DemandGen Award for Utilizing Marketing Automation to Fuel Corporate Growth in 2008. He is also a six-time finalist in the Marketing Excellence Awards competition of the Information Technology Services Marketing Association (ITSMA) and a 2005 and 2010 gold award winner.

Richard Krueger is founder and CEO of AboutFaceDigital, a social media marketing agency specializing in Facebook promotions. Recognized as an online marketing innovator, Mr. Krueger is also cofounder of Samepoint, LLC, a leading social media analytics company. He brings more than 20 years of experience to his roles at both companies.

Richard previously served as Chief Marketing Officer for Boonty, Inc., a worldwide digital distributor of casual games. Prior to that, he served as VP of Marketing and Business Development for Kasparov Chess Online, where he led marketing and brand licensing efforts for Garry Kasparov, the former world chess champion. Before his entrepreneurial career, Richard worked at several top-ten advertising and public relations agencies in New York City. He is a regular blogger and contributes numerous articles to advertising and PR trade journals.

Dedication

We dedicate this book to marketers everywhere who are in the middle of the biggest sea of change in marketing history. There's never been a better time to be a marketer, and tools like Facebook are rewriting the rules. We hope that by providing you with straightforward, step-by-step advice, as well as sharing our real-world experiences in marketing companies via Facebook, you'll become better at your craft and thereby take everyone to levels in marketing people have yet to explore.

We also hope that you keep your Facebook marketing efforts in perspective, and always put family and friends first!

Authors' Acknowledgments

This project couldn't have succeeded without the help and support of many people.

First, we want to express deep appreciation for our families, who support our passion for helping businesses and nonprofits use Facebook. We know that the time spent away from you can never be replaced.

We want to thank the superb team at Wiley, including Amy Fandrei, who originally reached out to us because of our blogs and held our hands through the entire process; Christopher Morris, our project editor, who kept us on track every step of the way and ensured the book conformed to *For Dummies* standards; and all the other Wiley folks behind the scenes who made the book possible.

Thanks to scores of bloggers, too many to list, who kept us informed about changes at Facebook and what they meant to businesses. Most of all, we want to thank Facebook founder Mark Zuckerberg and his team of young entrepreneurs and software developers for their vision in realizing the most popular online social network on the planet.

Publisher's Acknowledgments

We're proud of this book; please send us your comments at `http://dummies.custhelp.com`. For other comments, please contact our Customer Care Department within the U.S. at 877-762-2974, outside the U.S. at 317-572-3993, or fax 317-572-4002.

Some of the people who helped bring this book to market include the following:

Acquisitions and Editorial

Senior Project Editor: Christopher Morris

Acquisitions Editor: Amy Fandrei

Copy Editors: Heidi Unger, Teresa Artman

Technical Editor: Michelle Oxman

Editorial Manager: Kevin Kirschner

Editorial Assistant: Amanda Graham

Sr. Editorial Assistant: Cherie Case

Cover Photos © istockphoto.com/Daniel Vineyard (main image); © istockphoto.com/ erel photography; © istockphoto.com/ jonya; © istockphoto.com/H-Gall; © istock photo.com/MikLav © istockphoto.com/ Catherine Yeulet; © istockphoto.com/ Richard Frenchman; © istockphoto.com/ tola bayraktar; © istockphoto.com/dagmar heymans; © istockphoto.com/Leo Kowal; © istockphoto.com/Daniel Laflor; © istockphoto.com/Mark Bowden

Cartoons: Rich Tennant (`www.the5thwave.com`)

Composition Services

Project Coordinator: Katherine Crocker

Layout and Graphics: Carl Byers, Joyce Haughey, Corrie Socolovitch, Julie Trippetti

Proofreader: Melissa D. Buddendeck

Indexer: Palmer Publishing Services

Publishing and Editorial for Technology Dummies

    Richard Swadley, Vice President and Executive Group Publisher

    Andy Cummings, Vice President and Publisher

    Mary Bednarek, Executive Acquisitions Director

    Mary C. Corder, Editorial Director

Publishing for Consumer Dummies

    Kathleen Nebenhaus, Vice President and Executive Publisher

Composition Services

    Debbie Stailey, Director of Composition Services

Contents at a Glance

Introduction 1

Part I: Preparing for Success on Facebook 7
Chapter 1: Marketing in the Age of Facebook 9
Chapter 2: Researching and Understanding Your Target Audience 19
Chapter 3: Developing a Facebook Marketing Plan 27

Part II: Building Your Facebook Presence 49
Chapter 4: Getting Started with a Facebook Page 51
Chapter 5: Getting Noticed on Facebook with a Content Strategy 71
Chapter 6: Enhancing Your Facebook Page with Applications 83

Part III: Engaging with Your Customers
and Prospects on Facebook 99
Chapter 7: Going Public with Your Facebook Page 101
Chapter 8: Engaging with Your Fans 119
Chapter 9: Measuring Success with Facebook Insights 145

Part IV: Marketing beyond the Facebook Page 163
Chapter 10: Using Facebook Advertising to Promote Your Business 165
Chapter 11: Facebook Marketing for Local Businesses 195
Chapter 12: Setting Up Groups, Promotions, and Events 215
Chapter 13: Cross-Promoting Your Page 233
Chapter 14: Understanding and Using Facebook Social Plug-ins 247

Part V: The Part of Tens 273
Chapter 15: Ten Common Facebook Marketing Mistakes (And How
to Avoid Them) 275
Chapter 16: Ten Business Etiquette Tips for Facebook 281
Chapter 17: Ten (Okay, Eight) Factors for Long-Term Facebook
Marketing Success 285

Index 289

Table of Contents

Introduction *1*

About This Book 1
Foolish Assumptions 2
Conventions Used in This Book 2
What You Don't Have to Read 2
How This Book Is Organized 3
    Part I: Preparing for Success on Facebook 3
    Part II: Building Your Facebook Presence 4
    Part III: Engaging with Your Customers and Prospects
      on Facebook 4
    Part IV: Marketing beyond the Facebook Page 4
    Part V: The Part of Tens 4
Icons Used in This Book 5
Where to Go from Here 5

Part 1: Preparing for Success on Facebook *7*

Chapter 1: Marketing in the Age of Facebook 9

What Is Facebook and Why Is It So Popular? 10
Understanding the Marketing Potential of Facebook 12
    Leveraging the power of word-of-mouth marketing 13
    Marketing tools for all kinds of businesses 15
Understanding Why Your Business Needs a Facebook Page ... 16
    Attracting new fans that are friends of customers 17
    Changing first-time customers into repeat customers 17

Chapter 2: Researching and Understanding Your Target Audience 19

Defining Your Target Audience 19
    Understanding the marketing funnel 20
    Defining who your best customers are 21
    Selecting demographic criteria for your target audience ... 22
    Using personas to give your target audience personality ... 22
Researching Target Audiences with Facebook's Ad Tool 24

Chapter 3: Developing a Facebook Marketing Plan 27

Understanding What to Include in Your Marketing Plan.........................27
Developing Your Value Proposition: Why Should Customers
  Buy What You're Offering? 29
Understanding Your Audience..30
  Finding out what makes your fans tick 30
  Understanding what motivates your fans...31
Defining Your Marketing Goals 33
  Building your brand's awareness 34
  Driving sales 36
  Forming a community with a Facebook Group 37
  Listening to feedback 38
Developing Your Content Strategy...39
Monitoring and Reporting Page Activity 41
  Using Insights for Pages 41
  Creating benchmarks and setting goals...43
  Keeping an eye on key metrics 43
Integrating Your Online and Offline Campaigns 45
  Deciding on a media budget 47
  Hiring an online writer 47

Part II: Building Your Facebook Presence **49**

Chapter 4: Getting Started with a Facebook Page 51

Understanding the Differences between Pages, Profiles, and Groups....52
  Profiles are personal, not business 53
  Groups are for connection, not promotion 55
Creating a Facebook Page from Scratch...56
  Step 1: Uploading your profile photo 58
  Step 2: Inviting fans...60
  Step 3: Adding a description 60
  Editing your Facebook Page's thumbnail 60
  Limiting access to your Page until launch.......................................61
Providing Information about Your Business with the Info Tab................62
  Adding tabs to your Facebook Page...64
  Removing tabs from your Facebook Page 65
  Adding applications to your Facebook Page....................................65
  Editing the tabs on your Facebook Page 66
  Adding other administrators...68
Getting the Most from Facebook Marketing Resources 69
Understanding Facebook's Terms and Conditions 70

Chapter 5: Getting Noticed on Facebook with a Content Strategy...71

Understanding How Content Marketing Works on Facebook.................71
    Filtering a News Feed 74
    Understanding how EdgeRank affects visibility on Facebook 75
    Creating compelling content for your Facebook Page...................76
    Knowing your audience 77
    Staying on-message 78
Defining Your Posting Goals...78
Getting Fans Engaged 79

Chapter 6: Enhancing Your Facebook Page with Applications......83

Understanding Facebook Applications..84
Yeah, There's an App for That — but Where?....................................87
Using Third-party Custom Facebook Page Tab Services........................89
Choosing E-Commerce Applications for Your Page...............................90
Granting Access to Applications 92
Configuring Application Tabs on Your Facebook Page 93
    Changing tab names 93
    Removing an app from your Facebook Page.................................94
    Changing the order of tabs 94
Creating Custom Facebook Tabs with HTML 94
    Creating a custom Facebook tab with the Static HTML:
      iframes tab application..95
    Creating a hosted custom Facebook tab 95

**Part III: Engaging with Your Customers
and Prospects on Facebook.. 99**

Chapter 7: Going Public with Your Facebook Page...............101

Mapping a Launch Strategy for Your Facebook Page...........................101
Creating Enchantment on Your Facebook Page 102
Making Sure Your Page Is Ready 103
Adding Content to Your Page before Launch 104
    Adding photos 105
    Adding videos...106
Making Your Page Easier to Find..107
Using Friend Networks to Launch Your Page 108
    Telling your friends to share your Page with their friends 108
    Suggesting a Page to friends..108
    Promoting a Page via your profile 109
    Promoting your Facebook Page with the Tell Your
      Fans feature..110
    Tagging photos to promote your Facebook Page..........................111

Using Existing Marketing Assets to Launch Your Page 113
    Using your e-mail signature..113
    Using your e-mail list to get more fans..113
    Using printed marketing materials 114
    Using your blog to promote your Facebook Page 114
    Using your webinars to launch your Facebook Page 114
    Using YouTube to Promote Your Facebook Page............................115
Promoting Your Page in Your Store..116
Using Facebook's Sponsored Story Ads to Launch Your Page.............117

Chapter 8: Engaging with Your Fans. 119
Understanding What Engagement Really Means...................................120
    What engagement means for word-of-mouth advertising 120
    Understanding why people engage with businesses
        on Facebook..121
    Measuring engagement with Facebook Insights 121
    Configuring your Page Wall for maximum engagement.................124
Posting New Updates to Your Page...125
    Updating your status with the status update box.........................125
    Limiting the fans who can see your Page updates 127
Posting as a Page versus Posting as a Profile 129
    How to switch between posting as a Profile and posting
        as a Page..129
    Posting as a Profile should be a personal choice 131
    Knowing the difference between being helpful
        and being spam 131
Becoming a Ninja with Status Updates...133
    Understanding the research about what engages
        Facebook users...133
    Asking specific questions to engage fans 134
    Using quizzes to engage fans..135
Responding to Comments and Likes...135
Using Photos and Videos to Engage Fans...137
Using Webinars to Build Your Fan Base 139
Engaging with Your Fans with Your Mobile Phone..............................140
    Posting content and managing your Page Wall
        with mobile web browsers...140
    Posting content and managing your Page Wall
        with mobile apps..141
    How to post content and manage your Facebook Wall via SMS 141
    How to post content and manage your Facebook
        Wall via e-mail..142
Using the Facebook Subscribe Button on Your Profile 143

Chapter 9: Measuring Success with Facebook Insights **145**

Getting Analytical with Facebook Insights 146
Using Facebook Insights 147
  Understanding the two types of Likes your Facebook
    Page receives 147
  Accessing Page Insights 147
Exploring Facebook Page Insights 148
Understanding the Dashboard Report 148
Understanding the Page Posts report 150
Understanding the Likes Report 152
  Where your likes came from 152
  Understanding Like Sources 153
Understanding the Reach Report 154
  Understanding the Reach and Frequency graphs 154
  Understanding the Visits to Your Page reports 156
Understanding the Talking About This Report 157
Understanding the Check Ins Report 158
Exporting Data from Facebook Insights 159
Viewing Weekly Page Updates via E-Mail 159
Integrating Third-Party Analytics 160

Part IV: Marketing beyond the Facebook Page *163*

**Chapter 10: Using Facebook Advertising to Promote
Your Business** **165**

Introducing Facebook Ads...166
  Using Facebook Ads as part of your overall marketing mix.........167
  Understanding Facebook's targeting options 168
  Setting your budget 169
Creating Winning Ads...170
  Copywriting tips...170
  Choosing the right image...171
  Simplifying your offer 172
Creating a Facebook Ad...172
  Step 1: Design Your Ad...173
  Step 2: Targeting 175
  Step 3: Campaigns, Pricing, and Scheduling..............................179
Creating Multiple Campaigns 181
Devising a Landing Page Strategy for Your Ads 182
  Landing on a Facebook location 182
  Landing on a website page 183
  Revealing content on your landing page 183

Managing and Measuring Your Ad Campaigns with Ads Manager 185
    Viewing performance data..185
    Viewing campaign details 186
    Making changes to your daily budget 189
Understanding Other Facebook Ad Manager Features.........................190
    Accessing your Facebook Page from the Ad Manager 191
    Creating and scheduling Facebook ad reports 191
    Adding other users to your Facebook ad account 192
    Tracking payment transactions 193
    Managing ad creatives..193
    Learning about your business resources 194

Chapter 11: Facebook Marketing for Local Businesses 195
The Basics of Facebook Places 196
Understanding the Role of Location in Your Marketing Plan 198
    Knowing why your customers use location-based services 199
    Other location-based services 200
    Facebook Places versus Foursquare...201
    Facebook Places versus Gowalla 203
Getting Started with Facebook Places 204
    Claiming your Facebook Place 204
    Creating a Facebook Place..205
Promoting Your Business with Deals...206
Understanding Facebook Deals 207
Creating a Facebook Deal 208
Getting the Most from Your Deal..211
Promoting Your Deal..212
    Promoting your deal on your Facebook Page 212
    Promoting your deal with Facebook Ads......................................213
    Promoting your deal with other marketing channels 213

Chapter 12: Setting Up Groups, Promotions, and Events. 215
Discovering Facebook Groups 215
    Distinguishing Facebook Groups from Pages...............................216
    Finding a Group...218
    Joining a Group 219
    Accessing Groups you joined...219
    Participating in a Group...220
Creating Your Own Facebook Group 220
    Securing your Group's name 221
    Setting up your Group...221
    Deleting a Group 223
Creating a Facebook Promotion 223
    Understanding Facebook rules for promotions............................223
    Setting up a promotion 224
    Using third-party promotion apps...226

Hosting a Facebook Event 227
  Creating an event 227
  Editing your event 231
  Exporting your event 232
  Following up after an event 232

Chapter 13: Cross-Promoting Your Page 233

Making Facebook Part of Your Marketing Mix 233
  Choosing a custom Facebook username 234
  Cross-promoting your Page 236
Leveraging Your Facebook Presence via Your E-Mail,
  Website, and Blog 236
  Creating a Facebook badge for your website or
    e-mail newsletter 237
  Adding a Facebook Like Box to your website 239
Promoting Your Facebook Presence Offline 240
  Networking offline 241
  Placing the Facebook logo on signs and in store windows 242
  Referencing your Page in all ads and product literature 242
Optimizing Your Page 243
  Using search engine optimization to drive traffic 244
  Using Facebook Questions 245
  Driving more likes to your Page 245

Chapter 14: Understanding and Using Facebook
Social Plug-ins 247

Extending the Facebook Experience with Social Plug-ins 248
Adding the Code 254
Integrating Facebook Insights into Your Social Plugins 255
  Setting up your website as a Facebook application 255
  Integrating the Facebook's software into your website 257
Getting More Visibility with the Like Button 258
Allowing for Private Sharing with the Send Button 259
Leveraging Popular Content with the Recommendations Plug-In 260
Integrating Facebook's Login Button 262
Adding Comments to Your Website 263
Showing User Activities with the Activity Feed Plug-In 265
Liking the Like Box 267
Making Registration Painless with the Registration Plug-in 269
Personalizing a Site with the Facepile Plug-In 269
Engaging in Real Time with Live Stream 270

Part V: The Part of Tens 273

Chapter 15: Ten Common Facebook Marketing Mistakes (And How to Avoid Them) 275

Using a Profile to Market Your Business 275
Using a Group to Market Your Business 276
Setting an Ineffective Default Tab 276
Posting Shortened URLs 277
Winging It 277
Posting During Bad Times 277
Selling Too Much 278
Selling Too Little 278
Posting Lengthy Updates 278
Ignoring Comments 279

Chapter 16: Ten Business Etiquette Tips for Facebook 281

Don't Drink and Facebook 281
Keep It Clean and Civilized 282
Avoid Overdoing It 282
Dress Up Your Page with Applications 282
Respect the Wall 282
Be Careful When Talking to Strangers 283
Don't Be Afraid to Ignore a Fan 283
Deal with Your Irate Fans 283
Don't Forget Birthday Greetings 284
Maintain Your Privacy 284

Chapter 17: Ten (Okay, Eight) Factors for Long-Term Facebook Marketing Success 285

Learn the Language, Eat the Food 285
Understand Why People Share 286
Be Useful and Helpful 286
Listen to Your Fans 286
Consistently Participate 287
Appreciate and Recognize Your Fans 287
Measure and Monitor 288
Be Fearless and Creative 288

Index 289

Introduction

With more than 800 million active users and 250,000 new registrants every day, Facebook has become a virtual world unto itself. Harvard dropout Mark Zuckerberg originally started Facebook as a dorm room exercise to extend the popular printed college directory of incoming freshmen online, but he has since developed it into an international organization employing more than 2,000 programmers, graphic artists, and marketing and business development executives with offices across the United States as well as in Dublin, London, Milan, Paris, Stockholm, Sydney, and Toronto. These days, on average, more than 2 billion posts are liked and commented on, and more than 250 million photos are uploaded to Facebook every single day!

For many, Facebook is a social experience, a place to reconnect with an old college chum or poke a new friend. But in April 2007, Zuckerberg did something so revolutionary that its aftershocks are still being felt throughout the business web. He opened his virtual oasis to allow anyone with a little programming knowledge to build applications that take advantage of the platform's *social graph* (or network architecture). In that open software act, Facebook redefined the rules for marketers looking to gain access to social networks, and it will never be business as usual again.

About This Book

Facebook Marketing For Dummies provides you, the marketer, with in-depth analysis of the strategies, tactics, and techniques available to leverage the Facebook community and achieve your business objectives. By breaking down the web service into its basic features — including creating a Facebook Page for your business, adding applications for your Page, hosting an event, creating a Facebook group, advertising, and extending the Facebook platform to your website through social plug-ins — we lay out a user-friendly blueprint to marketing and promoting your organization via Facebook.

Foolish Assumptions

We make a few assumptions about you as the marketer and aspiring Facebook marketing professional:

- ✔ You are 14 years of age or older, which is a Facebook requirement for creating your own profile.
- ✔ You're familiar with basic computer concepts and terms.
- ✔ You have a computer with high-speed Internet access.
- ✔ You have a basic understanding of the Internet.
- ✔ You have your company's permission to perform any of the techniques we discuss.
- ✔ You have permission to use any photos, music, or video of your company to promote it on Facebook.

Conventions Used in This Book

In this book, we stick to a few conventions to help with readability. Whenever you have to enter text, we show it in bold so it's easy to see. Monofont text denotes an e-mail address or URL (for example, www.facebook.com). When you see an italicized word, look for its nearby definition as it relates to Facebook. Numbered lists guide you through tasks that must be completed in order from top to bottom; bulleted lists can be read in any order you like (from top to bottom or bottom to top).

Finally, we often state our opinions throughout the book. We're avid marketers of the social network medium and hope to serve as reliable marketing tour guides to share objectively our passion for the social network.

What You Don't Have to Read

This book has been designed to be a modular guide to Facebook marketing. You don't need to read the book in a linear fashion, chapter-to-chapter, but rather you can use the book as a research tool to help you market your company on Facebook. You can also use the index to find exactly the topics that are of most interest to you. We've incorporated real-life marketing scenarios to help you get a sense of what has worked and not worked for other marketers using Facebook. Following are some other helpful guidelines to using this book:

- ✔ Depending on your existing knowledge of Facebook, you may want to skip around to the parts and chapters that interest you the most.
- ✔ If as a marketer you have a good working understanding of Facebook, you can skip the first two chapters.
- ✔ If you want to set up a Page for your business, go directly to Chapter 4.
- ✔ If you have a Page and want to start going viral with your marketing, go directly to Part III.
- ✔ If you have a Page for your business and are interested in advertising and promoting it, go directly to Part IV.
- ✔ Don't read supermarket tabloids. They're certain to rot your brain.

How This Book Is Organized

We organized this book into five parts. Each part and the chapters within it are modular, so you can jump around from topic to topic as needed. Each chapter provides practical marketing techniques and tactics that you can use to promote your business, brand, product, or organization in the Facebook community. Each chapter includes step-by-step instructions that can help you jump-start your Facebook presence.

Part 1: Preparing for Success on Facebook

Are you ready to add Facebook to your marketing mix? Before you can answer that question, you have much to consider. Part I gives you an overview of some of the topics we discuss in detail in the book, such as how and why to build a presence on the social network, how to leverage content to build a fan base, how to put viral marketing features to work for you, and how to build a winning strategy for your business. You need to make a subtle mind shift along the way that we can only describe as being more open and transparent. Many companies struggle with this transition, but those that embrace it go on to have a new level of relationships with their customers and prospects.

Part II: Building Your Facebook Presence

All marketers young and old are looking to build a Facebook presence for their companies, small businesses, or clients. In this part, we show you how to secure a spot for your business on Facebook, how to design a great Page, and how to make promotions, groups, and events work for you. We also discuss how to cross-promote your Page and measure your Page's fan engagement activity.

Part III: Engaging with Your Customers and Prospects on Facebook

Here we discuss the strategies for going public with your Page. In this section you learn how to promote your Page, engaging fans, and measuring your campaign's success on Facebook. We show you specific strategies and tactics that have been proven to grow your fanbase and increase awareness of your Page. We also show you how to measure success on Facebook so that you can quickly find out what's working and what's not.

Part IV: Marketing beyond the Facebook Page

Part IV helps you create a new source of revenue for your business. We tell you how to advertise on Facebook by targeting a specific audience, creating and testing your ads, and then measuring your ads' success. We tell you how to use Groups, Events, and promotions to go beyond your Facebook Page. We also show you how to use social plug-ins to integrate Facebook into your website.

Part V: The Part of Tens

The chapters in this part give some quick ideas about how to conduct yourself on Facebook in a way that best meets your business goals, and what top business applications you can use on your Facebook Page. We also show you the most common mistakes to avoid.

Icons Used in This Book

This icon points out technical information that's interesting but not vital to your understanding of the topic being discussed.

This icon points out information that is worth committing to memory.

This icon points out information that could have a negative impact on your Facebook presence or reputation, so please read the info next to it!

This icon points out advice that can help highlight or clarify an important point.

Where to Go from Here

If you're new to Facebook and an aspiring Facebook marketer, you may want to start at the beginning and work your way through to the end. A wealth of information sprinkled with practical advice awaits you. Simply turn the page and you're on your way.

If you're already familiar with Facebook and online marketing tactics, you're in for a real treat. We provide you with the best thinking on how to market your business on Facebook based, in part, on our own trials and tribulations. You might want to start with Part II of the book, but it wouldn't hurt to take in some of the basics in Part I as a reminder and read about some of the new menus and software features. You're sure to pick up something you didn't know.

If you're already familiar with Facebook and online marketing tactics but short on time (and what marketing professional isn't short on time?), you might want to turn to a particular topic that interests you and dive right in. We wrote the book in a modular format, so you don't need to read it from front to back, although you're certain to gain valuable information from a complete read.

Regardless of how you decide to attack *Facebook Marketing For Dummies,* we're sure that you'll enjoy the journey. If you have specific questions or comments, please feel free to reach out to us via John's Facebook Page at www.facebook.com/inboundzombie. We'd love to hear your personal anecdotes and suggestions for improving the future revisions of this book. And in the true spirit of sharing on which Facebook is built, we promise to respond to each of your comments.

Occasionally, we have updates to our technology books. If this book does have any technical updates, they will be posted at www.dummies.com/go/facebookmarketingfd/updates.

Here's to your success on Facebook!

Part I
Preparing for Success on Facebook

The 5th Wave   By Rich Tennant

"I know it's a short profile, but I thought 'King of the Jungle' sort of said it all."

In this part . . .

Are you ready to market your company on Facebook? Part I talks about what to keep in mind when entering the world of Facebook marketing, such as how to define your target market on Facebook, how to add Facebook into your marketing mix, how to maximize the networking effect within Facebook, and how to develop a marketing plan that will best promote your business on Facebook.

Chapter 1

Marketing in the Age of Facebook

In This Chapter

▶ Understanding why Facebook is huge

▶ Getting acquainted with the marketing potential of Facebook

▶ Determining whether your business needs a Facebook Page now

*I*f Facebook were a country, it would be the third most populated in the world, just behind India and China. As of the publication date of this book, Facebook has more than 700,000,000 members worldwide.

Facebook continues to grow at a staggering rate because it fits the needs of both consumers and businesses. Consumers use Facebook to connect with friends, share photos, reunite with family members, and get recommendations for cool and useful products and services. All Facebook users have a Facebook *Profile*, which includes a main image or avatar; a *Wall* listing their latest activities and comments from friends; and a sidebar that includes tabs for photos, personal information, and other apps. Businesses use Facebook to reach out to these networks of friends and families by using Facebook's plug-ins to make their websites more "social," and by conducting highly targeted ad campaigns within the Facebook community. The primary tool for businesses is the Facebook *Page*, which looks very much like a Facebook Profile but includes features that allow businesses to publish content, to engage with fans who respond to that content, and to analyze the demographics of those fans.

Because Facebook provides features useful for both consumers and businesses, it has become an attractive platform for virtually all industries. Businesses are quickly learning how to use Facebook Pages, Facebook Applications, Facebook Ads, and Facebook plug-ins to achieve very specific business goals, such as:

✔ **Increasing brand awareness:** All size companies are penetrating Facebook's massive community with Facebook Apps and Facebook Pages.

✔ **Launching products:** Brands are using Facebook to test market products and to conduct Facebook ad campaigns as part of their overall product launch strategy.

✔ **Customer service:** More and more companies have realized that Facebook Pages are a very inexpensive way to enhance existing customer support channels, simply because resolutions to basic product issues or questions can be seen by many customers.

✔ **Selling products and services:** Businesses like Zipcar are selling their services on Facebook through the use of eCommerce applications that can be added to a Facebook Page.

This book shows you how you can achieve some of these business goals.

In this chapter, we give you an overview of why Facebook has gotten so huge, and how marketers are taking advantage of its potential. We also explain why you need to create a Facebook Page for your business.

What Is Facebook and Why Is It So Popular?

The social networking site Facebook was launched in 2004 by a kid at Harvard University named Mark Zuckerberg. It started out with the name "Thefacebook" (see Figure 1-1) and was available only for Harvard students, or anyone with a harvard.edu e-mail address. The social network spread quickly throughout Harvard because it was exclusive.

Although it was originally launched as a network for Harvard students, Facebook was eventually made available to students at other universities and then finally to anyone with access to a computer. Now, just a few years later, it has become the largest social networking site in history. As of the publication date of this book, Facebook has more than 800,000,000 users worldwide.

But it's not just the biggest social networking site in history. It's also the most active. According to Facebook

✔ 50%of its active users log on to Facebook every day

✔ The average user has 130 friends

✔ People spend more than 700 billion minutes per month on Facebook

By now, your mom is on Facebook. Most of your friends are on Facebook. You've connected with long-lost high school friends. You may have met your spouse on Facebook, and maybe even discovered who your biological parents are.

You might be wondering why Facebook and not Myspace or FriendFeed has gotten to where it is today. Although an entire book can written on this topic, it is worth exploring briefly here.

Figure 1-1:
Screen
shot of The
Facebook.
com as it
appeared
in 2004.

Here are a few reasons why Facebook has blown past all other social networks.

- ✔ **Facebook has used existing social connections to promote the platform.** From day one, the sign-on process has included inviting anyone you've e-mailed! Its assumption is that if you've exchanged an e-mail with someone, there's a good chance you have some kind of pre-existing relationship with that person, and would be more inclined to invite them to join you on Facebook.

- ✔ **Facebook is heavily covered by mainstream media.** Whether it's a newspaper article about a teacher getting fired for thoughtless comments about a student, or a TV interview with two siblings separated at birth but reunited on Facebook, not a day goes by without some kind of mention of Facebook in the news.

- ✔ **Facebook keeps us connected.** Young people famously use Facebook to stay connected, but they're not alone. One of the fastest growing segments on Facebook is people over 55. Many of them use Facebook to keep up with their children and sometimes grandchildren.

Facebook facilitates connection

Karen Graham and Tim Garman are brother and sister who were reunited after 40 years because of Facebook. Separated at birth and adopted by two separate families, they were only reunited when their younger sister, Danielle, began searching for them on Facebook.

After three months and more than a few dead ends, Danielle found the Facebook profile of Karen Graham's daughter. She messaged her with, "I think your mom is my mom's daughter," which eventually led to the reunion.

Today Karen and Tim are very close, and attend family gatherings around holidays and reunions.

Obviously the two had a desire to meet each other, but they lacked the means to find each other until Facebook provided the opportunity for connection.

Similarly, in 2011, John was able to meet an old friend he hadn't seen since high school. In middle school and high school, John was a very unpopular, shy nerd who was bullied by the "cool kids." Needless to say, he wasn't very excited to get friend requests from many of these classmates.

But with Clark, he said, *"Now that's someone that I'd be very interested in reuniting with!"* John remembered Clark as being extremely smart and creative. (The figure shows Clark (left) with John in Chicago.) They initially got connected through a Facebook Group someone created for their high school, and then arranged to connect in Chicago when John was there on business.

Understanding the Marketing Potential of Facebook

In the 1950s this gadget called the television exploded throughout American culture. At first, there were black-and-white TVs and then toward the end of the decade, there were color TVs in every middle-class living room. As more consumers started watching TV instead of listening to the radio, marketers had to adopt their strategies to the new medium. Successful ad executives and writers took the time to understand how TV fit within American culture. They researched how and why TV became a focal point for families at the end of each day (remember TV dinners?). They researched the ways men watched TV differently from women, and which television shows kids preferred on Saturday morning.

Only after this research were they able to create successful TV advertisements. They learned to condense their messages down to 30 seconds. They created ads with jingles that imitated popular TV themes, and effectively placed their products within popular shows.

In the same way, today's successful advertisers must research today's new medium — Facebook — to come to an understanding of how best to use it to market their brands.

If you're reading this book, there's a good chance you've heard about how brands like Harley Davidson and Starbucks, as well as thousands of small businesses and nonprofits that are using Facebook to market their products and services.

Through a variety of strategies and tactics, these businesses are tapping into Facebook to achieve a variety of objectives:

- ✔ They're increasing awareness of their brands through highly targeted Facebook ads.
- ✔ They're getting to know what their customers really want by having daily conversations with them.
- ✔ They're launching new products and services with Facebook Pages and custom Facebook applications.
- ✔ They're increasing new and repeat sales with coupons, group deals, and loyalty programs.

Part of the reason why these businesses are successful is that they understand Facebook is not just a static website — it's a way for people to connect and be heard.

Leveraging the power of word-of-mouth marketing

Word of mouth is the most powerful way to market any business. In fact, many studies have shown that consumers are more likely to make purchase decisions based on recommendations from people they know than from a brand's marketing materials. Each time a user likes, comments on, or shares content on Facebook, that action spreads out to their network of friends. This is how "word of mouth" happens on Facebook. (See Figure 1-2.)

According to a July, 2009 Econsultancy study, 90 percent of consumers online trust recommendations from people they know. And this makes perfect sense. Think about the last time you made a major purchase decision (a car, a TV, or even a contractor) — which influenced you more: an ad about that product or service? Or the experience of a friend who purchased that product or service?

Figure 1-2:
The Nature Conservancy benefits from the word of mouth marketing that's generated by 328 likes and 21 comments.

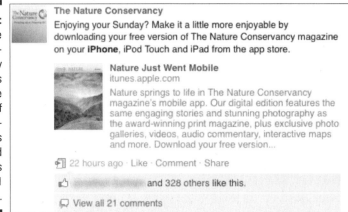

The most powerful aspect of Facebook is the deep ties among users. Large portions of friend networks are based upon work relationships, family relationships, or other real-life relationships. Some marketers refer to these connections as *strong ties,* meaning they go beyond the boundaries of Facebook. Such connections are in contrast to *weak ties* — online connections that lack stated common interests or goals.

Which would you be more influenced by: the Facebook friend with whom you went to college? Or the Facebook "friend" who sent a "friend request" simply because she met you at concert this past weekend?

Marketing tools for all kinds of businesses

Facebook offers marketers a number of unique ways to interact with customers and prospects, including the following:

- ✔ **Facebook Pages, Groups, Places, and Events:** Facebook Pages, Groups, Places, and Events are free for any business. These tools have the very same social features (including News Feeds, comments, and the capability to share links, photos, videos, and updates) that more than 700 million people use to connect with their friends on Facebook. In other words, Facebook allows businesses to connect with customers in the same way these customers connect with their friends. This "business is personal" paradigm has helped Facebook transform the way companies market themselves.

- ✔ **Facebook Ads:** Facebook Ads, which can be purchased on a cost-per-click (CPC) or cost-per-impression (CPM) basis, are increasingly popular because they enable marketers to reach as narrow or as wide an audience as desired, often at a fraction of the cost of other online media outlets, such as Google AdSense. (See Figure 1-3.) And because Facebook members voluntarily provide information about their personal interests and relationships (or friends), Facebook has a wealth of information about its members that advertisers can easily tap into.

The new Facebook marketing paradigm is rewriting all the rules. As marketers scramble to understand how best to leverage this powerful new communications channel, those who don't jump on board risk being left behind at the station.

Figure 1-3:
Facebook Ads like this one are an extremely cost effective way to target your exact customer based on a variety of factors.

Back to school at Walmart

From notecards to notebooks, Walmart has everything you need for back to school. Get low prices every day on everything on your list!

What's on your back to school list?
- ○ Clothes
- ○ A fancy calculator
- ○ Aspirin

8,060,358 people like Walmart.

Understanding Why Your Business Needs a Facebook Page

The best (and easiest) way for you to hang out a shingle for your organization on Facebook is to get a Facebook Page.

A Page serves as a home for your business, as well as a place to notify people about upcoming events, provide your hours of operation and contact information, display news, and even display photos, videos, text, and other types of content.

Pages also allow you to carry on conversations with your customers and prospects, providing a new means of learning more about what they want from your business.

Facebook Pages are visible to everyone online, regardless of whether that person is a Facebook member. This allows search engines, such as Google and Microsoft's Bing, to find and index your Page. This can improve your company's positioning in search results on those sites.

Here are a few important components that make Facebook Pages the core marketing tool for all kinds of businesses:

- **The Wall:** The Wall tab serves as the central component of a Page and allows you to upload content such as photos, videos, links, and notes. These actions generate updates and display as stories on your fans' News Feeds.

- **Like button:** When someone clicks your Facebook Page's Like button, she is expressing her approval of your Page. She becomes a fan of your Page, and a story appears in her News Feed, which is distributed to her friends who are then more likely to like your Page.

- **Status Update Field:** This is the box with the What's On Your Mind? text. If you want to push out a message, you can send a status update. Pages allow you, the Page administrator (admin), to send a limitless stream of updates (short messages up to 420 characters in length), which, in turn, appear in your fans' News Feeds.

- **Info Tab:** Here is where more detailed information about your company is located, including your location and website address.

- **Applications:** You can customize your Page with a host of applications (apps). Facebook offers a wide range of apps that you can use on your Page, anything from contest and promotion apps to RSS feeds from your favorite news services. (We discuss apps in detail in Chapter 12.)

Attracting new fans that are friends of customers

Facebook Pages include a Wall that allows you to publish content and engage with Facebook users to help you convert Facebook fans into first-time customers.

Marketers can use Wall updates — also called *stories* — to engage fans around relevant discussions. These updates appear in their fans' News Feeds, where the fans can either comment on or like the story. (See Figure 1-4.)

Figure 1-4:
Facebook
Page stories
like this one
appear in
the News
Feeds of
their fans.

These actions from fans — in the form of likes and comments — appear on their personal Facebook Profiles, and in the News Feeds of their Facebook friends.

When nonfans see those stories in their News Feeds, they can also comment on or like your Page story, and even visit your Page directly to engage with other stories and become a fan or a connection of Page.

Changing first-time customers into repeat customers

In marketing, getting people's attention and keeping it is paramount for success, and things are no different on Facebook. This principle applies to your current customers in addition to your prospects.

Once a customer has liked your Facebook Page, it's your job to nurture and grow your relationship with them by providing added value. In other words, you must use your Facebook Page to enhance the benefit that your customers get from doing business with you. You do this by continually posting interesting and relevant content on the Page, which we discuss in Chapter 8. For example, a car dealership can post auto-maintenance or travel tips— in addition to discounts on oil changes and other services — on its Facebook Page to turn a first-time customer into a lifetime customer.

Chapter 2

Researching and Understanding Your Target Audience

In This Chapter

▶ Determining your target audience

▶ Understanding your target audience

▶ Using personas to devise marketing methods and campaigns

▶ Researching your ideal customers on Facebook

S mart marketers, regardless of their medium, know that defining target audiences helps save time, money, and other resources. Small business owners know that paying for a full page ad in a national magazine or buying a 30-minute regional television spot is not a cost-effective way to reach specific audiences. The smart marketer knows who has bought from him in the past. He knows his customer's age, where she lives, what her lifestyle is, and more, and by knowing these things, he can target similar people through whatever marketing medium he chooses.

In this chapter we talk about how to define your target audience, how this understanding relates to Facebook, and how to exploit strong and weak ties within that target audience.

Defining Your Target Audience

Your *target audience* is the specific group of consumers to which your business has decided to aim its marketing efforts. If you think about your target audience in the context of everyone on the planet, you can see that defining your target audience prevents you from wasting money by identifying people who will never buy.

Understanding the marketing funnel

A useful model to help you understand and define your target audience is the *marketing funnel*. The marketing funnel shows the categories your customers fall into, and describes how those categories are related to each other — so-called *evangelists* or *advocates* are a subset of your loyal, repeat customers, for instance, and your repeat customers are a subset of more casual customers. The five marketing funnel categories group customers according to how well they trust you, do business with you, and recommend your products or services. (See Figure 2-1.)

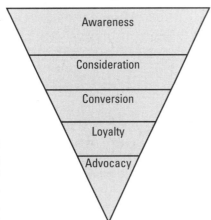

Marketing Funnel

Figure 2-1:
Diagram of the market-ing funnel.

The purpose of the marketing funnel is to help marketers develop specific marketing strategies for potential customers, new customers, repeat custom-ers, and raving fans. For example, car dealers could run different campaigns for different customer categories. New customers, such as new parents in the market for a minivan, could receive messages that include TV ads, newspaper ads, and content from a dealership's Facebook Page. Existing customers, on the other hand, would receive e-mails or direct-mail pieces offering discounts on oil changes and other specials.

In the marketing funnel, the marketplace is broken down into five behavior stages, or phases, as follows:

✔ **Awareness:** The people in this stage are aware of your product or ser-vice, but have yet to consider purchasing it. Awareness is created on Facebook though ads and friend networks.

✔ **Consideration:** The people in this stage are considering your product or service, but have yet to purchase it. This is the stage where the potential customer needs proof, testimonials, guarantees, and anything else that will instill confidence to proceed to the next stage.

✔ **Conversion:** The people in this stage have made the leap to purchase your product or service. At this stage, they are at the highest risk of experiencing buyer's remorse. In addition to your normal customer service channels (including e-mail, and phone), you want to actively monitor your Page Wall for customer questions and feedback.

✔ **Loyalty:** The people in this stage have decided to purchase your product or service repeatedly. They have done so because your product/service is of high quality and because they trust you.

✔ **Advocacy:** The people in this stage actively recommend your product or service to others. Smart Facebook marketers treat these people like gold, giving them special offers, additional discounts, praise, and recognition.

Defining who your best customers are

One of the first steps in developing a target audience strategy is to analyze your current customer base.

Of all your customers, think about the ones who keep coming back — the ones who consistently tell others about your business. Wouldn't it be great to attract more of these types of customers?

Of course it would be!

These are people who have already demonstrated that they're willing to pull out the credit card or give you cash for your products and services, and you already know that there's a huge difference between someone liking what you sell and buying what you sell.

From this perspective, you can begin to define your target audience as "the ideal person who you want to get your product or service in front of." It shares essentially the same characteristics as your best customers.

For example, let's imagine a Vespa scooter dealership in a college town. Through simple research, it discovers that its best customers are parents of students going to universities located around that dealership.

Rather than target everyone located within 50 miles of the dealership, then, it would be smarter to target only students (and their parents) who attend local universities. Its marketing resources would be best used for ads in university publications, local newspapers, and targeted Facebook ads.

Selecting demographic criteria for your target audience

Following are several factors that you should consider when creating a target audience:

- ✔ **Age:** The importance of age depends upon the type of product or service that you're selling. For example, if you sell driving lessons — that is, if you're a driving school — obviously you're going to target parents of children who are a specific age. On the other hand, if you're selling pizza, age may not be that important.

  One more important thing to think about with respect to age is that sometimes it's best to target a range of ages instead of a specific one. Marketers of clothing for pregnant women, for example, would target a range of ages; marketers of retirement funds, however, might pick a specific age.

- ✔ **Gender:** Is your product or service better suited for one gender over another? For example, Men's Wearhouse primarily sells clothing for men.

  If you must target a specific gender, be careful to consider who the buyers actually are (as this might not be readily apparent), such as wives who buy men's clothing as gifts for their husbands.

- ✔ **Location:** Is the location of your customer an important factor? Again a pizza shop primarily sells pizza to people who live in the neighborhood, but Amazon.com doesn't care where any of its customers live.

- ✔ **Interests:** Understanding your target audience's interests is very important because it allows you to sell additional, related products or services. For example, a store selling golf accessories could also sell golf lessons or getaways.

Demographic targeting should consider both the user of your product or service, and the buyer of your product or service. They might not be the same person.

Using personas to give your target audience personality

Demographic information alone won't help you understand what motivates your customers and prospects. Once you have a good understanding of the demographics of your target audience. you also should look at your customers' behaviors and beliefs, and the stages of life that they are in. This helps you better understand what motivates your prospects to actually buy your product or service.

For example, new parents tend to exhibit a specific set of beliefs and behaviors. Raising children and learning how to be good parents require focusing on or developing specific behaviors, including being thrifty, creating a secure home, being protective about the family, and choosing healthier eating habits.

How can you come to understand your target audience's behaviors? By using *personas*. Personas are your marketing campaign's imaginary friends. Playing with imaginary friends helps kids learn to interact with real people. Your personas will teach you to interact with a real audience. Think of a persona as an imaginary character that represents a member of your targeted demographic.

The purpose of personas is to encourage you to creatively come up with marketing campaigns and messages that resonate with your prospects.

You can develop personas by following these basic steps:

1. **Figure out who your customers are (by defining their needs, demographics, income, occupation, education, gender; do they volunteer, how much do they donate, and so on).**

2. **Create groups of customers that share a lot of the same characteristics. Include groups for new customers and repeat customers to help you understand why people buy from you in the first place, and why they come back to buy again.**

3. **Rank these groups in order of importance.**

   Home Depot, for instance, might rank professional builders higher than first-time DIYers.

4. **Invent fictional characters that represent each group. Add details such as age, occupation, marital status, kids, hobbies, interests, online activity, and more. Anyone who directly connects with your customers on a daily basis should be brought into this discussion (salespeople, tech support people, and so on).**

5. **Give these characters life by using a stock photo of an actual person and naming him.**

   This also makes it easier to create products and messaging that speak to this person. It might be tempting to skip this step, but don't. The more real you can make your personas, the more compelling your marketing will be.

6. **Finally, create a short back story for each persona.**

   For example, a food pantry might have the following story for "Beth," one of its volunteer personas:

"Beth is a 55-year-old empty-nester with two kids in college. She's a busy customer service manager at a local software company, but strongly believes in living a balanced and meaningful life. She also values contributing to her local community. When her kids moved to California to go to college, Beth began working at the local food pantry. This gives her a tremendous sense of happiness —_not only because she believes in giving back, but because she has new friends who she has over for dinner parties. For Beth, the food pantry is not at all about food — it's about living a meaningful life."

Researching Target Audiences with Facebook's Ad Tool

Facebook's Ad tool is primarily intended to be used by advertisers to create, launch, and manage advertising campaigns. (See Figure 2-2.) In Chapter 10, we go into great detail about creating Facebook Ads. In this chapter, however, we discuss how to use the Ad tool to research your target audience segments.

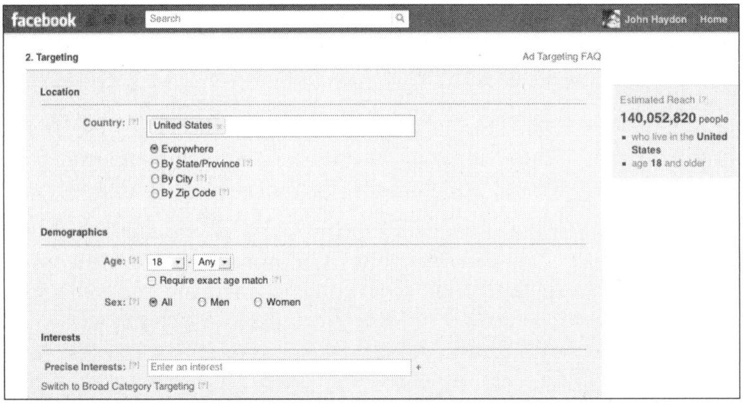

Figure 2-2:
Facebook's
Ad tool can
be used
to better
understand
your target
audience.

Using the Facebook Ad Manager as a research tool allows you to answer questions such as

- ✔ How many Facebook users near my business's location are married and between the ages of 35 and 39?
- ✔ How many fans of my competitor's Facebook Page live close to my business?
- ✔ How many of my target customers are already fans of my competitor's Facebook Page?

The following list describes several target segment criteria you can research in the Facebook Ad tool:

✔ **Location:** You can research a target audience based on where they live. (See Figure 2-3.) You can target broadly with countries, or even get as specific as cities. Note that if a city has no Facebook users living there, that city may not be available as a selection. (This is rare, however.)

Figure 2-3: Facebook allows you to target broad or specific geographic locations.

✔ **Age:** When a person first signs up on Facebook, that person's date of birth is required information. This allows you to see how many users are within a particular age range or are a specific age.

Always begin targeting with broad criteria, such as location, and add more specific criteria like interests. This allows you get a sense of the possible reach of people you can target on Facebook. As you add or remove targeting criteria in the Ad tool, the Estimated Reach number gets updated automatically. (See Figure 2-4.)

Figure 2-4: Facebook updates the estimated reach as you select target criteria.

✔ **Gender and Language (Advanced Demographics):** You can research a target audience based on their gender or on what language they speak. Note that if you don't make a language selection, the Ad tool automatically defaults to the official language of the country that the user is located in.

✔ **Relationship Status:** This selection allows you to research the number of people within a selected target audience based on their relationship status (see Figure 2-5).

Figure 2-5:
Facebook
allows you
to target
interests,
relationship
status, and
language.

Advanced Demographics		
Interested In: [?] ● All ○ Men ○ Women		
Relationship: [?] ☑ All ☐ Single ☐ Engaged ☐ In a relationship ☐ Married		
Languages: [?]	Enter language	
Enter language		

✔ **Likes and Interests:** Likes and Interests targeting allows advertisers to reach people based on the activities and interests they list in their Facebook profiles. This includes Pages they have liked and mentions of favorite movie stars, books, movies, or TV shows, as well as political views, employers, and job titles.

Keep in mind that researching Facebook Likes and Interests is very different from researching search engine keywords. For example, if you sell hiking shoes, you'd use "hiking boots" to research search engine keywords, but would use "backpacking" or "National Wildlife Federation" to research various Facebook audiences.

As you select keywords and phrases to target, Facebook automatically suggests additional Likes and Interests that other users have selected. As you add these keywords to your criteria, you'll notice that the Estimated Reach number updates to reflect the keywords you've added.

✔ **Networking Goals on Facebook:** Facebook allows users to indicate their primary motivations for connecting with others on Facebook. You can research these motivations by selecting the various selections under Interested In (refer to Figure 2-5). Although "dating" and "networking" are extremely broad definitions about networking goals, they can provide valuable insight that can be used for messaging. For example, if most people who like backpacking have also expressed an interest in dating, you can create messaging about backpacking as being a way to meet new people.

✔ **Education & Work:** Education & Work targeting is based on people who attend a specific school or work at a particular company. You can further target by current education level, major, and graduation year if applicable.

✔ **Connections:** In this section you can target fans, or friends of fans, and so on. Targeting people in this way can help you spread your message by word of mouth.

Chapter 3

Developing a Facebook Marketing Plan

In This Chapter

▶ Figuring out what to include in your marketing plan

▶ Developing your value proposition

▶ Getting to know your audience

▶ Identifying your marketing goals

▶ Creating engaging content and measuring your results

▶ Integrating your offline and online campaigns

*O*ne of the great things about Facebook is that it gives you access to a very large and growing audience at relatively low or even no cost. All that's needed is some sweat equity on your part, but that doesn't mean you shouldn't have a strategy for what you want to achieve for your business.

Whether you're a small business owner, an artist, a celebrity, or you sell a well-known (or soon to be well-known) product or service, you need to think about who your audience is and what they want. This chapter helps you decide what message you want them to receive and which Facebook tactics will get them to interact with that message.

Understanding What to Include in Your Marketing Plan

Social networks represent a shift in the way that people use the Internet. Rather than just search for information, Facebook members can search for and interact with like-minded people who have similar interests.

Traditional marketing methods like print or TV ads are limited in that they can only shout at, so to speak, your customers to get them to buy something.

This approach doesn't work in a social network like Facebook because the users expect dialogue. For this reason, a shouting approach isn't only less effective than other methods — it might even work against you.

Over time, even marketing on Internet media has undergone a dramatic evolution. Websites once represented a kind of one-way communication, one in which visitors could only view content. This was followed by blogs and forums, which allowed visitors to comment on content, and then networks like Myspace and Facebook came along and really gave friends the ability to connect with each other. Finally, tools like Twitter and Foursquare allowed for real time conversations with all people (not just friends), and even to share their real-world locations within those conversations. (See Figure 3-1.)

With Facebook and other social networks, your business can take advantage of technology that promotes your business by word of mouth. For example, when a Facebook user becomes a fan of your company's Page, confirms attendance at your Facebook event, or installs your application on his profile, these actions are automatically turned into stories that appear on the user's Wall. In essence, the user passes along your marketing message to other Facebook members, expanding word-of-mouth awareness of your business — without any extra effort.

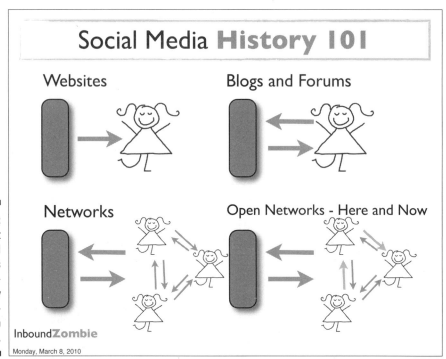

Figure 3-1:
The advent of social networks has influenced how people connect with brands.

Before you can take full advantage of the marketing power of Facebook, you need to put together a Facebook *marketing plan,* which is a structured way to align your strategies with your objectives. Here are the general steps for creating your plan:

1. Develop your value proposition.

2. Understand your audience.

3. Define your marketing goals.

4. Develop a content strategy.

5. Monitor and measure your Page activities.

6. Integrate your online and offline campaigns.

The rest of this chapter explains each of these steps in more detail. By putting these steps into practice, you can begin to put your marketing strategy in place by the end of this chapter.

Developing Your Value Proposition: Why Should Customers Buy What You're Offering?

When developing a formal marketing plan, the first thing you need to consider is your organization's *value proposition,* or *Unique Selling Proposition* (*USP*), which describes how your company is different from the competition and why people should do business with you. You may have a different value proposition for each audience segment you target, or for each product or service you offer. Your marketing plan should detail the ways in which you plan to communicate these values to your target audience.

To understand your value proposition, answer the following questions:

✔ **How are you different from your competitors?** By knowing your competition and what separates your offering from theirs, you can begin to develop your *product differential,* a key ingredient that goes into your value proposition. So what makes your product or service different from — and better than — your competitors? The answer to this question is what sets you apart from them. Do you offer a longer free trial of your product than your competitors? Do you have the ability to tailor your service to meet your customers' exact needs? Whatever that difference is, exploit it.

✔ **What value do you provide to your stakeholders?** *Stakeholders* are your customers, shareholders, employees, partners, and anyone else impacted by your company. Understanding the value you provide is key in developing your messaging and communications strategy. By having a clear picture of what you want to accomplish with your marketing plan, you open a world of opportunities for your business. The key is communicating this to your stakeholders. When your employees know your brand messaging, they can pass that information on to your customers in the form of knowledge and better service. When your stakeholders know you have a clear plan of action, they'll be more comfortable with the direction that you're taking the company, which leads to greater support for your future ideas and plans.

✔ **What are your big-picture goals?** Some goals are more obvious than others. They could include increasing company sales or driving more traffic to your website, both of which can be done when you clearly define and communicate your value proposition. Some aren't as obvious, such as improving your company's reputation or creating a more friendly face for the brand. Whatever your company's goals, make sure all of your Facebook marketing activities align with these goals.

Understanding Your Audience

Whatever your business goals, always assemble the best information that you can about your audience. The better you understand the culture and viewpoints of your audience — what they like and don't like, where they spend their time, and what information sources they rely on — the more effectively you can capture their attention and deliver your message. Understanding the lives of your customers and prospects is key when communicating your business or product to them.

Finding out what makes your fans tick

Facebook provides some powerful insights into your fans. In fact, identifying and then reaching a specific audience has never been this exact and cost-effective. The Facebook Insights tool helps you find out more about who visits your Facebook Page, including a demographic and interest breakdown of your fans, and the Facebook ad-targeting capabilities make it relatively easy to get your message to the right target audience within Facebook.

Understanding your fans' psychographic profiles is an important element in knowing who they are. *Psychographic* variables (such as music a user loves, politicians he endorses, or causes he supports) are any qualities relating to a user's personality, values, attitudes, interests, or lifestyles. These variables are in contrast with *demographic* variables (such as age and gender) and *behavioral* variables (such as usage rate or loyalty) and can help you better understand your customer segments.

Gathering this information can be fairly easy if you know where to look and how to go about doing it. For example, ask your customers to fill out satisfaction surveys or a quick questionnaire through your e-newsletter or website. Another option is to search Facebook for some companies similar to yours and read through the comments posted by *their* fans to see what makes them return to those companies.

Psychographics is exceptionally relevant in any discussion of social networks because your target audience is more likely to interact with you along the lines of their interests, values, and lifestyles. Examples of this can be seen in Facebook apps similar to *iLike,* which integrates users' favorite music and makes recommendations on their Profiles. Another example is Tom's of Maine, a company that produces all-natural personal care products such as toothpaste and soap. Tom's of Maine takes advantage of the fact that many people are concerned with making positive changes to their communities and the environment and are "going green." In fact, its site has an entire tab devoted to fundraising outcomes and that creating positive change starts with each individual.

Refer to Chapter 2 for more on developing personas to understand your target market.

Understanding what motivates your fans

After you understand your target customers, you need to understand what motivates them. Customers want to feel as though they're receiving special treatment on Facebook. They want to know that their support is important to you and that their concerns are being heard. But most of all, they want something in return for their attention and loyalty. Facebook members love free stuff, special discounts, and promotions.

It's not surprising that Facebook members are looking for real value in the form of informative and engaging content from marketers on Facebook. Much like in Google Search, in which users are further down the intent-to-purchase road by the very nature of their searches, Facebook users aren't necessarily looking for specific products and services to purchase. That's why marketers need to grab their attention through special offers.

Special incentive offers can be found throughout Facebook in the form of ads on Facebook Pages. In Figure 3-2, Ann Taylor offers a 30 percent discount just for becoming a fan of its Facebook Page.

Figure 3-2:
Ann Taylor offers fans a discount promotion but requires they like the Page to redeem it.

Although pricing discounts serve as good incentives for some, savvy marketers want to provide value in different ways that reinforce their proposition value. For example, the Hallmark Channel allowed its fans to create multimedia tributes to their moms around Mother's Day and then tied those tributes into its premiere of *Meet My Mom,* an original Hallmark movie. Through a dedicated Meet My Mom tab on Hallmark's Facebook Page, as shown in Figure 3-3, users uploaded testimonials to their mothers for all to see and comment on. The promotion was advertised on the Hallmark Channel and via its website and Facebook Page. Within its first week of running the promotion, the company added 5,000 new fans, bringing its total number of fans to just more than 65,000.

Figure 3-3:
The
Hallmark
Channel
provided
tools to
allow fans
to create
multimedia
tributes to
their moms
to honor
them around
Mother's
Day.

Defining Your Marketing Goals

After you have a better understanding of the makeup of your Facebook audience, you need to define a few goals for your Facebook marketing strategy. You may have other objectives for your business, but these are the four we found are the most common:

- Building your brand's awareness
- Driving sales
- Forming a community of people who share your values
- Listening to feedback about your brand

We discuss each objective in more depth in the following sections, but keep in mind that these objectives aren't mutually exclusive but rather can be used in combination. You can start with one method and advance your strategy in other areas as you go along.

Building your brand's awareness

The concept of branding can be traced back in history to the early Romans, but the practice that always stuck with us was early livestock farmers branding their cattle with branding irons so they could be recognized by the farmer and his neighbors, so that when the animals wandered, everyone would know who owned them. Branding was a way of distinguishing their product from other products that looked very similar.

These days, things are very similar. A *brand* is how you define your business in a way that differentiates you from your competition; it's a key element in defining your marketing goals. With a Facebook Page, you can build awareness of your brand with all your current and prospective customers.

A Facebook Page serves as the home for your business on Facebook, and it should be created with your company's brand and image in mind. It's a place to notify people of an upcoming event; provide hours of operation and contact information; show recent news; and even display photos, videos, text, and other types of content. A Facebook Page also allows for two-way interaction between you and your customer, providing her a place to post messages, It's also a great feedback loop for you to find out more about your customers' needs.

After you've created your Page (as shown in Figure 3-4), here are a few ways to let people know about it and start building awareness of your brand:

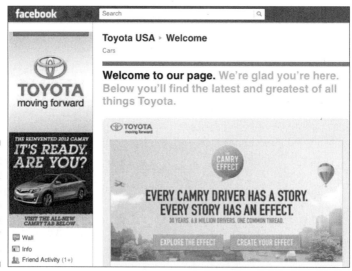

Figure 3-4: Facebook allows you to create a Page to market your business.

✔ **Reach out to your Facebook friends.** Your best place to start promoting your Facebook Page is with existing Facebook friends! You can do this by using the Invite Friends feature on the right side of any Facebook Page.

✔ **Reach out to existing customers, friends, and contacts outside Facebook through your normal marketing channels**. Let these folks know that your business has a Page on Facebook. For example, you can send them an e-mail blast or include the address for your Page in a printed newsletter or flyer. Something as simple as "Join us on Facebook!" does the trick.

✔ **For those customers and friends with Facebook profiles, utilize the share link located on the left side of your Page.** There's no doubt that the people you interact with on Facebook would love to know that your business has a Page. Don't be shy about spreading the word. After all, Facebook makes it easy for you, so put those links to good use.

To use the Invite Friends feature, just click the Invite Friends link on the right side of your Page and then select the friends you want to send a notification to, as shown in Figure 3-5.

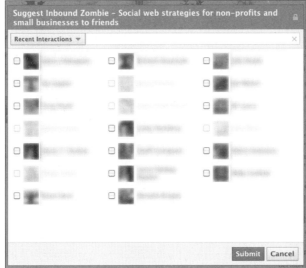

Figure 3-5:
Use the
Invite
Friends link
to send a
notification
about your
Page.

Chapter 4 discusses many more strategies and tactics for promoting your Facebook Page.

Driving sales

Whether you're a local, a national, or an international business, Facebook can help you drive the sales of your products and services. As another potential sales channel, you can leverage the social network in a number of ways to achieve your sales objectives:

✔ **Communicate special offerings and discounts and provide an easy path to purchase with a simple link to your company website.** Some larger retailers bring the entire shopping cart experience to Facebook. For example, 1-800-Flowers.com launched a tab within its Facebook Page, shown in Figure 3-6, that links directly to its shopping site.

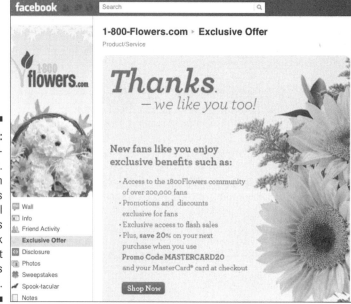

Figure 3-6: 1-800-Flowers.com displays special offers on its Facebook Page that link to its website.

✔ **Target your audience with a Facebook ad campaign.** In addition to creating a free Facebook Page, many marketers are also discovering the potential in Facebook as a cost-effective advertising medium. You can test and launch targeted ad campaigns that employ traditional direct marketing techniques, such as ads with engaging copy and pictures that capture a reader's attention. The most successful offer is an incentive that appeals to your audience. (We discuss advertising in more detail in Chapter 11.)

✔ **Create a Facebook event to generate buzz about a product.** For example, you can hold a new product launch party or a wine tasting for potential customers, and you can throw a Facebook-only event for fans and allow them to network as well. (See Chapter 14 for a discussion of Facebook Events.)

Forming a community with a Facebook Group

One of the best uses of a social network is to build a *community* — that is, a group of people who share the same interests and passion for a cause. No matter what your marketing goals are, forming a community takes some effort. We generally think it's arrogant for marketers to feel they can build a community that people will flock to — the proverbial "build it, and they will come" model. However, with a Facebook Group in addition to a Page for your business, that very model is possible.

A *Facebook Group* is a page that's based on shared interests or goals. With a Group, you can create a community focused on an existing cause that matches your business goals, and you can give your Group members the tools to communicate with each other on Facebook. Another reason to create a Group is if you have an interest or hobby outside of your business that you want to share with others. For example, if you own a hardware store and have a passion for building furniture, you can start a Group for the purpose of uniting people who share your love of woodworking. A Group is a great place for you and other Group members to share tips and tricks for practicing your craft.

You can also build a Facebook Group around a cause related to your brand. For example, Lee National Denim Day supports breast cancer awareness and the search for a cure, as shown in Figure 3-7, and who doesn't like to wear denim? Calling attention to a cause Lee is passionate about, shows its customers that it's not all business all the time and that Lee takes the time to support a charitable cause.

Spirited discussions are prominent in Facebook Groups, so plan for someone in your company — perhaps a product expert or someone on the communications team — to lead regular discussion threads weekly, monthly, or even bimonthly. Keep in mind, though, that you probably want people coming back to the Group more often than monthly, but less often than weekly. For example, weekly updates from your Group might be too much for your fans to handle because most people have loads of information coming at them from multiple sources like News Feeds and would prefer not to be bombarded with frequent messages. Remind them every three weeks or so to come back to your site, just to keep your Group fresh in their minds.

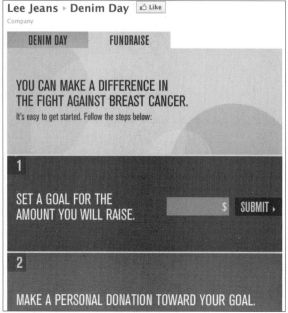

Figure 3-7:
Lee National
Denim Day
to support
breast
cancer
awareness.

Listening to feedback

You can listen to feedback from Facebook members in a number of ways:

- ✔ **Monitor discussions in your Group.** As discussed in the preceding section, a Facebook Group lets you create a community and have discussions with your members, but a noteworthy byproduct of forming a Facebook Group is the ability to get feedback. For example, the next time you think about launching a new product or service, consider having the members of your Group (in addition to fans of your Page) weigh in on it before it goes to market. And don't worry about a delay in getting the product to market; it takes only a few days to get feedback from members. Of course, you have to build up your member base before you can tap into it.

Facebook doesn't publish Group discussions to Internet search engines. Therefore, they aren't *indexed,* which is how a search engine finds its information. This may change, but currently, you can't find Facebook Groups via an Internet search.

- ✔ **Search for discussions about your brand.** Facebook is fertile ground for open, honest, peer-to-peer discussions about your business. Just plug any search terms related to your business into the Facebook search box and see what comes up. You might be surprised to find other fan Pages devoted to your brand.

To search terms, type your keywords into the main search box at Facebook.com and filter by Pages or Groups on the left-hand side.

✔ **Review postings on your Wall.** Facebook users can post comments, questions, and even suggestions to your Page's Wall. Make sure you closely monitor those as well and respond appropriately and in a timely manner.

Developing Your Content Strategy

Keep in mind that content drives engagement. How can you tailor your content to appeal to your fans? What assets do you already have (such as videos, tips, customer testimonials, and so on) that will enhance your brand while delivering real value to your fans? In essence, you need a content strategy to make Facebook and other social media work for your business.

When developing your content strategy, look at your different channels of communication your website, Facebook Page, Twitter presence, e-newsletter, and so on and then decide which content is right for each channel. For example, you may realize that your Twitter followers want a different stream of updates than your Facebook fans, and your website visitors would be better served with more product-focused content. Because you want different types of engagement across all your channels, the content you publish needs to address each audience's needs and concerns.

Here are some ways to develop your content strategy on Facebook:

✔ **Post to engage users.** Although some content you post will be purely informative in nature, such as broadcasting a particular price promotion to your fans, *engagement posts* are designed to garner feedback and participation from your fans. The key is to engage your fans and solicit responses from them so that you can benefit from the viral effect: Every time a fan comments on your Facebook Page, a story publishes to her News Feed, which will end up on her *friends'* News Feeds.

So tactically, these stories provide links back to the original post and often generate additional traffic to the content. In this way, your fans invite others along for the ride. But there's also another reason to foster fan participation: to build an engaged community, one comment at a time.

✔ **Provide discounts and special offers.** As we touch on earlier in this chapter, Facebook marketers are discovering great success through extending discounts, special offers, and giveaways to attract Facebook fans. Ads that generate the greatest responses on Facebook offer something of perceived value for very little effort on the member's part. Often, these offers are based on a prerequisite, such as the completion of a form or clicking the Like button.

When developing a promotion, keep in mind that the offer must interest your target audience. Sometimes, the offer doesn't even have to be tangible, but merely the chance to have a shot at glory. In Figure 3-8, Klondike appeals to its fans' competitive nature, offering them a chance to beat their friends' scores in the *Bar Slinger* video game. The Page even shows their high scores.

Figure 3-8: Klondike created games that challenge fans to beat their friends' high scores.

✔ **Deliver content in a format accessible to your audience.** When developing your content strategy, it's important to consider the range of media at your disposal. Facebook allows you to publish content in a number of formats (including photos and videos), making this content accessible directly through Facebook with a click of the mouse. Why not take advantage of the convenience of having everything in one easy-to-access location?

Likewise, if your fans enter into a dialogue on your Facebook Page's Wall, continue to use Facebook as your communications channel. Don't reach out to that individual on Twitter, LinkedIn, or some other social network unless requested to do so by the fan (otherwise, you could seem too aggressive). Maintaining a consistent approach to communicating with your Facebook fans will keep them fans for the long term.

The culture of Facebook is formed by young, digitally fluent adults who understand when they're being talked at versus engaged in a conversation. So the key isn't to interrupt them with a continuous stream of messages, but to instead use content to encourage participation. By creating a steady stream of rich content, you can engage the right audience and get them to interact with your brand. For more on fine-tuning and implementing your content strategy, check out Chapter 5.

Monitoring and Reporting Page Activity

The last piece of the puzzle for an effective marketing plan is taking the time to monitor and measure your Page activities. Only through careful analysis can you figure out what content resonates with your audience, and because actions within Facebook are measurable, your Page's metrics, or *key performance indicators,* can give you lots of insights into your fans' interactions with your Page.

A marketing campaign is only as good as your ability to measure it. The number of people who like your Page aren't worth anything to your business if you can't peel away the layers to gain greater meaning into their actions. You need to translate those analytics into real-world lessons that you then apply to your content. If you don't see any performance changes, it might be time to rethink your content strategy.

Facebook provides some powerful analytic tools to help you discover what's really happening on your Page. The following sections discuss just a few things to keep in mind when taking stock of your Facebook Page's analytics.

Using Insights for Pages

Facebook has an internal analytics system through which you can gain a greater understanding into your visitors' behavior when interacting with your Page. Facebook Insights is available for free to all Page admins and is located in the left sidebar of your Page. www.facebook.com/insights. By understanding and analyzing trends in your user growth and audience makeup as well as content consumption and engagement, you gain valuable, well, insights to how your fans interact with your Page. You'd be wise to pay attention to your Page's Insights.

Facebook Insights focuses on three areas of data: your fans, your reach, and how Facebook users interact with your content, as shown in Figure 3-9. (We explore these in greater detail in Chapter 9.) Insights provides information on the demographics of your audience and tracks the growth of fans on your

Page and the number of likes and comments your content has received. By keeping tabs on some key metrics, such as the increase in the number of fans over the previous week or the number of interactions following a particular post, you can get an idea of what works and what doesn't. For example, if you notice that a number of fans have opted out of being a fan after a particular post, you might draw a correlation between the content you posted and the drop-off rate.

Figure 3-9:
Facebook Insights provides metrics on how your fans interact with your Page.

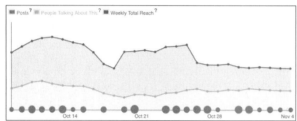

We suggest that you check out your Insights metrics regularly and stay on top of increases in engagement numbers and activity. Also, keep track of which posts people respond to and which ones they don't. If you don't see any performance changes, it might be time to rethink your content strategy.

The Insights Dashboard shows you an aggregate of your geographic and demographic information about your fans, who you are reaching, and who is engaging with your Page without identifying any individual's location or demographic, as shown in Figure 3-10. This is a great way to find out who your audience is.

Figure 3-10:
Facebook Insights also offers geographic and demographic data on your audience makeup.

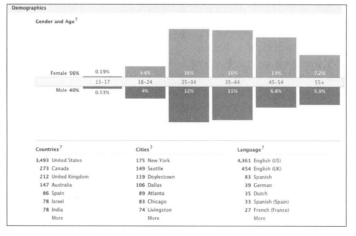

Flying blindly into your Facebook marketing plan is a fool's journey. The more you know about how and what your fans react to, the easier it is to tailor your content to the audience, giving it more of what they want.

Creating benchmarks and setting goals

As we've discussed, your Facebook efforts are indeed measurable. You need to have an idea of where you stand at the beginning of your efforts to compare it with where you end up at the end of a promotion, ad campaign, event, or other activity. By creating *benchmarks,* or the key indicators that define your Page's activity level, you can gauge your progress. Without knowing how many fans your Page had prior to a promotion, how can you calculate the success of the campaign? For example, take note of the number of views each specific tab on your Page gets, which can be found under the Users link on your Insights page. Are there certain tabs, such as your Photos tab, that get more views than others? Make it a point to update the content on the other tabs to see whether this increases their views. If views increase, you know that your fans are looking for you to update *all* of your tabs more frequently, not just your Wall.

In addition to benchmarks, set goals attached to your various Facebook marketing efforts. For example, Japanese electronics manufacturer JVC set a goal to acquire as many fans as possible over a 60-day period through a daily contest promoted via Facebook Ads. The contest required that members like its company Page before entering the contest. The promotion proved so successful that JVC saw an increase in fans from fewer than 1,000 at the outset of the contest to more than 34,000 in 30 days.

Although anticipating the success of a campaign or particular post prior to going live with it is difficult, by forecasting the outcome, you have to consider the results at the outset of your planning. Therefore, you can better manage your co-workers, and more importantly, your boss's expectations.

Keeping an eye on key metrics

The Facebook Page performance metrics that are important to you are, in part, determined by what your goals are. If your goal is to drive clicks to an external website, tracking referrals from your Facebook Page is an important indicator for you. Likewise, if your goal is to drive engagement, the number of comments associated with your content is most likely the metric you need to measure. But most of all, you need to take this data and translate it into real-world insights to make it valuable.

Here are nine key metrics to consider when tracking the performance of your Facebook presence:

- ✓ **Views:** A fundamental measurement is the number of views or visitors your content receives, and your Facebook Insights page is the place to go for this information. Understanding where people spend their time on your Facebook Page gives you a good idea of what information they find valuable.

- ✓ **Comments:** The number of comments you receive for a particular post is a great way to track performance. This also helps you identify which posts resonate with your fans. Typically, the more comments a post receives, the more interested your fans are in that content. Insights provides your Page's comment activity in an easy-to-read graph.

  When measuring the number of comments, don't forget to consider the sentiment of those comments. If all the comments are negative in nature, you could have a backlash if you produce similar posts.

- ✓ **Clicks and downloads:** If you post downloadable content or a link to content on an external website, it should always be trackable. Several URL shorteners, such as bitly (`http://bit.ly`) and Tiny.cc (`http://tiny.cc`), provide third-party click-through metrics on any link you shorten through their service. This is an excellent way to track the interest in a particular link or download.

- ✓ **Length of visits:** The amount of time someone spends on your Facebook Page is a strong indicator of your fans' interest, or lack thereof, in your content. Although Facebook doesn't provide these types of metrics at this time via Insights, you can install a third-party analytics tool on a Facebook Page to provide this data. Google Analytics (`www.google.com/analytics`), for example, offers a tracking service for free that you can integrate into your Page with a little technical knowledge; see Chapter 9 for details.

- ✓ **Shares:** If your content strikes a chord with your fans, chances are your fans will share the content they find valuable with their own network. By monitoring (with Insights) the number of times content you post is shared, you can get a good sense of what's of interest to them.

- ✓ **Inbound links:** Although linking is more common on external websites, Facebook Pages are linked to by bloggers, media outlets, search engines, and people who are generally interested in your Page. Searching Google using your Page URL as a search term tells you how many sites link to your Facebook Page. Typically, the more links to your Page, the better.

- ✓ **Unique versus repeat visitors:** Tracking *unique* (or new) and repeat visitors is a good indicator as to how valuable your content is to keep them coming back for more. Pay special attention to the increase in the number of repeat visitors over time because this lets you know whether your content strategy pays off. This is another metric that you can track with Google Analytics.

✔ **Brand mentions:** If you're doing a good job marketing your business on Facebook, chances are it'll have a spillover effect across other social media outlets. A number of free social media search sites track brand mentions, such as social mention (http://socialmention.com), and OneRiot (www.oneriot.com). Make a point to run a search of your company name on these sites on a regular basis. Monitoring what people say outside Facebook provides numerous insights into your marketing effectiveness.

✔ **Conversions:** A *conversion* occurs when a visitor undertakes a desired action, such as completing a transaction on your website, filling out a registration form, subscribing to your e-newsletter, or signing up for an event. Conversions are one of the strongest metrics you can measure and track. If you look at it as a ratio of total visitors to those who have converted on a particular action, the higher the percentage of people who undertake that action, the better.

One of the most important metrics not represented in this list is the good old-fashioned practice of listening to your fans. Paying attention to their comments, discussions, and communications helps you better align your content strategy with their interests. If you're not getting the kind of helpful feedback to make this analysis, just ask them. Fans love to share their thoughts and opinions with marketers, and sometimes all they need is a little prodding.

Integrating Your Online and Offline Campaigns

When you start to solidify your Facebook marketing strategy, you may question what support systems and resources you need or wonder how to integrate your social network marketing strategy with your existing marketing plans. In this section, we make some suggestions on how to support the effort without overloading you or your marketing team.

There's no reason why you can't leverage your existing offline campaigns with a social network, but be sure that you incorporate the campaigns into Facebook the right way. That is, include all elements of your campaign on Facebook. If you're throwing an event or starting a campaign, for example, mention it to your Facebook fans. Pretty much anything you currently do can be digitized and used on your Facebook Page.

Here are some ways that you can integrate your offline campaigns with your Facebook marketing activities:

✔ **Promote face-to-face events.** You want people to attend your event, right? Mention your event on your Page and even link to any outside information you've posted, such as on your website. Better yet, create a Facebook Event and get a head start on your head count with those RSVPs that are going to come rolling in via your Page. (See Chapter 7 for more information on setting up events within your Facebook Page.)

✔ **Adapt advertising campaigns to use for Facebook ads.** Just be sure to make the campaign more social and conversational in tone by creating short, attention-grabbing headlines and utilizing eye-catching pictures. Remember, you have a limited number of characters to use in a Facebook ad, so make every character count.

✔ **Sell products in the Facebook Marketplace.** This is the classifieds section of the Facebook Platform, and you can find it at `http://apps.facebook.com/marketplace`. Here you can post help wanted or services offered ads, as well as sell everything from collectibles to houses to vehicles. The best part about this is that it's a tab that you can easily add to your Facebook Page so that all your fans know exactly what you're selling on the Marketplace without having to go to the page and search.

✔ **Adapt promotions so that they have a social element and drive awareness of your brand.** Everyone likes free stuff, and people like to win contests. When your fans know you're running a promotion with a cool prize, they're more likely to not only enter the promotion but also refer their friends to your Page.

✔ **Compare research within Facebook to offline efforts.** Have you found that you have a better response rate to your Facebook marketing activities than, say, sending out a direct mailer? Did you find that you got more visits to your website because of something you posted on your Page than phone calls from prospective customers as a result of your mailers? Take some time to view both your online and offline marketing results to get a clear picture of what's working and what isn't. After you compile this information, you can focus more closely on what gets you the most results.

The following sections explain how to evaluate your media budget and take inventory of your content assets.

Deciding on a media budget

Believe it or not, the cost of the technology used for social network marketing is rather low. For example, a blog costs nothing to start, a podcast can cost up to $2,000, a wiki can cost up to $6,500 per year, and a video can cost up to $15,000. Your Facebook Page is free, but a private, branded app on Facebook can cost up to $100,000.

Unlike traditional media (print, TV, and radio) that can cost big money, social networks' upfront costs are very little. A blog or Facebook Page costs nothing to start, but the real (and potentially large) cost is creating a steady stream of rich content to fill these new media channels.

You can also use an online marketing budget calculator like the one at `http://digitalmarketingcalculator.com` to help you determine what percent of your marketing budget should be spent on online ads, social and search engine optimization (SEO).

We recommend dedicating up to 25 percent of your traditional media budget to nontraditional media. This gives you a healthy budget to experiment with for advertising, apps, and promotions, and for creating content to be successful in social networks like Facebook Pages.

Hiring an online writer

To create a steady stream of rich content that attracts the right audience, plan to have access to some additional, perhaps dedicated, writing resource for all your social content needs.

Social writing is a unique skill because the writing needs to be conversational. Headlines need to be provocative and entice the reader into wanting to know more. Above all, body copy needs to have a colloquial tone without a trace of sales- or marketingspeak.

We recommend hiring a separate writer for social network marketing content unless you happen to be one. Most people tend to think they can use the same writing resource for research papers, fact sheets, brochures, website copy, e-mail copy, and social content. This is a dangerous practice. Having someone who truly understands the medium can help tailor existing content, and writing new content helps to ensure that you always put your best foot forward. A great resource for finding web copywriters is `http://jobs.problogger.net`.

Part II
Building Your Facebook Presence

The 5th Wave   By Rich Tennant

"Jim and I do a lot of business together on Facebook. By the way, Jim, did you get the sales spreadsheet and little blue pony I sent you?"

In this part . . .

All marketers are looking for ways to put Facebook to work for their companies, small businesses, or clients. Part II shows you how to start a Facebook Page for your business, create tabs that engage your fan base, and promote your Page to get more likes. We also help you create a long-term content strategy for your business to develop more conversations and engage with potential customers.

Also in this part, you find out how to virally build your fan base throughout the Facebook platform, and we discuss how to use apps to add functionality to your Facebook Page.

Chapter 4

Getting Started with a Facebook Page

In This Chapter

▶ Introducing Facebook Pages for your business

▶ Creating and customizing your Facebook Page

▶ Getting the most from Facebook's marketing resources

▶ Understanding your business and Facebook's terms and conditions

*F*acebook Pages give your business a presence on Facebook where you can promote your products or services. Facebook Pages are the business equivalent of a Facebook member's profile. Members can like your Facebook Page, find out about specials and promotions, upload content (photos, videos, and links), and join other members in discussions through commenting. You can also add branded custom tabs with various features to engage customers, capture e-mail addresses, and even sell your products or services, such as the one offered by Fuddruckers, a restaurant chain. (See Figure 4-1.) You can post updates to your Page connections (users who like your page) to keep them engaged and informed. With all these features as well as exposure to thousands of potential customers, the Facebook Page has become a central tool in the marketing toolbox of thousands of brands.

In this chapter, you find out what Facebook Pages are all about and what that means for your business. We walk you through creating a Facebook Page and give you tips on how to set up your Page so that you convert more visitors into fans. We also help you understand how to make the most of Facebook marketing resources.

Figure 4-1:
Fuddruckers
enhanced
its brand
with a
custom tab
application.

Understanding the Differences between Pages, Profiles, and Groups

One of the most common mistakes businesses make when they start using Facebook is to use the wrong Facebook tool. Many start by creating a *Profile,* which is really intended for people to share personal information on Facebook. Or, they start by creating a *Group,* which is intended for people to connect with each other around very specific goals and interests.

Each of these Facebook tools serve a very different purpose:

- **Profiles:** Profiles represent people. They allow Facebook users to connect with friends, upload and share videos and photos, and store a user's activities over time. If you use Facebook for personal purposes, you are using a Profile.

- **Page:** Pages represent businesses, brands, nonprofits, public figures, and celebrities. They allow you to create awareness of your product or service within the Facebook community, engage with customers and products, and even sell your products or services.

- **Groups:** Groups allow people (Profiles) to organize around shared goals or topics of interest. People can join Groups — Pages can't.

Many businesses start with the wrong Facebook tool because they may be used to using a Profile and not know anything else, or they got no clear direction from Facebook or a marketing expert. Lucky for you that you're reading this book!

Profiles are personal, not business

Unlike Profiles (where the number of friends is limited to 5,000), Facebook doesn't limit the number of people who can like your Page. This makes sense because no human being could actually be friends with an unlimited number of people. A business, on the other hand, might suffer under such limitations. Your business can post updates to on your Page Wall at any time, without any concern of a limitation on the number of people you can reach. From your business's perspective, Page *connections* (users who like your page) are like e-mail subscribers, with Facebook providing the infrastructure for you to reach those subscribers via internal e-mail notifications, message updates, and Wall updates.

Here are four more key differences between a Facebook Page and a Facebook Profile:

- ✔ **Profiles don't have any marketing analytics.** Facebook Pages give marketers a powerful tool — Insights — that allows you to see how users engage with your Facebook Page.

- ✔ **Friending a Profile is very different from liking a Page.** When Facebook users send friend requests, they're essentially asking that user for access to her photos, her list of friends, her phone number, her relationship status, and other very personal information. Facebook Pages offer no functionality for marketers to unknowingly cross this social boundary (see Figure 4-2). Facebook users don't want to share this info with your organization. Asking a user to like your Page, on the other hand, doesn't cross any such boundary.

  Facebook now allows Profiles to activate a subscribe feature, allowing Facebook users to opt in to Public updates from that Profile. (Read more in Chapter 8 about engaging fans.)

- ✔ **Using a Facebook Profile to market your organization is a violation of the Facebook Terms and Conditions.** (www.facebook.com/terms.php). More specifically, Facebook forbids the use of Profiles to post "unauthorized commercial communications" or "use your personal profile for your own commercial gain."

  This means that even after you spend a lot of resources to build up a large amount of friends — say 5,000 — Facebook can simply delete your profile.

- ✔ **Facebook Profiles have bad search engine optimization (SEO).** The last key difference between Facebook Pages and Profiles is that Facebook Pages are public by default. This means that anyone can search and find your Page with the Facebook search engine and with Internet search engines (such as Google and Yahoo!), thereby helping your business gain visibility and broadening your audience beyond just Facebook.

Figure 4-2:
Facebook
Profiles
require
friend
requests
for access;
Facebook
Pages
require
users to like
the Page.

If you created a profile to market your business and want to switch to a Page, here's the good news: Facebook gives you the opportunity to convert your existing Profile into a Page. When you do so, your Profile picture will remain, and all your friends will become fans of the new Page.

When converting a Profile to a Page, though, all other information will be removed. So if you opt for this conversion, make sure you save any Wall updates, videos, photos, and other types of content onto your hard drive so that you can put those onto your new Page.

After you convert your profile to a Page, you can't revert back to a Profile.

To begin converting a Profile into a Page, go to `https://www.facebook.com/pages/create.php?migrate` and then follow the steps for creating a Facebook Page outlined later in this chapter. (See Figure 4-3.)

Figure 4-3:
Convert a
profile into
a Page.

Groups are for connection, not promotion

Another very common mistake businesses make is to create a Facebook Group to market their products or services. The problem with this is that Groups are intended for Facebook users to connect with each other — not to receive notifications about promotions or new products.

Last year, Facebook released some very interesting information about how people use Facebook Groups: Most Groups are very small, and are used as tools to communicate with people in real-life social circles. For example, an extended family can use Facebook Groups to more easily keep in touch with each other in a single location.

Now this isn't to say that businesses shouldn't use Groups. Marketing Profs, an online learning site for marketing, uses Groups to answer questions and keep in touch with students who have participated in its courses. Epic Change, a nonprofit organization, uses a private Facebook Group to prepare and manage online campaigns with top supporters (see Figure 4-4).

Figure 4-4:
Epic Change
uses private
Facebook
Groups to
organize
its top sup-
porters
who help
them launch
online
campaigns.

Groups are valuable, then, but here are three reasons why Facebook Groups aren't as good as Facebook Pages for your business:

✔ **Groups offer no capability to add custom applications.** One thing that people love about Facebook Pages is that you can add a lot of custom tabs to conduct polls, create photo contests, and collect e-mails, among other ways to keep prospects and customers connected. You can even add storefront e-commerce applications to a Facebook Page!

 ✔ **Facebook groups have very limited viral features.** When Facebook users join a Group, they're not necessarily interested in sharing their activities within that group with all their friends. When users post updates in Groups, they're not automatically shared on their Wall (like they are in Pages).

 ✔ **Facebook Groups have no hierarchy.** All members within a Facebook Group are generally seen as being equal players who all contribute to a common cause or interest. This is different from Facebook Pages where brands set the agenda for the Page. Because of this, the members — not a brand — should dictate what topics are discussed.

In Chapter 12, we go into more depth about Facebook Groups. For now, just know that they're not the best choice for marketing your business.

Creating a Facebook Page from Scratch

Here are the steps to create a Facebook Page. We recommend reading through all the steps before you begin.

1. **Go to** www.facebook.com/pages/create.php.

2. **Select the business type that best describes your business.**

   You can choose from six types of Facebook Pages (see Figure 4-5):

   • *Local Business:* Local Pages are meant for businesses that would benefit from a strong local market presence: a breakfast cafe, a pizza shop, or an advertising agency.

   • *Company, Organization, or Institution:* These Pages are meant for larger national businesses, which could include nonprofit organizations or large companies. Apple or Dell are good business-to-consumer examples; Avaya and Oracle are good business-to-business examples.

   • *Brand or Product:* These pages are meant for large brands. Think Starbucks and Coca-Cola.

   • *Artist, Band or Public Figure:* These Pages are good for politicians, artists, TV celebrities, or a musical group: for example, Jimmy Kimmel, Barack Obama, or Lady Gaga.

   • *Entertainment:* These Pages are meant for brands and companies in the entertainment industry, like Broadway shows and cable TV networks.

   • *Cause or Community:* Community Pages are intended for fans who like a topic or experience, and are owned collectively by the community connected to it. An example of a Community Page can be found at `https://www.facebook.com/pages/Hugging/115576608453665`. Because you want to have administrative control over your business presence on Facebook, we don't recommend using a Community Page as a primary way to market on Facebook.

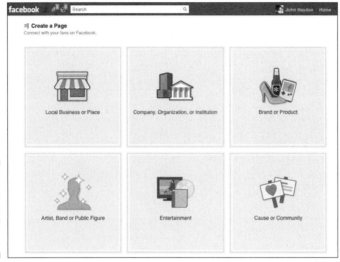

Figure 4-5: Facebook offers six types of Pages.

3. **Type your business name in the Company Name field to secure your organization's name on Facebook.**

   When you name your Page, it becomes permanent after you've acquired 100 fans, so make sure you choose a name that you want your fans and customers to associate with your business (see Figure 4-6). The name of your Page should communicate exactly what kind of business you are. If it doesn't, add a word or two to convey this.

4. **Select a category for your Page.**

   Depending upon the Page type you select (refer to Figure 4-5), you have a variety of choices regarding your Page category. Choose a category based on how your customers think about you rather than how you think about your business. For example, a Museum of Science has chosen "Museum" as its category even though its executive director might think of the museum as a nonprofit, which is another category choice.

   Although you can always change the category of your Facebook Page, try to get this right from the start.

Figure 4-6:
Select the
name and
category
of your
Facebook
Page.

5. **Select the check box below the name of the Page to accept the Facebook terms.**

   Selecting this check box certifies that you are the official representative of the business, organization, entity, or person that's the subject of the Facebook Page and that you have the necessary rights to create and maintain the Page (refer to Figure 4-6).

6. **Click the Get Started button.**

   Congratulations! You just created your Facebook Page. The next sections will show you how to upload a main image and add your business information.

Step 1: Uploading your profile photo

Your first step in creating a new Page is to upload a profile photo. A good way to start making your Page unique is to upload your company logo or a photo of your product. This picture represents your business on Facebook, so make it a good one. If you're a services company, you can have photos of happy people using your service.

You can upload photos in JPG, GIF, or PNG formats only. Pictures are resized to 180 pixels wide and 540 pixels high so to create a clear image, make sure your image is at least those dimensions. The maximum file size is 4MB.

To upload the first picture for your Page, follow these steps:

1. **Click the Upload an Image link on the Step 1 tab.**

   The Upload a Profile Picture dialog box appears. (See Figure 4-7.)

2. **Browse to the picture you're looking for and then click the Open button to start the upload process.**

Figure 4-7:
Uploading
your avatar
is as easy
as upload-
ing a photo
to any
website.

You can also import a photo directly from your website. To do this, just click the Import a Photo link, enter your website URL in the pop-up window (see Figure 4-8), and then click the Import button.

Figure 4-8:
Facebook
allows you
to import
an image
directly from
your
website.

A thumbnail version of your profile picture gets created automatically. It will be seen all over Facebook, so you want it to look its best. However, because the image is created automatically, your image won't always get placed correctly in the thumbnail.

Later (after you complete Step 3) you can scale your image so that it fits better within a thumbnail. For more on this, see the section, "Editing your Facebook Page's thumbnail," later in this chapter.

Step 2: Inviting fans

The second step in creating a brand-new Page is called Get Fans. This step allows you to invite your Facebook friends to become fans of your Page, and import your existing e-mail contacts to promote your Page. Because your Page really isn't ready for prime time yet, we recommend skipping this step. After you add applications, a custom welcome message, and configure the Wall settings, you'll be ready to promote your Page.

Step 3: Adding a description

The third step in creating your Page is to enter your website (which would be done already if you imported an image) and a short description of what your company does. (See Figure 4-9.) Fill out this description to the best of your ability for now. Later, in the section "Providing Information about Your Business with the Info Tab," we go over this and other information in greater detail.

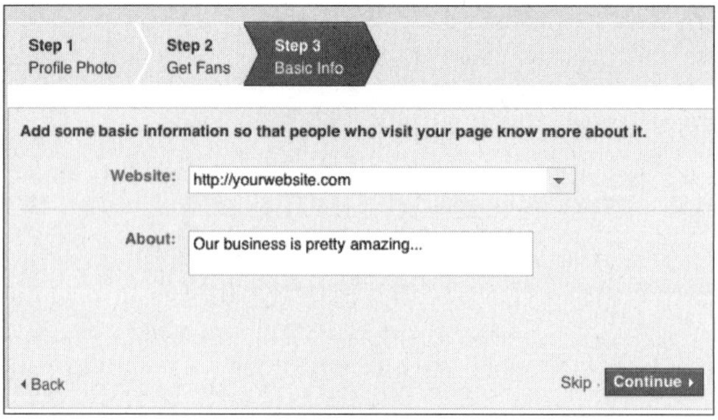

Figure 4-9:
List your website and add a short description of what your company or organization does.

Editing your Facebook Page's thumbnail

When you first create your Page, a thumbnail version of your profile picture is created automatically. This thumbnail image is important: It will be seen all over Facebook, so you want it to look its best. However, because the image is created automatically, your image won't always get placed correctly in the thumbnail. You can scale your image so that it fits better within a thumbnail simply by following these steps:

1. **Mouse over your Profile picture and click the Change Picture link.**

2. **On the next page, click the Edit Thumbnail button under your Profile picture and move the image to your liking in the pop-up window (see Figure 4-10).**

3. **When you have your thumbnail positioned to your liking, click Save.**

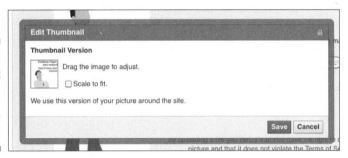

Figure 4-10:
You can edit the thumb-nail version of your avatar.

Limiting access to your Page until launch

Before you go live with your Page, you might want to consider limiting the access to admins only until you're ready to launch your Page.

You do this by clicking Edit Page on the top right and then selecting the Unpublish Page check box on the Manage Permissions tab (see Figure 4-11). Setting your Facebook Page to unpublished hides it from all users, including your customers and prospects. Only the administrators of the Page will be able to view it while it's unpublished. Your Page won't be visible to users until you change this setting back to published.

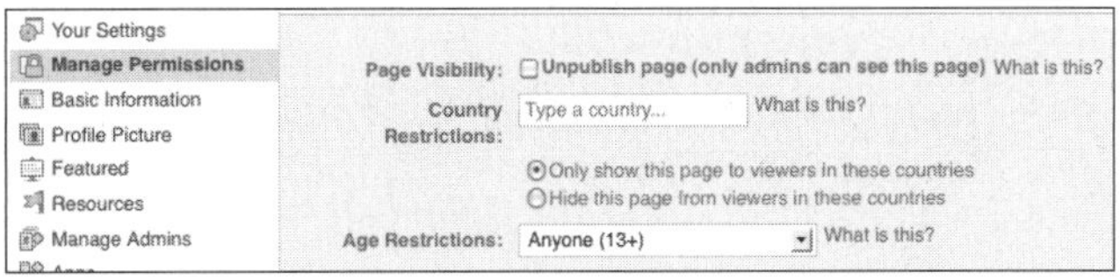

Figure 4-11:
You can keep your Page hidden from view by selecting Unpublish Page.

Providing Information about Your Business with the Info Tab

The Info tab contains detailed info about your business. Which individual details appear in these sections depends on which category and business type you chose when you created your Page. To add or edit information about your business, simply click on the Edit Page button on the top right of your Page and then select the Basic Information tab in the admin panel (as shown in Figure 4-12.)

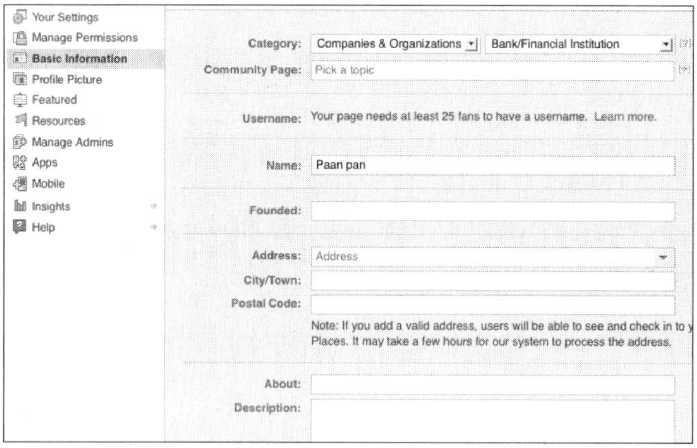

Figure 4-12:
You can edit your Info in the Basic Information section of your Page's admin panel.

Here's a general rundown of the various sections:

- ✔ **Basic Info:** Here you enter your basic contact information, such as a business address and phone number, as well as hours of operation. For example, for bands, this would include band member names and type of music.

- ✔ **Web site:** Add your website's URL.

- ✔ **Company Overview and Description:** Add your company's boilerplate text on who you are and what you do. Or, you can add content that is more social and less "corporate" to give your Page more personality.

- ✔ **Mission:** Add your mission statement. You don't have to enter one if you don't have one, or you can make up something provocative.

- ✔ **Products:** Add a listing of your products or services.

Be sure to click the Save Changes button when you're finished entering information on the Info tab.

Facebook Pages are public, and these fields can help you with the SEO of your Page. So, fill them with content that contains the keywords under which you wish to be found on a search engine.

Setting Page access allows you to restrict access to your Facebook Page by country: U.S., Canada, U.K., Australia, and several others. You can also restrict access by age: Anyone (13+); People Older Than 17, 18, 19, or 21; and Alcohol-Related (which represents the legal drinking age where the user resides). Restricting by age is something you may want to consider if you're a local bar or a tobacco brand.

To access your Page permission settings

1. **Click the Edit Page button on the top right of the Page.**

2. **Click the Manage Permissions tab on the left menu. (Refer to Figure 4-11.)**

3. **Select any of the following settings to restrict access to your Page:**

   • *Country Restrictions:* List the countries you want to restrict access to.

   • *Age Restrictions:* Make a selection if you want to restrict access to your Page based on the user's age.

   • *Wall Tab Shows:* Choose between All Posts or Only Posts by Page to determine which posts appear by default on the Wall. (See Figure 4-13.)

Figure 4-13:
Fans see posts by Page or all posts on the Wall depending on how you configure it.

   • *Default Landing Tab:* From the drop-down list, choose the tab a user will land on. (See Figure 4-14.)

   By default, this setting is set to Wall, but you can change it to any tab. This is a good way to test different landing pages to see which one is most effective.

Figure 4-14:
You can
also select
a default tab
as well as a
default Wall
view for
your Page.

• *Posting Ability:* Select these check boxes to allow anyone to post comments, photos, and videos to your Wall. You can also allow fans to tag other users in photos on your Page (see Figure 4-15).

Our advice is to allow as much interaction as you can with your fans, so be sure to select these check boxes. However, if you're in a heavily restricted industry and have a specific legal requirement to maintain control of your message, you might want to restrict your visitors' ability to contribute.

Figure 4-15:
You can
select a
variety of
ways to
allow fans
to engage
with your
Page's
content, and
post to your
Wall.

Posting Ability: ☑ Users can write or post content on the wall
☑ Users can add photos
☑ Users can add tags to photos by The Nonprofit Facebook Guy
☑ Users can add videos

4. **Click the Save Changes button.**

You can change these settings anytime.

Adding tabs to your Facebook Page

Facebook makes further customizing your Page through the use of tabs easy. *Tabs* are, in essence, additional pages that enhance your Facebook presence. Facebook provides some preset tabs that add additional functionality to your Page, including an Events tab, a Video tab, a Links tab, and a Notes tab.

To add one of these tabs to your page, follow these steps:

1. **Click the Edit Page icon at the top right of your Facebook Page.**

2. **In the admin panel of your Facebook Page, select Apps.**

3. **To add one of these apps to your page so that it shows up in your left sidebar, click Edit Settings and then click Add in the new pop-up window. (See Figure 4-16.)**

Figure 4-16: You can add or remove tabs on your Facebook Page.

Removing tabs from your Facebook Page

If you're not using an application on your Facebook Page, it's best to remove that tab from your Page's sidebar. You can do this easily by following the steps in the preceding section, and clicking Remove instead of Add in step 3.

Adding applications to your Facebook Page

In addition to applications that are included with your Facebook Page (photos, videos, notes, links), you can also select from thousands of free and premium applications on the market. These applications allow you to add further functionality to your Page, like promotions, videos, and e-commerce. One way to do this is to search Facebook for an application and add it to your Page by following these steps:

1. **Type the name of the application in the Facebook search bar at the top your screen.**

   If you don't have a specific application in mind, simply search for the type of application you're looking for. For example, type in the word *video* to search for video applications, select See More Results to see all of the results, and then filter by Apps on the left panel (as shown in Figure 4-17).

Figure 4-17:
Filtering
searches
by Apps.

2. **From the application profile Page, click Add to My Page in the left sidebar.**

3. **Click the Add to Page button next to your Page from the pop-up window (see Figure 4-18). If you're an admin for more than one Page, a pop-up window appears that lists all the Pages you administer.**

4. **Go to your page and configure the application. Each application will have a different process for configuring it. (For example, a video application might ask you to add video URLs and whether to display multiple videos in a grid layout or a single video.)**

Figure 4-18:
Adding an
applica-
tion to your
Facebook
Page from
an applica-
tion profile.

Editing the tabs on your Facebook Page

You can edit the tabs that appear in the left sidebar of your Facebook Page in several ways: Change the names of the tabs, delete tabs, or change their order. The following sections describe how to do each.

Changing the names of your Facebook page tabs

Whether you can change the name of a Facebook tab depends upon the application. For example, custom third-party tabs often allow you to change the name, but standard Facebook Page applications (such as photos, notes, and links) don't allow you to change their names.

To change the name of a Facebook page tab, click Edit Page on your Page to go to the admin panel. Then follow these instructions:

1. **Select the Apps link.**

2. **Click Edit Settings for the tab that you'd like to rename.**

3. **In the pop-up window, change or edit the name of the tab in the Custom Tab Name field (see Figure 4-19).**

4. **Click the Save button, and then the Okay button to close the window.**

Figure 4-19:
You can edit
the name
of many
custom
tabs and
third-party
applica-
tions.

Removing Facebook page tabs

There may be times when you want to remove tabs from your Facebook page. For example, you might decide to try out a third-party application to conduct a photo contest, but then find a better application for your purposes. Deleting these applications and tabs from your Facebook page is fairly simple:

Click the Edit Page button on your Facebook Page to go to the admin panel. Then follow these instructions:

1. **Select the Apps link.**

2. **Click the blue X to the right of the tab or application that you'd like to remove.**

3. **Click the Remove button in the confirmation pop-up window.**

After you delete applications from the back end of your Facebook page, the corresponding tab in your Page's sidebar will automatically disappear.

Changing the order of your Facebook page tabs

To change the order of your Facebook page tabs, simply click the Edit link below the list of tabs below your Profile image on your Facebook page, and then drag and drop them into the desired order (as shown in Figure 4-20).

The Wall, Info, and Friend activity tab cannot be reordered and are grayed out.

Figure 4-20: Reorder your Page tabs by dragging them.

> Wall
> Info
> Friend Activity
> Free Facebook Video T
> Latest Articles
> Questions
> Photos
> **DONE**
>
> **2,131**
> like this

Adding other administrators

Facebook Pages can include multiple administrators. We recommend adding other admins on the page for several reasons:

✔ Additional administrators can share the workload of managing Facebook Page.

✔ Having additional administrators on the Page helps ensure that comments will be replied to quickly. The last thing you want is to be left waiting for the only administrator of your Facebook Page to come back from vacation.

✔ Additional administrators can help promote your Facebook Page through their personal networks.

Adding admins to your Facebook Page takes just three steps:

1. **Go to your admin panel (by clicking the Edit Page button on your Page).**

2. **Select the Manage Admins tab, as shown in Figure 4-21.**

3. **Enter the e-mail address of the person whom you want to add as an admin. (If this person is your Facebook friend, simply enter her name.)**

   Admins have full control over your Page, so make sure you know this person very well!

Figure 4-21:
Adding
admin-
istrators
can make
managing
Facebook
Pages
easier.

Getting the Most from Facebook Marketing Resources

Probably the best resource on Facebook for marketers is the Facebook Marketing Solutions Page (`https://www.facebook.com/marketing`). This Page includes several useful tabs for marketers, including a Videos tab with great educational videos, an API Developers tab for API developers, and a Resources tab for average Joes like us. The Resources tab includes the following areas:

✔ **Educational Videos:** At the top of this Resources tab, you'll see the latest videos on using Facebook for marketing.

✔ **Facebook for Business:** This links to an Educational area for businesses with resources on using Facebook Pages, and using Facebook Social Plugins.

✔ **Webinar Center:** This links to an area where you can sign up for on-demand webinars on a variety of Facebook marketing topics.

✔ **Step-by-step Guides:** Throughout the Resources tab are links to downloadable PDF documents on a variety of topics, including marketing best practices, using Facebook ads, crisis response guidelines, and using Facebook Insights.

In addition to Facebook, you should check out other amazing websites, including the following:

✔ **Social Media Examiner:** This website helps businesses use social media tools like Facebook, Twitter, Google+, and LinkedIn to connect with customers, generate more brand awareness, and increase sales. The articles are written by Facebook marketing thought leaders like Mari Smith and Amy Porterfield. Go to `www.socialmediaexaminer.com`.

✔ **Inside Facebook:** Another amazing online resource for both Facebook developers and marketers. It publishes about two or three articles per day that are written by a variety of Facebook experts. Go to www.insidefacebook.com.

✔ **The Nonprofit Facebook Guy:** John Haydon publishes this website for small- and medium-sized nonprofits. Go to www.nonprofitfacebook guy.com.

Understanding Facebook's Terms and Conditions

If you're a business owner, one thing that you care about, in addition to marketing your business, is protecting your business. This is why you need to understand Facebook's terms and conditions, found at www.facebook.com/terms.php.

These terms and conditions set guidelines around some following areas:

✔ You are responsible for the content you post on Facebook. Any copyright violation or other legal consequences are your responsibility.

✔ Anyone younger than 13 cannot use Facebook.

✔ You cannot misrepresent your relationship with Facebook to other people.

✔ You cannot spam users on Facebook.

✔ Facebook reserves the right to delete any of your content, and even delete your account if you violate the terms of service.

You'll have nothing to worry about if you read the terms of service and practice common sense business ethics. If you do this already (which hopefully you do), then the terms and conditions should be of little concern, and you can focus your efforts on building your business with Facebook!

Chapter 5

Getting Noticed on Facebook with a Content Strategy

. . . .

In This Chapter

▶ Understanding how Facebook users filter content

▶ Posting with a purpose

▶ Developing a response strategy

. . . .

*I*n the new Facebook marketing paradigm, organizations are just waking up to the fact that in addition to the products and services they sell, information is one of their core offerings. And, in fact, information may just be the most important one. Facebook marketing starts with giving valuable and interesting information to your customers; it's a social media marketer's new currency.

This is why a content strategy is probably the most important strategy for marketing on Facebook. A *content strategy* consists of the plan, goals, and tactics you'll use to decide what content to post on your Page, when to post it, and how to measure its effectiveness.

In this chapter, we help you understand why content is important and how to create remarkable content.

Understanding How Content Marketing Works on Facebook

To understand marketing content on Facebook, you first must understand the News Feed. In Figure 5-1, you can see that Page stories are displayed on my home News Feed right where John logs in every day to connect with friends and businesses he likes.

Figure 5-1:
Facebook
users view
updates
from friends
and Pages
primarily in
their News
Feed.

When you publish content on a website, visitors have to go to that specific web page (a single location) to view that content. But when you publish an update (otherwise known as a "story") on a Facebook Page, fans won't view your story in a single, static location; they'll view it in their News Feed (as shown in Figure 5-2) — where it must compete with updates from other businesses (Facebook Pages) and from their friends. In fact, according to the comScore study (May, 2001) "Social Essentials," users are 40 to 150 times more likely to engage with content on News Feeds than to visit your actual Facebook Page.

Figure 5-2:
Content on
Facebook is
consumed
differently
than a
traditional
website.

To reinforce the fact that the News Feed is home base for Facebook users, the comScore study also shows that Facebook users do most of their content sharing on the News Feed: 27%, as shown in Figure 5-3.

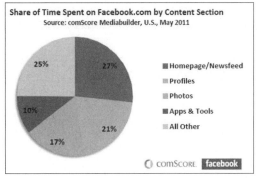

Figure 5-3: Users share content the News Feed 27 percent of their total time on Facebook.

Here are three reasons why Facebook users make their News Feed their homebase on Facebook:

- ✔ **The home page:** The News Feed is the first thing all Facebook users see when they log in.
- ✔ **Convenience:** In this one location, Facebook users can share content or catch up on updates from Pages they've liked, family connections, co-workers, and friends.
- ✔ **Filtering:** In their News Feed, Facebook users can choose to filter content by friend lists. For example, they can choose to only view stories from close friends. When they filter by Friends lists, they will still see stories about your Page that friends have created (by liking or commenting on posts, liking your Page, and so on.)

If you've been using Facebook for a while now, you've probably seen a lot of noise in your News Feed. By *noise*, we mean *sheer quantities of information not relevant to you.*

We all have the old high school friend (call her "Maria") who found us years later on Facebook and who now posts fire-hose barrages of pictures, videos, and comments about her latest crochet creations to our Facebook Page. Because we are nice people, we don't want to offend her by unfriending her. Instead, over time, we've learned to "tune out" Maria's Facebook updates.

The collective effect of such nuisances has been to create a society of people with advanced filtering abilities, people like your customers and prospects, who constantly fine-tune their abilities to scan web content for only the useful stuff. This means that instead of reading your 1,000-word article, your prospects will probably just

- ✔ Read the title.
- ✔ Scan any subheadings.
- ✔ See whether anyone has recommended your article.
- ✔ Scan the first paragraph.
- ✔ Scan the last paragraph.
- ✔ Look at the pictures.

How users filter content on Facebook includes these same strategies, but instead of viewing a single web page with a few related articles (that is, your website), they're scanning photos, videos, links, and status updates all having to do with unrelated topics. Plus there's the added pressure of all this content getting pushed further down in the News Feed with every passing moment. You can begin to see that being concise, relevant, and interesting are key success factors in getting the attention of customers and prospects on Facebook.

Filtering a News Feed

After a user logs into Facebook and views his News Feed, he can filter it down to specific types of content. As shown in Figure 5-4, Facebook users can choose to see only the content from specific friend lists or photos.

Figure 5-4: Facebook users can filter their News Feed by selecting specific lists of friends.

In addition to updates from their friends and Pages they've liked, Facebook users will also choose between viewing Highlighted Stories or Recent Stories as the default view at the top of their News Feed (see Figure 5-5).

Figure 5-5:
Facebook
users can
choose
Highlighted
Stories or
Recent
Stories as
the default
view for the
top of their
News Feed.

If a user chooses Highlighted Stories, Facebook pushes the most important content to the top of her News Feed. If she chooses Recent Stories, Facebook simply presents the most recent stories from Pages and friends.

Facebook also aggregates popular topics such as political news and popular movies within a single post. (See Figure 5-6.) This is Facebook's attempt at promoting "trending topics," which is something Twitter has done for years.

Figure 5-6:
Facebook
automati-
cally groups
posts on
popular top-
ics (such as
the SXSW
Festival)
into a single
post.

Understanding how EdgeRank affects visibility on Facebook

Just because someone becomes a fan of your page doesn't mean that she is seeing your Page content in her News Feed. This fact bears repeating:

Someone who becomes a fan of your page doesn't automatically see your Page content in her News Feed. For example, a sneaker company that attracts new fans in exchange for a 20% discount but fails to post updates that are interesting and engaging to fans will find a hard time nurturing and growing a vibrant fan base. Their Page updates will slowly disappear from their fans' News Feeds because of the Facebook EdgeRank algorithm.

EdgeRank is a value that Facebook uses to determine how content will rank within in a user's News Feed. Facebook hasn't publicly disclosed this formula used to derive this value. In general, though, updates with a low EdgeRank value will show up lower in a user's News Feed than updates with a higher value (if they show up at all), and updates with a high EdgeRank value may show up within a user's Highlighted News.

Three factors determine EdgeRank:

- How interesting is your Page's content? In other words, how many shares, likes, and comments has a specific Page story received?
- What kind of mix of types of engagement does your content get? For example, does the story have hundreds of likes but no comments?
- How recent and consistent are your updates?

From a marketing perspective, this means that you not only have to acquire fans, but you have to keep them interested — which isn't always easy.

Creating compelling content for your Facebook Page

Creating, aggregating, and distributing information via your Facebook Page helps build trust between you and your customers; however, if that information is off-topic or irrelevant, it can also weaken that trust. Providing relevancy is the key. For example, if you sell antiques, don't post links to blog posts about scrapbooking, even if that's a hobby of yours. And, of course, on Facebook, it's easy to find out what sorts of content your customers are looking for: You can always ask your customers directly about the types of content they want, so that you can make your Page more useful to them.

Keep in mind that creating relevant content that resonates with your audience is part science, part art:

- On the science side stands *Facebook Insights,* which is a set of metrics that quantifies how people interact with your content. If something works based on the response it receives, by all means, produce more content similar to it. (Facebook Insights is discussed at length in Chapter 9.)

✔ On the art side of the equation, your content strategy also requires an element of creativity. Even if you simply repurpose other people's content (such as by linking to articles or videos — see Figure 5-7), you must be artfully selective to determine what's worth sharing with your customers.

Figure 5-7: Link to relevant YouTube videos to share entertaining and valuable information.

Inbound Zombie - Social web strategies for non-profits and small businesses

_____ talks about why you need a Page instead of a Group.

Grandma Mary on Facebook Fanpage vs. Group for your Business
www.youtube.com
http://www.GrandmaMaryShow.com/ Find out whether you should create a Fanpage or a Group to promote your small or home business. Also find out exactly how you ...

2 seconds ago · Like · Comment · Share

Knowing your audience

Before you can deliver content relative to your customers' lives, you need to understand the psychographics and demographics of your audience. Who are these folks? What interests and motivates them? What can they learn from you that will make them more valuable to their organization?

Here are some questions to ponder when deciding whether your content is on-message and relevant to your audience:

✔ Does the content address your audience's questions, concerns, or needs?

✔ Does it inspire or entertain your intended audience?

✔ Does it help users complete a specific task?

✔ Will it help influence a decision?

✔ Does it motivate the user in some way?

✔ Does it bring your brand to life or add a positive spin in some way?

Read Chapter 2 on understanding your target audience for more on this topic.

Content and conversations can significantly contribute to making a *conversion* — getting a user to take a specific call to action, such as signing up for a newsletter or liking a Page.

Staying on-message

According to the traditional marketing model, from awareness and knowledge come desire and action. However, with Facebook, the rules have changed. Everyone and everything is connected, so any engagement you do through your Page doesn't go away. After you post something on your Page, fans may use your advice or they may pass the videos you uploaded on to others. Therefore, you have to maintain a common message, or theme, throughout all your updates to ensure that you always accomplish the goals you set out for yourself in your Facebook marketing plan, whether it's brand awareness or increasing sales.

An easy way to stay on message with your Facebook fans is to develop a posting calendar based on topics for each day of the week. For example, an auto repair shop can post based on the following schedule:

- ✔ **Monday:** Safe driving tips

    Get fans to share their tips as well.

- ✔ **Tuesday:** Do-it-yourself repair tips

    Tell fans to ask questions in the comments.

- ✔ **Wednesday:** Discounts and specials

- ✔ **Thursday:** Recommendations for day-trips for the weekend

    Get fans to share their favorite driving destinations as well.

- ✔ **Friday:** Show and tell

    Get fans to post pictures of their cool cars.

Publish content based on what the reader needs or wants, not what the company needs or wants.

Defining Your Posting Goals

People are drawn to Facebook content for various reasons. Some folks come for the discounts. Others consume and recommend (or *like*) content that informs or entertains them. And still others are attracted to more anecdotal or everyday life updates. One thing is for sure: Even within a group of like-minded individuals, people have differing opinions as to the kind of content they enjoy and share.

Compelling content doesn't magically appear, though. It requires planning, creativity, and an objective. Content without a goal doesn't help you sell more products, build awareness for your cause, or promote your brand.

Your content needs to align with the business goals of your organization. Some basic goals may include

- ✔ Driving traffic to your website
- ✔ Building your brand
- ✔ Improving customer service
- ✔ Generating leads
- ✔ Increasing ad revenue
- ✔ Adding e-commerce to your online marketing efforts

If your content strategy includes incentives — such as coupons, giveaways, and promotions — you need to translate that into a very clear and straightforward call to action (or goal). You may have several converging goals behind your posts, such as to let people know about an event as well as provide an incentive for those who RSVP to attend.

The following section examines some motivational goals to consider when you publish content to your Facebook Page.

Getting Fans Engaged

Engagement is the name of the game on Facebook. By *engagement,* we mean to solicit a response or action by your fans. This engagement from your fans could be commenting on a post, liking something, contributing to a discussion topic, or posting photos and videos. You want fans to interact with your Page for several reasons:

- ✔ You can build a relationship with fans through dialog and discussion.
- ✔ The more activity generated on your Page, the more stories are published to your fans' News Feeds, which drives more awareness to the original action and creates a viral marketing effect.

How do you get your fans to engage with your Page? That all depends on your audience and the subject matter of your Page. Here are some helpful hints to encourage fan engagement through your content:

- ✔ **Show your human side.** All work and no play makes for a very dull Page. People like to share the more human side of life. For example, many people take part in "take your child to work day" or even "take your dog to work day." If you participate in one of these, post a picture of your child or pet, and then add a note that they're doing a great job at helping Mom or Dad at work. Ask your fans whether anyone else takes advantage of this opportunity, and encourage them to post pictures as well.

✔ **Ask your fans what they think.** In the Facebook paradigm, Page admins actively solicit feedback from those connected to their Page. Be direct and ask fans what they think of your organization, new product, or position on a topic. For example, the Brain Aneurysm Foundation regularly asks its fans to share their personal experiences with the condition, as shown in Figure 5-8.

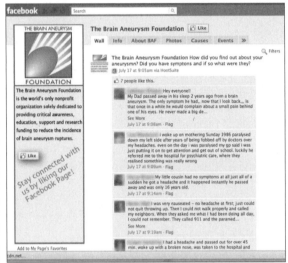

Figure 5-8:
The Brain Aneurysm Foundation asks fans about their personal experiences.

✔ **Tell your fans how much you appreciate them.** Don't underestimate the goodwill to be gained by saying thanks. Thanking your fans for their questions or complimenting them on their comments can go a long way in social media circles. The clothing retailer Lands' End is known for its exceptional customer service, and its fans aren't afraid to tell everyone about it! Lands' End participated in National Customer Service Week, and the fan response was incredible. As shown in Figure 5-9, Lands' End thanked its fans for the response.

✔ **Highlight a success story.** Another tactic that appeals to vanity is to highlight a peer's success. She'll be sure to thank you for the attention. Your other fans will appreciate hearing about one of their own making good. Many companies on Facebook run a Fan of the Month promotion and foster engagement by soliciting entries.

✔ **Share your tips and insights.** People are always looking for information that helps them do their jobs better. Don't underestimate your knowledge and what you have to share that's valuable. Sharing helpful tips is some of the best engagement around. Technology blog Mashable does a great job at providing a steady stream of tips to its Facebook fans, as shown in Figure 5-10.

Figure 5-9:
Clothing
retailer
Lands' End
thanked
fans for
their kind
words as it
celebrated
National
Customer
Service
Week.

Figure 5-10:
Mashable
updates its
fans with
a steady
stream of
tech tips.

✔ **Provide links to relevant articles and research.** You don't have to be a prolific writer to be valuable to your fans. By posting links to relevant articles, videos, resources, and research, you build your credibility as a content aggregator.

✔ **Ask your fans what they think of something and test their knowledge using quizzes and polls.** Again, appealing to the ego factor, quizzes and polls are popular tactics on Facebook. Mentos, the popular chewy fruit candy, regularly creates lighthearted polls using the popular Facebook Poll Daddy Polls app. One of these polls was titled, "In the Fruit Pack of Mentos, Which Flavor Do You Save for Last?" This poll served the double purpose of allowing Mentos fans to share their opinions while also showing the company whether one flavor was preferred. Its marketing team can then use this information to better target future Mentos Page content and promotions.

For more on engagement, see Chapter 8.

Chapter 6

Enhancing Your Facebook Page with Applications

In This Chapter

▶ Introducing Facebook applications

▶ Finding applications

▶ Adding applications to your Facebook Page

*F*acebook applications (apps) have become powerful tools for marketers. When you install them on your Facebook Page, they can serve a variety of functions, and they really add some sizzle to your business's Facebook presence.

Facebook now has more 7 million apps and websites integrated with its Platform, most of which were created by individuals and third-party companies. And every month, more than 500 million people use an app on Facebook or experience the Facebook Platform on other websites. If you've ever entered a contest on Facebook or signed a petition, you've used a Facebook app.

There are hundreds, if not thousands, of Facebook Page apps designed to add specific functionality to your Page. Whether you want to add a slide presentation via the SlideShare app, or post content from a blog that you write or admire via the NetworkedBlogs app, apps can help you customize your Facebook Page.

Apps are also becoming an important advertising and branding vehicle tool within Facebook. Brands like Fuddruckers have developed apps that can be used by any of their franchisees (see Figure 6-1). Facebook has developed a platform for apps that's easy to use, so more and more types of industries can leverage Facebook for their businesses.

This chapter introduces you to the world of Facebook apps, shows you how to find useful applications, and how to add them to your Facebook Page.

Figure 6-1:
Fuddruckers
enhanced
its brand
with a
custom tab
application.

Understanding Facebook Applications

Facebook apps are just software modules you can install on your Facebook Page that add a unique functionality to further engage your audience with your brand.

Often this added functionality is displayed and contained within a separate tab on your Facebook Page. For example, in Figure 6-2, the Hyundai Facebook Page has a Shopping Tools tab, which is obviously a nonstandard tab — one that is not included when you create your Facebook Page. (For more on tabs, see the upcoming section, "Using Third-party Custom Facebook Page Tab Services.")

Figure 6-2:
Hyundai
enhanced
its Facebook
Page with
a Shopping
Tools tab.

Apps can take on many different forms, from video players to business cards to promotions. Facebook offers countless apps for marketers that provide business solutions and promote the business enterprise.

Some apps are designed to help you promote your website or blog, stream a live video conference, or show customized directions to your office. Also, third-party developers are licensing and selling apps focused on the business market, including promotional apps from Wildfire Interactive, lead-generation apps from Involver, customer-service apps from Parature, and apps that encourage user participation from Buddy Media and TabSite.

Here are a few examples of some apps that can add useful marketing functionality to your Facebook Page:

- **YouTube Video app:** If your company has sales videos, messages from the CEO, or product demonstration videos posted to YouTube, add them to your Page for all to see. One of the best applications for this is Involver's "YouTube for Pages" app. (See Figure 6-3.)

- **NetworkedBlogs app:** Promote your latest blog posts (or those from any blog) on a custom tab within your Facebook Page, which also publishes posts to your News Feed. In Figure 6-4, you can see that John's latest posts are displayed on the Inbound Zombie Facebook Page.

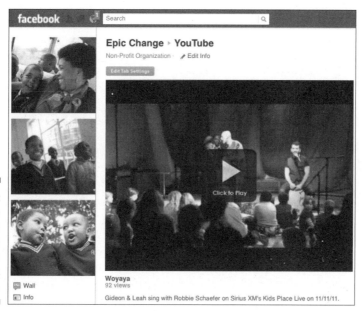

Figure 6-3:
The YouTube app on the Epic Change Facebook Page.

Figure 6-4:
The
Networked
Blogs app
appears on
the Inbound
Zombie
Page.

✔ **Sweepstakes applet:** This app helps Page admins create and manage a sweepstakes. From creating the sweepstakes template to reviewing entries, GOSO's Sweepstakes applet makes sweepstakes management a breeze. Visit www.goso.com/applets for more info.

✔ **Woobox coupons:** This application allows marketers to offer fan-only coupons on a Facebook Page, and even require the user to Like multiple Facebook pages before being issued a coupon. Visit http://woobox.com/vouchers for more info. See Figure 6-5.

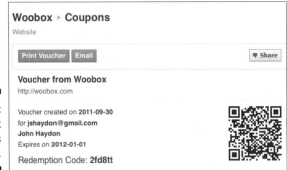

Figure 6-5:
Woobox
Coupons
app.

✔ **Woobox Group Deals:** Woobox also offers an excellent Groupon-style application for Pages, and even automatically generates a coupon code for your shopping cart. Visit http://woobox.com/groupdeals for more info.

✔ **Reveal tabs:** Reveal tabs, or *"like-gates,"* are tabs that allow admins to hide content from nonfans, and then when they Like the page, the content is revealed. Content that's revealed could be anything from articles, to coupons, to premium videos. These applications are usually a basic component of most third-party application vendors.

Many Facebook marketers rely on apps to make their Facebook presence stand out from the competition and to add engaging elements with which their fans can interact. (You can find more examples in the upcoming section, "Choosing E-Commerce Applications for Your Page.")

As we say in Chapter 3, you should clearly define the goals of your Facebook Page before investing time and money in additional applications. For example, a nonprofit with the goal of raising money via its Facebook Page should focus on adding an app that supports that goal. Or a museum with the goal of engaging fans around its current art exhibits should consider a Facebook Page app that allows it to post photos of its most popular artwork that Facebook users can discuss.

Also, a word of caution about adding too many applications: If you're like most people, you want to add the latest fancy app to your Facebook Page. You add one, and then another, and before you know it, your Page looks like downtown Tokyo!

Two more thoughts about adding apps:

✔ **Less can be more.** Too many apps could drive away visitors who get blinded or confused by an abundance of shiny objects.

If visitors don't know what to do, they'll leave.

✔ **Nothing is permanent.** The good news about Facebook apps is that you can try them out for free (even most premium apps have free trial periods), and remove them if they don't work for your goals.

Yeah, There's an App for That — but Where?

When searching for an app, you need go no further than Facebook itself. Search Facebook, peruse Facebook Groups, or search AppBistro.

Here's how insanely easy is it to search Facebook for an application and add it to your Page:

1. **Type the name of the application in the Facebook search bar at the top of your screen.**

   If you don't have a specific application in mind, simply search for the type of application are looking for. For example, type **video** to search for video applications.

   A list of potential matches appears.

   Once you find the application, click on the link and go to the application profile page.

2. **From the application profile Page, click Add to My Page in the left sidebar.**

3. **Click the Add to Page button next to your Page within the pop-up window (see Figure 6-6). If you admin more than one page you will see them all in this pop-up window.**

   Go to your page and configure the application. Of course, each application will have a different process.

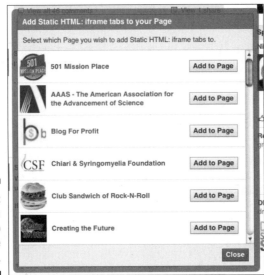

Figure 6-6:
Adding a useful app to your Page is easy.

A few active Groups on Facebook are aimed specifically for marketers seeking to understand how to use Facebook Pages. One Group we like is Facebook Fan Page Owners (www.facebook.com/groups/pageowners). You can use the Group's search function to search for conversations about useful Facebook Page applications (see Figure 6-7).

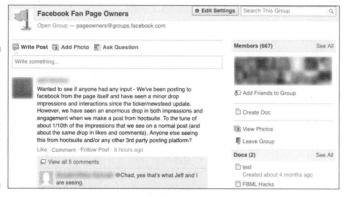

Figure 6-7:
Facebook
Groups
are often
a great
resource for
app recom-
mendations.

Appbistro (`http://appbistro.com`) is an online marketplace for Facebook Page applications. The applications are rated and reviewed by app users and the Appbistro staff. The site includes previews and installation instructions. Some of these apps are free, and some are paid. (See Figure 6-8.)

Figure 6-8:
Business-
focused
apps
directory
Appbistro
offers third-
party apps
to help cus-
tomize your
Facebook
Page.

Using Third-party Custom Facebook Page Tab Services

Over the past few years, hundreds of companies have appeared that offer online services to create custom Facebook tabs. Many of these companies include a lot of marketing tools, like the ones mentioned earlier, which can be added to a custom tab.

Online custom tab services like FanPageEngine (http://fanpageengine.com) and Pagemodo (www.pagemodo.com) typically offer a tool or wizard that you can use to create custom Facebook tabs without requiring you to know HTML or other complicated web technologies. The price range of these services can range anywhere from $5 to more than $250 per month, depending on how many Facebook fans you have, which apps you want to use, or other factors.

Some of the more popular services include

- ✔ **FanPageEngine:** This service allows you to easily create Facebook custom tabs with a drag-and-drop wizard. You can add pictures, video, HTML, and create a reveal tab. Find out more at http://fanpageengine.com.

- ✔ **ShortStack:** This service allows you to create custom tabs with contests, sweepstakes, videos, pictures, HTML, and slideshow widgets. You can also set the visibility of tabs and sections within tabs to be seen by fans, nonfans, and even admins. Find out more at www.shortstack.com.

- ✔ **Pagemodo:** With its really good and professional templates, this tool makes it very easy for users to create great-looking custom tabs quickly and easily. Find out more at www.pagemodo.com.

- ✔ **TabSite:** TabSite allows you to create custom tabs with a drag-and-drop wizard, and offers a wide variety of widgets like an RSS widget, a Google Maps widget, and an e-mail opt-in form. Find out more at www.tabsite.com.

All these solutions range in price from free to $300 per month, depending upon variables like the number of fans, the number of apps you want to add to your page, and the complexity of features. The most important thing when deciding on which company to use is the functionality it offers, and the designs. All have a gallery and a list of clients.

Choosing E-Commerce Applications for Your Page

Brands are beginning to realize that in addition to being a powerful marketing platform, Facebook also offers a huge opportunity to make money directly from the Facebook users by using e-commerce applications. Plus, using an e-commerce app on your Page allows you to easily measure your return on investment.

Here are a few of the more popular Facebook e-commerce applications:

✔ **Ecwid:** This is a free shopping cart for both Facebook Pages and websites. Ecwid currently has more than 100,000 sellers, and provides a single web-based interface to manage multiple shopping carts. Learn more at `www.ecwid.com`.

✔ **Payvment:** This Facebook e-commerce solution brings together sellers and shoppers in a Facebook shopping mall marketplace. (See Figure 6-9.) The app has an admin area in the back end of your Facebook Page so you can manage your storefront tab, products, and sales. Payvment has more than 1 million Facebook users. Learn more at `www.payvment.com`.

Figure 6-9:
The Payvment shopping mall on Facebook.

✔ **ShopTab:** This e-commerce Facebook application is easy to use for both Page admins and customers. The app directs customers from Facebook to your website so you don't have to pay extra shipping fees or taxes. They also have an app for nonprofits that allows for multiple levels of donations. Learn more at `www.shoptab.net`.

✔ **VendorShop:** This is a free shopping cart app that admins can set up directly on their Facebook Page. A PayPal checkout service is used for payments, and you can offer fan-only discounts. Learn more at `www.vendorshopsocial.com`.

✔ **FundRazr:** This e-commerce app allows nonprofits, school teams, and other organizations to collect donations on a Facebook Page. (See Figure 6-10.) You can also sell tickets for events, manage customers, and allow fans to share campaigns with their friends. Learn more at `http://fundrazr.com`.

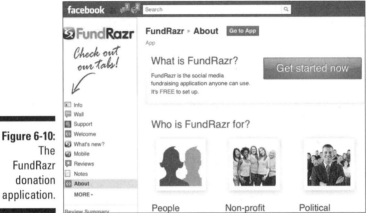

Figure 6-10:
The
FundRazr
donation
application.

Granting Access to Applications

Third-party apps are required by Facebook to ask users for permission to their e-mail, News Feed, or other important information.

If you have more than one Page, the Request for Permission page lists the various Pages and asks you to specify the Page on which you want to install the app (see Figure 6-11).

Figure 6-11:
Third-party
apps are
required
to ask
Facebook
users for
permission.

If you don't want to grant the app access to your information, click the Don't Allow button. However, you can't use an app for which you haven't approved permissions.

After you click Allow and select the Page where you want the app installed, you will then be prompted to follow additional installation instructions specific to that application.

Configuring Application Tabs on Your Facebook Page

There are several ways that you can edit the application tabs on the left sidebar of your Facebook Page. You can change the tab names, delete tabs, and change the order of your tabs.

Changing tab names

Okay, maybe not. Whether you can actually change the name of a Facebook tab depends upon the application. For example, custom third-party tabs often include the capability to change the name, but standard Facebook Page applications — like Photos, Notes, and Links — don't.

To change the name of your Facebook Page tabs

1. **Click Edit Page on your Page to go to the admin panel.**

2. **Select the Apps tab.**

3. **Click Edit Settings for the tab that you'd like to rename.**

4. **In the pop-up window, change or edit the name of the tab in the Custom Tab Name field (see Figure 6-12).**

5. **Click Save, and then Okay to close the window.**

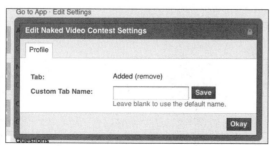

Figure 6-12: You can edit the name of many custom tabs and third-party applications.

Removing an app from your Facebook Page

If you want to delete an app from your Page, follow these steps:

1. **On your Page, click the Edit Page link.**

2. **On the next page that appears, click the Apps tab on the left.**

3. **In the Added Apps section on the right, find the application that you want to delete and then click the X button to the right of the app, as shown in Figure 6-13.**

Figure 6-13:
Click the X button to remove an application.

x buttons

Facebook displays a dialog box asking whether you're sure you want to remove the app.

4. **Click the Remove button in the bottom of the pop-up window to delete the app.**

You can't remove some Facebook apps, such as Video, Notes, or Photos, from your Page. These core apps are instrumental to the Facebook experience, and Facebook developed them internally.

Changing the order of tabs

You can also delete or change the order of tabs right under your Page's main image by clicking on Edit below the sidebar links. After clicking Edit, you can delete a tab just by clicking the X to the right of a tab. You can also move tabs by dragging them into the desired order.

Creating Custom Facebook Tabs with HTML

If you're well versed in web technology and want to design your own custom tabs from scratch, you can do so through either of these two methods:

✔ Use the Static HTML: iframe tabs application.

✔ Pull a custom webpage through an iframes application and add it to your Page.

The next two sections describe these in more detail.

Creating a custom Facebook tab with the Static HTML: iframes tab application

If you know even basic HTML, creating a custom tab is easy with the Static HTML: iframes tab application (`www.facebook.com/apps/application.php?api_key=190322544333196`). This application allows you to add a custom tab to your Facebook Page by entering HTML directly into the application after it's added to your Page (as shown in Figure 6-14). To do this, from the application profile click on the Add to My Page link in the left sidebar, and then, in the resulting pop-up window, click the Add To Page button next to the Facebook Page to which you want to add the app.

Figure 6-14: A custom tab using the Static HTML: iframes tabs app.

Custom tab

Creating a hosted custom Facebook tab

The second way to create your own custom tab is to pull a hosted webpage into an iframes app and add it to your Facebook Page. Here are the steps to add a custom iframes tab to your Facebook Page.

Adding a self-hosted custom Facebook app to your Facebook Page requires a significant amount of knowledge of PHP, HTML, and Facebook's Developer tools. We recommend that you find someone to help you if you don't know how to do this.

1. **Create an HTML or PHP file and upload it to your web server. Make sure that the width of this web page doesn't exceed 520 pixels. A Facebook iframe app will display this webpage as a tab in your Facebook Page.**

2. **Go to the Facebook Developer's site (**`http://developers.facebook.com`**), create an account if you don't have one yet, and then click Apps at the top.**

3. **Select Create New App in the upper right.**

4. **Fill in the App Display Name field (shown in Figure 6-15) with the name of your application.**

   This is a unique name for the application you are creating. Because only you will see this info, you can simply use the name of your custom tab.

   Leave the App Namespace field blank for now. (You can always fill it in later.)

5. **Click Continue.**

Figure 6-15:
The first
step in
creating a
Facebook
app is to
name it.

> **New App**
>
> App Display Name: [?]
>
> App Namespace: [?] You can update this later
>
> ☐ I agree to the Platform Privacy Policy.
>
> Please note that your app name cannot contain Facebook trademarks or have a name that can be confused with an app built by Facebook.
>
> Continue   Cancel

6. **Fill in the captcha on the next screen and then click Submit.**

7. **On the next page (shown in Figure 6-16), fill in the App Namespace so that you can edit the app from the Apps area of your Facebook Page.**

8. **Click App on Facebook (in the menu at the bottom of this page).**

   Two fields — Canvas URL and Secure Canvas URL — appear, as shown in Figure 6-17.

9. **In the Canvas URL field, enter the URL to the directory for the web page you created in Step 1.**

If the web page is in a folder called MyFacebookApp, the URL for the directory will be

```
yourdomain.com/myfacebookapp/
```

Do not include the name of your web page in the URL (that's next).

Figure 6-16:
Add an App
Namespace
to your
application.

Figure 6-17:
Complete
the Canvas
URL fields.

10. **In the Secure Canvas URL, enter the Secure URL for the web page you created in Step 1.**

11. **Click the Page Tab tab link at the bottom of this page (as shown in Figure 6-18).**

12. **In the Page Tab Name field, enter the name of your Facebook Page tab.**

    This will be the tab name seen by Facebook users.

Figure 6-18:
Enter the
name of
your tab and
page URLs.

Page Tab	
Page Tab Name: [?]	
Page Tab URL: [?]	
Secure Page Tab URL: [?]	
Page Tab Edit URL: [?]	
	Save Changes

13. **In the Page Tab URL, enter the full URL for the web page you created in Step 1.**

    For example

    ```
    yourdomain.com/myfacebookapp/CoolPageTab.html
    ```

14. **In the Secure Page Tab URL, enter the Secure URL for the web page you created in Step 1.**

15. **Click Save Changes.**

16. **Under Related Links (the left side of your application Page), click View App Profile Page.**

17. **At the application profile page, add the application to your Facebook Page by following the same instructions outlined for adding the Static HTML: iframes tab application to your Page (earlier in this chapter).**

18. **Edit your app settings in the Apps section of the admin panel of your Facebook Page, as described in Chapter 4.**

To change the content on this tab, you need to edit the web page you created on your server.

Part III

Engaging with Your Customers and Prospects on Facebook

The 5th Wave   By Rich Tennant

"I know Facebook is great and you want to be a part of it. But you're my mom - you <u>can't</u> be my 'friend.'"

In this part . . .

Part III discusses strategies for going public with your
Page, promoting it, engaging fans, and measuring your
campaign's success on Facebook. You discover how to
optimize content for your specific fan base, promote your
page, and target your ads to a very specific audience — and
then create and test those ads to ensure their success. We
explore the Facebook tools that help you measure and optimize your advertising campaign and then obtain insight
into your customers from their interactions with your Page.

Chapter 7

Going Public with Your Facebook Page

In This Chapter

▶ Making sure your Page is ready for prime time

▶ Making your Facebook Page easy to find

▶ Getting fans fast through your existing friend network

▶ Using e-mail marketing, webinars, and Sponsored Story ads

*A*fter you've created a Facebook Page that you're happy with, it's time to begin promoting your Page. The power of using a Facebook Page for marketing exists in Facebook's social graph — the interconnection of people and the things they like. But at this point, you have zero presence on Facebook, which means you're starting off from a standing start.

In this chapter, we show you how to use existing marketing assets like direct mail, e-mail lists, and your website to give you that initial push you need to send your Page off into the Facebook stratosphere. You'll learn why it's important to create awesome content that is optimized for Facebook users, and why you need to create unique content for your Page. You'll also learn strategies like using incentives and hidden content (content accessible only by fans) to increase fan conversions. Finally, you'll learn how to use other channels like blogs and YouTube to promote your brand new Facebook Page.

Mapping a Launch Strategy for Your Facebook Page

Many marketers refer to the initial stage of a promotion as a *launch,* whether it's a book, the newest model of a car, or an event. A launch might include a widely covered announcement of a highly anticipated product, like the latest iPhone, or a launch could be free samples to promote the opening of a local restaurant. But in all cases, a launch is the beginning — the birth.

Launch is an appropriate word when you think about it, and launching a Facebook Page is very similar to launching a rocket ship in that they share the same basic stages:

- ✔ **Preparation:** Like a rocket ship, a Facebook Page requires a strategy to steer its course. It also needs a main image, applications, and a welcome tab that provides function and features for Facebook users.

- ✔ **Countdown:** You should set goals for your Page and have a deadline in mind for when you want to launch your Page. This essentially forces you to prepare and get everything lined up for success.

- ✔ **Initial thrust:** Starting with zero Facebook fans is like being a rocket ship that has to fight gravity by thrusting up away from the earth. This is where you might use assets like a huge e-mail list, or an announcement at a conference of a special "attendees -only" promotion on your Page. Throughout this chapter, we show you several strategies for leveraging existing marketing assets.

- ✔ **Second-stage thrust:** After you've acquired a fair amount of Facebook Page fans and have achieved a healthy amount of engagement on the Page, you can fire off a second round of thrusters. This includes things like using Facebook-sponsored ads to leverage your fans' social graph, or conducting a cross-promotional campaign with another Facebook Page.

- ✔ **Orbit:** At this stage, you're no longer fighting a gravitational force. Instead, you're slightly ahead of a tipping point. What's critical at this stage is the ability to navigate and continuously refresh your attitude and creativity so that fans stay interested.

Creating Enchantment on Your Facebook Page

The first step in creating a Facebook presence is to create an identity in the form of a Page. You want to carefully follow all the recommendations for creating a Facebook Page that we outline in Chapter 4, plus have a well-planned content strategy. In other words, you want to create enchantment with your Facebook Page so that fans are naturally inspired to share your Page with others.

The Brain Aneurysm Foundation (www.facebook.com/bafound) has an application on its Facebook Page that allows Facebook users to upload a photo of a loved one to a "Memorial" gallery or a "Survivor" gallery and then share their photos with friends. (See Figure 7-1.) This campaign has boosted fan engagement and has also driven more traffic to its website.

Figure 7-1:
The Brain
Aneurysm
Foundation
engages
Facebook
users with a
photo
application.

Here are a few questions you should consider to help set your Facebook Page apart from your other marketing channels:

✔ How can you bring your business's unique voice to life in a compelling and personal way?

✔ In what specific ways do your current customers like to connect with your business? What content do they find useful, valuable, or interesting?

✔ In addition to building awareness for your business, how important is it for you to use Facebook to drive sales?

The clearer you are about the answers to these questions, the clearer your brand messaging will be to Facebook users.

Making Sure Your Page Is Ready

Before you launch your Page, you want to make sure that it's ready to make a good first impression, which is often the only impression you get a chance to make. We recommend that you review Chapter 4 to make sure that you have include the following on your Page:

✔ **Pick a good name for your Page.** You can boost your search engine rankings by choosing a Page title that includes your brand.

✔ **Display an attractive avatar or main image that reflects your brand.**

✔ **Set a custom welcome tab as your default tab.** Remember, having a custom welcome tab greatly increases your fan conversion rates.

✔ **Remove any tabs you're not using.**

✔ **Create a short URL at** `http://facebook.com/username.`

✔ **Add a few posts to your Page.** That gives new fans something to engage with once they arrive.

Adding Content to Your Page before Launch

Before you do an initial promotion of your Facebook Page, you have to seed it with photos, videos, and links that new fans can comment on and Like. Again, when fans engage with your Page stories, their friends see that activity. This is a fundamental way that awareness about your business will slowly (but surely) penetrate the vast network of Facebook users.

Two charts within the Insights application show the relationship between engagement on your Page updates and how that engagement is seen by their friends. The Talking about This graph (on the left in Figure 7-2) shows the number of Facebook users engaging with your Page, and the Viral Reach graph (on the right) shows how their friends see that engagement.

Figure 7-2:
You can clearly see how friends of fans engaging with your Page content can see that content.

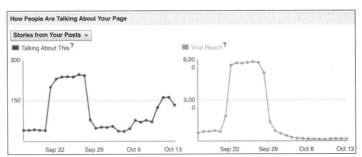

Adding photos

Facebook allows you to upload an unlimited number of albums and up to 200 photos per album to your Facebook Page. You can reorder photos, rotate them, and acknowledge Facebook members by *tagging* (identifying) them in the photo. We explain how to tag a photo later in the "Tagging photos to promote your Facebook Page" section.

To upload a photo, follow these steps:

1. **Click the Photo link at the top of your page.**

2. **Click the Create an Album button.**

   Facebook prompts you to select the images you want to upload and then allows you to name the album and enter the location where the photos were taken, as shown in Figure 7-3.

   Use images and photos that communicate who you are and what your business is about, and that inject personality into your Page. Be sure you select photos you want potential customers to see, not the holiday party where everyone had a few too many cocktails!

3. **Click the Create Album button.**

   Here you can add captions to the photos, tag people in them, organize your album, change the album's details (including the name and location), and delete the album altogether.

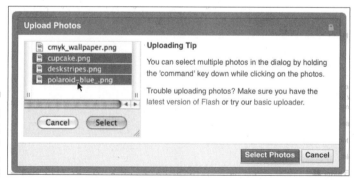

Figure 7-3:
Uploading
new photos
for a Page.

You can take a photo with a camera and immediately upload it to Facebook if you have that camera attached to your computer or you're using a smartphone equipped with a camera.

Adding videos

You can add a video to Facebook just as easily as you can add a photo (which we discuss in the preceding section). You can either upload or record a video — we tell you how to do both in this section. Adding videos is a great way to, for example, introduce yourself and your employees through short interviews or footage from your most recent company party or trade show. Again, be sure that anything shown on the video shows your company in a positive light!

You can add a video to your Wall by uploading one from your hard drive, a CD, or another storage device. All video must be less than 1,024MB and shorter than 20 minutes. You also need to agree to the Facebook Terms of Service, which stipulate that you own the videos you're placing on Facebook.

Publishing a video as you're recording it requires that you have a webcam attached to your computer or a smartphone from which to record and upload the video. Many computers have a built-in webcam, but don't despair if you don't have one. You can easily connect a webcam to your computer by using the provided cables.

To upload an existing video file to your Page, follow these steps:

1. **Click the video camera icon underneath the status update box.**

   If you don't already have a Video tab visible on your Page, click the double-arrow sign (>>) at the right end of the tab bar, and then click Video in the list that appears.

2. **Click the Upload button and then browse your hard drive to find the video file that you want to upload.**

   While the file uploads, you can tag people as well as add a title and description.

3. **Click the Save Info button.**

   As the video uploads, you get a message that it's processing, and you're given the option to be notified when it's done. At this point, you can edit the info you entered, delete the video, or go back to the Video tab.

If you want to record your own video, you need a webcam and a good microphone either in or attached to that computer. If your computer has what it takes, follow these steps:

1. **Click the Video icon at the top of your Facebook Page.**

2. **Click the Record a Video with a Webcam button.**

   A dialog box appears, asking you to give Facebook access to your camera and microphone (you'll notice an option for you to hide this notification in the future).

3. **Click Allow and then click the Close button to close that dialog box and access the camera window.**

4. **Click the Record button to begin filming.**

   The Record button is red with a white dot and is right underneath your video screen.

5. **When you're finished, click the Stop button, which is the black button with the white square.**

6. **Click Play or Reset.** Play lets you review the video. Reset allows you to rerecord the video.

7. **Write a comment about the video.** You'll notice an option to "Say something about this video" underneath your video before selecting the Share button, which puts it on your Wall.

   Clicking Save takes you to the screen where you can add tags, a title, and description for your video, as well as choose a thumbnail that will represent the video on your Page.

8. **When you're finished editing the settings, click the Save button.**

   Your video is posted to your Page for all your fans to enjoy!

Making Your Page Easier to Find

Anyone, whether a Facebook member or not, can access your Facebook Page. People can find your Page by using Facebook's internal search, as well as search engines such as Google and Microsoft's Bing. But what you might not know is that a Facebook Page can actually improve your search engine rankings, so people can more easily find both your Facebook Page and your website.

All Facebook Pages are public, and therefore, search engines like Google can index them. Build a positive image for your brand and engage readers so that they engage with you and return often.

By publishing a steady stream of links to your company's blog posts and other pages of your company's website within Facebook, you allow search engines to more easily find you, which is also known as *search engine optimization (SEO)*. Simply by having a Facebook Page, you increase the number of relevant links to your site and therefore your site's SEO.

Just adding links to your Facebook Page is not enough — those links need to include relevant keywords related to your business. Additionally, the content within the linked article should have relevant keywords. For example, an auto repair garage would post links to articles about do-it-yourself auto-repair tips on its Facebook Page. In other words, tossing a bunch of keywords together to make your Page is not enough.

There's a lot more to say on this topic — too much to include here. If you'd like more in-depth coverage, check out *Search Engine Optimization For Dummies* by Peter Kent (Wiley).

Be sure that your Page contains many uses of the keywords that can best help you appear in the search engines. For example, if you're a professional photographer, make sure you use keywords like *wedding photography* or *photography in Atlanta* to help capture the people who are specifically in the market for your services. Some good places to use these keywords are in your Info tab as well as in any notes you post. Also, be sure that you provide all the necessary contact information, such as your address, as well as your company's website and blog addresses.

Using Friend Networks to Launch Your Page

As we mention at the beginning of this chapter, one challenge of launching a brand new Facebook Page is the lack of awareness of your Page within Facebook. The first step many admins take in launching their Page is to leverage their existing friend networks. This can be done by using personal friend connections you've developed via e-mail and on your personal Facebook profile.

Telling your friends to share your Page with their friends

The Share link, which appears at the bottom of the left column on any Page, lets people invite their Facebook friends or a list of Facebook friends to check out your Page.

Suggesting a Page to friends

People who have become friends with you on Facebook may not know you have a Page set up specifically for your business. Facebook makes it easy for you, as a Page admin, to let them in on the good news.

To do so, follow these steps:

1. **Click the Invite Friends link on the right side of your Page.**

   The Suggest to Friends dialog box appears, as shown in Figure 7-4.

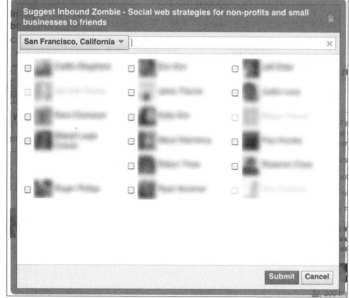

Figure 7-4:
Sharing
your Page
with friends
using the
Invite
Friends
feature.

2. **Either scroll through your friends' pictures and click those you want to invite or type their names in the Search All Friends box at the top to find a specific friend quickly. (You can narrow your results by using the drop-down menu on the left to sort by Networks, Locations, and Recent Interactions.)**

3. **Click the Submit button at the bottom of the dialog box.**

   The Success dialog box appears, letting you know your recommenda-tions have been sent. Now get ready for all your new Likes to come roll-ing in!

People you promote your Page to who aren't already Facebook members need to join Facebook first to be able to Like or comment on your Page.

Promoting a Page via your profile

The Share link, which appears at the bottom of the left column on your Page, lets you post a description of and link to any Page (even if you haven't cre-ated it) to your personal profile to let all your Facebook friends know about it, and you can express how you feel about that Page by adding a personal message. (Make sure you're logged into your profile.) If your target custom-ers are businesses, for example, what better way to showcase your work than by promoting the Facebook Pages of the businesses you have worked with, and then take it a step further and add a message, such as

I had the pleasure of working with ABC Company on the corporate photography for its XYZ product. What a great, knowledgeable bunch!

Follow these steps to post a Page to your profile:

1. **Click the Share link at the bottom left of the Page.**

   The Post to Profile dialog box appears.

2. **Input a message about the Page.**

   Your message can be up to 800 characters in length, but we recommend that you keep it short and sweet. Less than 80 characters is best!

3. **Click the Share Page button.**

Promoting your Facebook Page with the Tell Your Fans feature

When your Page is new, you can send up to 5,000 invitations to Like your Page by leveraging your current e-mail contacts with the Tell Your Fans feature. You can import contacts directly from supported e-mail web services or upload them through a contact file. The tool is available to admins of any new or smaller Pages, and can help businesses convert their e-mail database they've built for years into a Facebook audience.

To use the Tell Your Fans feature on your Page, follow these steps:

1. **In the Edit button at the top right of your Facebook Page, click Resources in the left sidebar.**

2. **Click the Tell Your Fans link. Choose one of the networks as shown in Figure 7-5.**

   If you select Other Tools, you're prompted to upload Microsoft Outlook Express, Thunderbird, Apple Mail, or other types of files.

3. **Log in to your selected network when promoted and click Find Friends.**

   The Authenticating window appears. Depending on how many contacts you have, this might take a while.

4. **Either import all contacts or select specific friends and click Send Invitations.**

   A confirmation message like the one in Figure 7-6 appears.

Figure 7-5:
Facebook
allows you
to send
requests
to like your
Page to
your Skype,
Yahoo!, and
other net-
works.

Figure 7-6:
The confir-
mation box
appears.

Tagging photos to promote your Facebook Page

Tagging (identifying and labeling the name of) a fan in photos, videos, or notes directly links your Page to an individual Facebook user. When you tag someone, the person who's tagged then receives a Facebook notification, an e-mail notification, or both, depending upon her Profile settings. That user has the option of approving the tag or not.

By tagging you not only share that tag with your fans, but it also appears on the Wall of all those fans' friends, which gives you immediate credibility with the friends of your fans.

To tag a friend or fan in a photo or video, display the photo or video and then follow these simple steps:

1. **Click the Tag Photo (or Video) button to the right of the image.**

   The cursor turns into a plus sign (+).

2. **Click the face of the person or Page you want to tag.**

   A box appears below the cursor where you can start typing a friend's name, as shown in Figure 7-7.

3. **Select the name of the friend or Page that appears in the picture or video, and then click the Tag button.**

Figure 7-7: Tagging a photo on a Facebook Page.

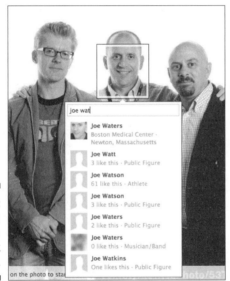

Be sure to take as many photos as possible at in-person events and shoot as many videos as you can so that you can post and tag them accordingly.

You can obtain a suitable photo to include on your Page by conducting a promotion to find the best new product or service idea or even the most creative use of your products. Then, take a photo of the winner with your company's CEO and tag the winner in the photo on Facebook. (To find out how to host your own Facebook promotion, see Chapters 11 and 12.)

When you tag a fan in a photo, that person can delete the photo from his profile by clicking the Remove Tag link next to the profile name.

Using Existing Marketing Assets to Launch Your Page

After you attract that initial boost of personal friends to your Page as described in the preceding section, it's time to start promoting your Page using other tactics.

Using your e-mail signature

Imagine if each e-mail you sent in the course of doing business each day included a link to your Facebook Page! Adding an anchor link in your e-mail signature that connects with your Facebook Page is relatively easy to do in most e-mail programs, such as Outlook, Gmail, and Apple's Mail program. If you use Gmail, WiseStamp (www.wisestamp.com) has an awesome Firefox add-in that adds a Like button to your e-mail signature so that people can Like your Page and continue reading your e-mail.

 One factor that influences whether someone becomes a fan of your Page is the number of current fans your Page has. Getting as many new fans as possible creates a kind of social validation for these future fans.

Using your e-mail list to get more fans

You can promote your new Facebook Page many different ways, but the easiest way to get new connections is to use your e-mail list — an asset that you've been growing (hopefully) over the past few years.

Facebook users want to share useful information with their friends and click the Like button on Pages that will help them achieve that goal. But if they get an e-mail that says, "We're now on Facebook; please Like our Page," they'll probably delete it unless they are your hard-core, number-one raving fan.

When e-mailing your current list about your Facebook Page, keep the following tips in mind:

✔ Keep the focus on the value to the recipient, not your business.

✔ Write the e-mail in the second person, using *you* and *yours* to speak directly to the customer.

✔ Present the benefits in a concise list of bulleted items.

✔ Tell recipients that they'll meet others on the Page with similar interests and ideas. This way, they'll feel like they're joining a community, and not just another Facebook Page.

Using printed marketing materials

The best way to promote your Facebook Page in print (such as with annual appeals or newsletters) is with a custom URL. (See Chapter 4 for info on how to create one.) A custom UL is much shorter than the default Facebook Page URL, which no one would ever take the time to type in from a printed page.

You should use this custom URL on every single piece of printed material.

Using your blog to promote your Facebook Page

Write a blog post that elaborates on the launching of your Page, followed by a series that elaborates on a comment someone wrote on your Wall. Include a link to your Page and/or a comment.

Using your webinars to launch your Facebook Page

If your business does webinars on a regular basis, make your Facebook Page Wall the place where follow-up questions are answered.

For example, CharityHowTo, shown in Figure 7-8, does this regularly with free webinars each month and has used this strategy almost exclusively to acquire more than 5,000 fans in just a few months!

Figure 7-8:
Charity-
HowTo uses
its Facebook
Page Wall
to answer
questions
from reg-
istrants
who attend
their free
educational
webinars.

Using YouTube to Promote Your Facebook Page

As you might know, YouTube is the top video-sharing website in the world. Posting videos on YouTube is a way to promote your business to millions of people. If you already have a presence on YouTube, you can leverage that presence to drive traffic to your Facebook Page.

For example, a company called Blendtec posts a series of whimsical, mock game show videos, called Will It Blend?, on YouTube to promote the power of its products. In Blendtec's excellent Will It Blend? Facebook video (see Figure 7-9), the nerdy, engaging host demonstrates the product in a funny way and then announces a contest for potential fans to share — on Blendtec's Facebook Page — their ideas of things to blend.

It's an ingenious promotion of its Facebook Page, and you can find it here: `www.youtube.com/watch?v=4lQ1Pz_O-j0`.

And if have a YouTube brand channel, you can annotate your video with a link to your Facebook Page.

Figure 7-9: Blendtec uses YouTube to promote its Facebook Page.

Promoting Your Page in Your Store

When people visit your business and have a great experience, they naturally want to share that experience with their friends. This type of word-of-mouth advertising has been going on for eons. When you launch your Facebook Page, make sure that you're promoting it in your store. If people check in to your place on their mobile devices, those posts provide additional exposure for your business on the News Feed. (See Chapter 11 for more info on "checking in.")

Here's an example of using an in-store promotion to promote a Facebook Page:

Cashiers at iParty (a party supply store) handed out bingo cards to customers before Halloween, which drove in-store traffic to catch a daily drawing on its Facebook Page (as shown in Figure 7-10).

Make sure you create a custom username URL for your Facebook Page at `http://facebook.com/usernamehttp://facebook.com/username`. This short URL takes up less space on printed materials and other signage.

Figure 7-10:
iParty's
Facebook
Page pro-
moting its
Halloween
Bingo cards
available in
stores.

Using Facebook's Sponsored Story Ads to Launch Your Page

Another way to acquire Facebook fans is to use Facebook Page Like Sponsored Story ads to promote your Page to the friends of your existing fans.

Sponsored Stories are Facebook ads that appear in Facebook users' News Feeds. The powerful thing about Facebook Sponsored Story ads is that they leverage the "social graph" — the Facebook friend networks. These ads show up on the right column of various pages on Facebook. The types of ads available include: Page Likes (where a Facebook user Likes a Page), Page posts (which displays posts from a Page), and Page post Likes (which displays Likes on Page posts).

Facebook Sponsored Like Story ads are different from traditional Facebook ads in four ways:

✔ Sponsored Stories can be targeted to friends of current fans. This takes advantage of the idea that "birds of a feather flock together."

✔ Sponsored Stories display the user's friends who have already Liked your Page, such as "John, Bill, and Barbara like the National Wildlife Federation." Facebook users are more likely to take action when they see that their friends have already taken that action.

✔ Users can Like the Page directly in the Sponsored Story . This eliminates any abandonment that might occur between the Sponsored Story and your Facebook Page (shown above).

✔ Fans acquired are displayed in the Fans report within Facebook Insights. This allows you to see how these Sponsored Story ads compare to other methods of acquiring fans.

For more on using Sponsored Story ads, see Chapter 10.

Chapter 8

Engaging with Your Fans

In This Chapter

▶ Understanding what engagement means for your business

▶ Measuring engagement on Facebook

▶ Strategies and tactics that increase engagement

*A*fter you create a Facebook Page (see Chapter 4 for details on how), you can start building a strong fan base for your Page. Social networking is a "quantity game," meaning that the amount of time you spend networking has a huge effect on the results you receive. In this way, using Facebook isn't that different from in-person networking. For example, when you attend a networking event, you'll likely build your credibility in the group and add to your number of contacts.

However, Facebook is also a *quality* game. Say that you attend 50 events instead of just 1. If you don't offer valuable information and interaction, people won't be inclined to support your agenda or even remember you. If all you do is hand out your business card to as many people as possible, all they'll remember is the moment when someone interrupted them.

If you instead offer a solution to a problem they brought up during your conversation, though, they'll not only remember you, but they might repay the favor by referring you new business. This is why creating useful content and conversation on your Facebook Page is a paramount marketing paradigm.

In this chapter, we show you the strategies and tactics that generate conversations, instead of unknowingly creating annoying and off-putting interruptions. These tactics give you a way to listen to your customers and prospects, help to build awareness of your brand, drive your sales, and form a community of people who share your values and your business with their friends.

We also discuss how to generate the best Wall stories by writing text updates, adding photos and videos, and starting discussions. Finally, we show you how to leverage your existing friends and customers, both within and outside Facebook, and how to find new business prospects within the Facebook community.

Understanding What Engagement Really Means

If you've been reading up on how to market your business with social media, you've no doubt run across the word *engagement*. Like the word *love*, engagement is one of those words that means less and less the more it's used.

To some, engagement means publishing interesting and creative content with little interest in understanding or listening to one's customers or prospects. To others, engagement is all about conversation: asking questions, replying to comments, expressing appreciation to fans, and so forth.

The truth is that it's both. You have to publish interesting content, but you also have to understand what your fans are interested in.

What engagement means for word-of-mouth advertising

Before we go any further on this topic, we must remind you that good engagement is nothing more than good communication. As with in-person networking events or conferences, engagement — meeting your customers, getting to know them, and inspiring them to take action — takes time and effort. Online or off, people are still people, which means no shortcuts to building healthy relationships with your customers and prospects. That said, engagement means something slightly different from each party's perspective.

So from your standpoint, engagement includes the strategies to motivate your customers to talk about your business. You also want them (hopefully) to trust you enough to tell you when they have a problem, or when they love what you do.

You want fans to interact with your Page for two reasons:

- ✔ You can build a relationship with your fans through dialog and discussion.

- ✔ The more activity that's generated on your Page, the more stories that will be published to your fans' News Feeds, which drives more awareness to the original action and creates a viral marketing affect.

Always stay on message, meaning make sure that the content relates to your business in some way. And consider keeping your links on the positive side. No need to associate negative news with your business.

Understanding why people engage with businesses on Facebook

A recent study by *The New York Times* concluded that consumers are more likely to buy from brands and businesses that they feel listen with social media. From your customers' standpoint, engagement means nothing more being heard. Facebook — and all social media — allows customers to converse directly with brands and businesses. When they have a problem with your product or service, they want to feel like there is a real, live person behind the Facebook Page listening to their concerns.

Measuring engagement with Facebook Insights

In one sense, engagement is a feeling of connection between customer and business. However, you can't determine that your marketing efforts are giving you the expected return based on just feelings — and this is why you measure.

In practice, the meaning of engagement is found in clicks and visits to a website, but it's also found in Wall conversations, Page mentions in status updates, replies within comments threads, and the general sentiment expressed in all actions that can be measured with the Insights analytics tool included with every Facebook Page. As you can see in Figure 8-1, Facebook Insights allows you to see how each post has performed.

Figure 8-1:
Measure
fan engage-
ment
received for
each Page
update.

Date ?	Post ?	Reach ?	Engaged Users ?	Talking About This ?	Virality ?
10/31/11	Happy Halloween!	611	166	23	3.76%
10/25/11	What does "Talking About...	54	9	2	3.7%
10/24/11	Click like if you wish it wa...	781	24	16	2.05%
10/21/11	This graph basically show...	736	159	15	2.04%
11/1/11	Knowing what fans prefer...	758	19	12	1.58%
11/1/11	A very useful attitude for ...	829	31	13	1.57%

What's amazing about Facebook is that marketers can measure engagement by tracking a combination of the following actions:

✔ **Liking, sharing, or commenting on a Page story.** In the table shown in Figure 8-1, you can view more details about likes and comments by clicking on any data point in the Talking About This column.

✔ **Playing a video or viewing a photo.** In the table shown in Figure 8-1, you can view more details about video plays, photo views, and more by clicking on a data point in the Engaged Users column.

✔ **RSVPing to an event associated with your Page.**

✔ **Tagging your Page in an update (otherwise known as *mentions*).** In the table shown in Figure 8-1, you can view mentions by clicking on any value in the Talking About This column.

✔ **Inviting friends to like your Page.**

Here are four Facebook Insights reports that show you how engaged your Facebook fans are. (Facebook Insights is covered in detail in Chapter 9.) You should make a habit of regularly viewing these four reports on your Page.

To access these reports, first go to your Facebook Insights reports by clicking the Insights icon in the left sidebar of your Facebook Page, as shown in Figure 8-2. When you do this, you can access any of the following four reports.

✔ **The Talking About This graph:** Click the Talking About This subtab under Insights, scroll down to the How People Are Talking about Your Page section, and then select Stories from Your Posts from the drop-down menu, as shown in Figure 8-3. The resulting Talking about This graph (on the left) shows you how many Facebook users have either Liked or commented on your Page story over a specific amount of time.

✔ **The Viral Reach graph:** The graph on the right in Figure 8-3 shows you *viral reach,* which is the number of people who saw the actions displayed in the graph on the left. Figure 8-3 shows very clearly how engagement spreads through Facebook, like a sound and its echo.

Figure 8-2: Insights, the analysis tool included in all Facebook Pages, can be accessed directly on your Facebook Page.

Insights icon

✔ **The Page overview report:** Click the Insights icon again, and you're taken to a graph (see Figure 8-4) showing you how updates to your Page are followed by increases in engagement and awareness. The purple dots on the bottom of this graph indicate how many times you posted updates on a particular day. The green (middle) line shows how many people engaged with content on your Page, and the top blue line shows how many people saw content related to your Page. With this graph, you can see the way your Page updates cause people to respond (by, say, commenting, sharing, and so on), and also the way those responses are then seen by those people's friends.

✔ **The post-level report:** Scroll down below the Page overview graph to see a report listing your most recent Page updates and some statistics about how those updates have performed. In this post-level report (see Figure 8-5) are several columns, including information such as the date you posted the update, an excerpt from the update, how many users engaged with that update, and how many people were "Talking About" that update. The rightmost column is Virality, which show the percentage of the people who saw your update that actually took action with it. (In other words, the Virality value is the Talking About This value divided by the Reach value.) If you rank this list by Virality, you can quickly determine which updates were the most engaging with users — and from this information, you can start to define trends about the content on your Page that people reacted to the most.

Figure 8-3:
Talking about This and Viral Reach reports reflect engagement around your Page.

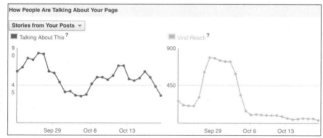

Figure 8-4:
The Page overview report shows the relationships among content, engagement, and awareness.

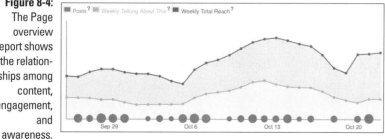

Figure 8-5:
See which
of your Page
updates
have
received the
most com-
ments and
Likes.

Date ?	Post ?	Reach ?	Engaged Users ?	Talking About This ?	Virality ? ▼
10/10/11	📹 This video covers four differe	1,134	191	109	9.61%
10/06/11	🖼 How will you inspire the worl	1,264	130	30	2.37%
10/15/11	🔗 You've got to watch this vide	1,500	81	32	2.13%
09/30/11	🖼 Happy Friday! Click "like" if	1,333	32	21	1.58%
10/07/11	🔗 Seven ways to be eternally	78	9	1	1.28%
10/14/11	🖼 Facebook Page WIFM	247	23	3	1.21%
10/20/11	🖼 This made me laugh...	1,439	124	15	1.04%

The more active Facebook users who are around your Facebook Page — that is, the more they view posts, Like posts, comment on posts, and so on — the further your marketing message will spread throughout Facebook. Friends of your Facebook fans who aren't already fans are exposed to your Page each time their friend (who is a fan) comments or Likes your Page updates.

Because real engagement with fans grows over long periods of time, choose weeks or months for your ranges of data in Insights. In other words, don't bother tracking this information on a daily basis.

Facebook uses the EdgeRank algorithm, which determines whether fans will see your content in their News Feeds. One of the biggest factors in this algorithm is the prevalence of comments and Likes each of your Page stories receives. Facebook Insights shows you how you can post updates that receive more Likes and comments.

Configuring your Page Wall for maximum engagement

In addition to commenting and Liking your Facebook stories, your fans can also post their own updates on your Page and tag photos from your Page provided that you configured your Wall to allow fans to do so. If you choose not to allow fans to share content on your Facebook Page, you'll limit the extent to which fans can connect with you on Facebook, and that will have a negative effect on your EdgeRank.

To configure your Wall so that fans can post content, simply follow these steps:

1. **Log into Facebook and go to your Facebook Page.**

2. **Click Edit Page to the right of your page name.**

3. **In the admin section of your Facebook Page, click Manage Permissions.**

4. **Select all the Posting Ability options (see Figure 8-6).**

Figure 8-6:
Enable Wall
settings
for your
Facebook
Page here.

If your business is new to social media marketing, allowing anyone on Facebook to post content on your Page might seem scary. This feeling is understandable, but often unwarranted. What you will find is that by engaging criticism directly on your Facebook Page, you'll create a positive image about your brand. Also, as we discuss later, you have ways to moderate profanity or offensive language on your Facebook Page.

Posting New Updates to Your Page

Maintaining a steady stream of content helps you attract new members from the Facebook community as well as interact with them. This fresh content also helps keep your existing fans interested and engaged. Also, every time you update your Page, Facebook publishes a story in the News Feed.

Updating your status with the status update box

The most common place to publish an update on your Facebook Page is at the top of your Page Wall. Five types of updates can be published; for details on how to post these updates, see Chapter 7.

✔ **Status:** In the status update box at the top of your Facebook Page, you can write an update to your fans (in the box where it says `Write some-thing`; see Figure 8-7).

Figure 8-7:
Facebook
allows
admins
and fans to
publish text
updates on
Page Walls.

> Wall   Inbound Zombie - Social w... · **Everyone (Most Recent)** ▾
>
> Share: 📄 **Status** 📷 **Photo** 🔗 **Link** 📹 **Video** 📊 **Question**
>
> Write something...

✔ **Photo:** You can publish photos directly to your Facebook Page by clicking the Photo link above the status update box. You can upload a photo directly from your desktop, take a picture directly from your webcam, or, if you have multiple photographs, create a Photo Album (see Figure 8-8).

✔ **Link:** Facebook allows you to share links on your Page Wall along with comments about that link (see Figure 8-9).

✔ **Video:** You can also publish videos to your Facebook Wall by uploading them from your desktop or recording a video from your computer's webcam (see Figure 8-10).

Figure 8-8:
Page admins and fans can share photos in a variety of ways.

Figure 8-9:
Page admins and fans can share links.

Figure 8-10:
Page admins and fans can share videos in a variety of ways.

✔ **Question:** Finally, Facebook allows Page admins to post poll questions by using the Question feature on their Page. (See Figure 8-11.) To post a question, simply click the questions icon at the top of your page, enter a question, enter choices for answers, decide whether you want fans to add their own responses, and then post the question.

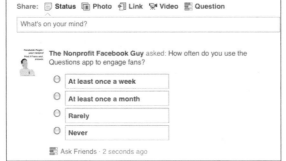

Figure 8-11: Facebook admins can create simple polls with the Questions application.

A status update of just text requires nothing else to be shared. When sharing photos, videos, and links, however, Facebook allows you to comment on that content. In addition to comments, you can also decide who will see that comment. The following steps show you exactly who will see it:

1. **Click the Status, Photo, Link, or Video link above the status update box.**

2. **Enter your message in the status update box, upload your photo or video, record your video, or add your link in the link field.**

   If you choose to upload a photo or video, you must specify the photo or video file to be uploaded. To do so, in the window that appears, search your computer for the correct file and double-click on it.

3. **For photos, videos, and links, click the Attach button.**

4. **If you want all your fans to see the content, click Share.**

Limiting the fans who can see your Page updates

You can choose to share Page updates with fans that live in a specific geographic location, or speak a specific language. For example, a national hotel chain shares promotions about a specific location only with fans in the city where that hotel is located.

You do this by publishing updates to a specific group of your Facebook fans. Just follow these steps:

1. **Choose Customize from the Public drop-down list (see Figure 8-12).**

   The Choose Your Audience window appears (see Figure 8-13).

2. **If you want to publish the update to fans in a specific geographic location, type that location (the country) in the Location field.**

3. **Select the appropriate radio button (see Figure 8-14) to narrow your specification by state or city, as follows:**

   • *Everywhere:* Publish to all fans in that country

   • *By State/Province:* Publish to all fans in a specific state

   • *By City:* Publish to all fans within a specific city

   If you select By State/Province or By City, simply begin typing in the name of that state or city until it appears in the list of suggestions.

4. **To publish the update to fans who specified a language other than English as their primary language on Facebook, enter the name of that language in the Languages field.**

   Again, just begin typing the name of the language, and then select it from the resulting list of suggestions.

5. **Click OK.**

Figure 8-12:
Page admins decide which fans can view an update in the Public drop-down list.

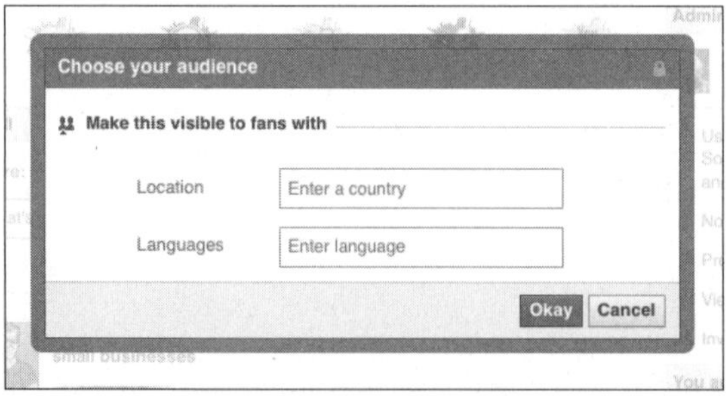

Figure 8-13:
Limit the visibility of updates to specific geographic locations.

Figure 8-14:
Target fans
on your Wall
by select-
ing State/
Province or
City.

Posting as a Page versus Posting as a Profile

Facebook Pages allow admins to post content as the Page identity or as a personal Profile. This allows admins to have the flexibility to express both the brand voice and their personal voice.

For example, admins of the National Wildlife Federation Facebook Page are invested and interested in conservation issues outside of their job description. They participate in nature-related activities on the weekends and after work because they sincerely care about protecting wildlife. As Facebook admins, they can post updates on recent legislation impacting wildlife conservation, and follow up those posts with personal comments as individuals.

How to switch between posting as a Profile and posting as a Page

To post as a Page, simply go to your Facebook Page (make sure you're logged in) and then click Post as [name of your page] in the right-hand side of your Facebook Page (Figure 8-15).

After making this switch to posting as a Page, you can comment and Like stories from other Pages (you must Like their Page first), Post updates on other Pages that you've Liked, mention other Pages in updates on your Page, and tag other Pages in your photos.

In Page mode, you can also view your Page's News Feed. Your page's News Feed, which is different from your profile's News Feed, will show you the latest updates from all the Pages that you've Liked as a Page. You can also comment and Like these updates directly in your News Feed in the same way you would if you were logged in with your personal profile (see Figure 8-16).

Figure 8-15:
Facebook
Pages allow
admins
to switch
between
posting as
their Page
or posting
as a Profile.

Figure 8-16:
When
logged in as
a Page, you
can view
the latest
updates
from Pages
you've Liked
as a Page.

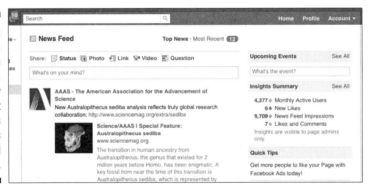

Note that in the menu bar of Facebook (at the very top of any Facebook page, you can also view the latest notifications about fan activity, notifications about new fans, and a high level overview of your page insights (see Figure 8-17).

Newest fans

Notifications

Figure 8-17:
Facebook.
com
displays
valuable
information
for page
admins
when they
are logged
in as a page.

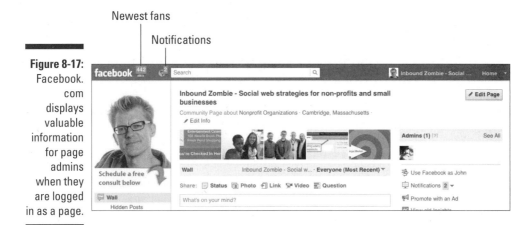

Figure 8-17: Facebook.com displays valuable information for page admins when they are logged in as a page.

Posting as a Profile should be a personal choice

Deciding whether Facebook admins should post as their personal profile is a choice you should make, not one mandated by your boss. The reason is that when someone posts on a Page as a profile, that person is potentially opening herself up to friend requests from fans, which may be unwanted. Privacy of one's personal profile should always be respected by managers, and this should be a personal choice.

That said, if an admin is a recognized thought leader, trusted pundit, or well-known member of your Facebook Page community, allowing him to post as a Profile will only enhance the relationship fans have with your organization.

Knowing the difference between being helpful and being spam

Just because you can post on another Page as a Page doesn't mean it's always the smartest thing to do. Many Facebook marketers make the common mistake of posting to another Page in an attempt to promote their business, but the result is that they come across as spam. And like with e-mail and other social platforms, Facebook users have only a certain tolerance for spam. Two factors can determine whether your post on another Page will be perceived as spam:

✔ **The community doesn't know you.** As a Facebook Page marketer, you may believe that the content you're posting on another Page is quite obviously useful. For example, an owner of a pet supply store running a promotion on cat food might think there is nothing harmful about posting info about the promotion on a local animal shelter's Facebook Page. Still, many of that Page's fans will perceive that post as unwanted and self-promoting.

✔ **The community doesn't trust you.** If Facebook fans on another Page don't know you, they probably don't trust you because you haven't yet established a bond of trust with them.

The obvious solution here is to become a trusted member of that Page community before even thinking about promoting your own agenda.

One way to do this is to reply to posts on that Page in a way that contributes to that post's topic and supports the Page's agenda. In the pet supply store example, the store owner could improve his standing on the animal shelter's Facebook Page by replying to, say, a post about a new dog up for adoption, and in his comments, provide fans useful information about that breed. The more the pet supply store owner follows the strategy, the more he (and his store) will get noticed by fans of that Page.

Another way to do this is to promote the other Page's agenda on your own Facebook Page by mentioning that Page in status updates, as shown in Figure 8-18.

Figure 8-18:
Posting as a Page on another Page could be perceived as spam if not done correctly.

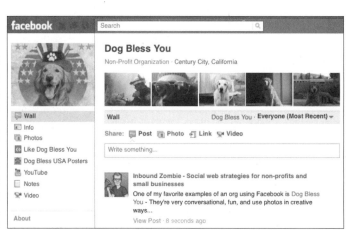

Becoming a Ninja with Status Updates

Engagement is the name of the game on Facebook, and the brands that do it best know how to be creative with their updates. Before we get into the tactics and strategies, take a look at what works and what doesn't work.

Understanding the research about what engages Facebook users

A lot of research has been conducted about what actually works and what doesn't work on Facebook. One study by Buddy Media called "Strategies for Effective Facebook Wall Posts: A Statistical Review" (`http://forms. buddymedia.com/whitepaper-form_review-strategies-for- effective-facebook-wall-posts.html`) goes into great detail about the types of Page stories that get the most engagement. The following list offers some notable conclusions from that study:

- ✔ **Shorter text updates get more engagement.** The study found that updates with fewer than 80 characters had a 27 percent higher engagement rate than longer updates. Like you, most Facebook users are busy people with little time to read lengthy status updates. Posting shorter updates ensures that people will respond.

- ✔ **Posting updates outside normal business hours can increase engagement.** The study found a 20 percent higher rate of engagement for posts made during these hours. Most Facebook users check their personal Facebook Page updates in the early morning and after work. Posting an update during these hours ensures that you're toward the top of your fans' News Feeds!

- ✔ **Posting updates at the end of the week increases engagement.** Buddy Media found that the best days during the week for engagement were Thursdays and Fridays, which is, according to Facebook, when the Happiness Index peaks. How are Thursdays and Fridays different from the rest of the week? The weekend is almost here! When people are happy, they're much more open to engaging with friends and brands on Facebook.

Asking specific questions to engage fans

Asking questions is the easiest way to get Facebook users commenting. Having said that, keep in mind that Facebook fans don't like homework. If they have to spend time trying to understand a question, they'll be less likely to answer it. The more specific and concise your questions, the more likely they will get more comments. The following list shows some examples of the types of questions that Facebook fans tend to prefer:

- ✔ **Yes or no:** This obvious type of question is very easy to answer. It also serves as a way to collect market research information about potential offerings.

- ✔ **True or false:** This is another type of question that works really well. Always begin these questions with *True or False*. Facebook users will be more likely to answer if they know that a simple answer is all that's required.

- ✔ **Questions about photos:** Share a photo and ask your fans to comment. For example, an animal rights organization could post a photo and ask, "What's wrong with this picture?"

- ✔ **Poll questions:** Facebook's new Question feature makes it easy to create polls on your Page. Plus, such polls are better than simple Wall posts at increasing awareness about your Page.

- ✔ **Preference questions:** When you were in college, did you prefer essay questions or multiple choice questions? (That's what we thought. Nobody likes essay questions.) The same goes for Facebook users.

- ✔ **Fill-in-the-blank:** These types of questions also make less work for Facebook users. When you ask these, always begin with *Fill in the blank*. Facebook users will be more likely to answer a question if they know what's expected. And everybody knows how fill-in-the-blank questions work.

- ✔ **Attendance questions:** Ask who's attending an event. You can pose this question to fans located near an upcoming event. Bonus points if you share a link to your Facebook event.

- ✔ **Favorite moments:** Ask those who attended the event to share a favorite moment: If you're a national organization that held an event in Chicago, you can target an update to those attendees asking to share their impressions. This will mainly get responses from your core fans, but will give less-active fans a deeper look at your organization's culture.

- ✔ **Tips:** Ask fans for tips. This one works well if you're looking to create a sense of community among your Facebook fans.

Using quizzes to engage fans

Photos, Videos, Links, and Text updates often a wide variety of content for fans, but sometimes try something different. Quizzes and polls are popular tactics on Facebook to keep fan engagement diverse and interesting.

T3, a UK-based website about tech, regularly creates polls using the popular Facebook Poll Daddy Polls app. One of these polls ("Which [online video] game will be better?") received more than 88,000 votes (see Figure 8-19). This poll served the dual purpose of allowing fans to share their opinions, and of showing the companies who sell these video games which games were preferred. Those companies' marketing teams can use this information to better target future content and promotions.

Figure 8-19: Use a poll app to keep fan engagement diverse and interesting.

Responding to Comments and Likes

When fans ask you a question or are interested enough in what you're saying to post a comment on your Wall, they have invested time in the interaction. Not responding or acknowledging them in some way makes it seem like you're ignoring them. Who wants to give their money to a company that ignores them even before a sale takes place? If a user asks you a question, respond to it. If you receive a compliment, thank the person and reinforce your commitment to creating exceptional customer experiences. If you receive a negative comment, ask how you can improve the overall experience.

In short, every time someone reaches out to engage with your Page, engage with that person in return. Failing to reciprocate can potentially backfire or cause less revenue.

Although generally you want to respond to comments within 24 hours, in some cases — such as with an irate customer who is never going to be happy with anything you might say — you may be better off not responding at all. Trying to decide when and when not to respond can be tricky, so here are some tips to help you make this decision:

- **If a mistake was clearly made on your part, respond and correct the situation quickly.** Apologies can go a long way as long as you explain that steps are being taken to correct the situation.

- **If someone leaves a negative comment about something that never actually took place or is based on incorrect facts, correct him.** Always be polite because often people don't realize they've made an error. If you don't respond, however, this misconception could spread and escalate.

- **Try to salvage a bad situation.** If you made a mistake and think you can put a positive spin on a bad experience or convince the customer to give you another chance, a response is appropriate to right the perceived wrong.

- **An irate person may never be satisfied, so you may be better off not doing anything.** Sometimes people direct their frustration with the world toward you and your Facebook Page. To know if you're dealing with such a person, take a look at the other comments she's made. You may conclude that it's better for you to not to enter a fight you're never going to win. Instead, invest your time and efforts where you can have a positive result.

- **Don't engage in a fight you can't win.** Sometimes a response does more harm than good. A negative comment or review can have a devastating effect on a company's online reputation. However, you don't want to engage in a back-and-forth that will uncover more cracks in the armor, so to speak. Often in these situations, just take a passive role as opposed to going for the jugular.

- **Don't let anger derail your response.** Although the saying, "It's not personal, it's just business," is good in principle, it's a lot harder in practice. Disparaging Facebook comments can really make you angry. Rather than rattle off a negative response, either have someone else who is less emotional about the situation respond or sit on the sidelines and wait until your emotions calm before responding. An angry response can go a long way in damaging your relationship with the customer and can have a spill-over effect on all who read it.

Using Photos and Videos to Engage Fans

The old saying about a picture saying a thousand words couldn't be more true than on Facebook. Pictures and images are the types of content that consistently receive the most engagement.

A great example of a Facebook Page that uses photos to engage fans is Dog Bless You (`https://www.facebook.com/exploredogs`). When they post photos, they always add a funny or interesting comment to solicit a response.

After you share a photo (as shown in Figure 8-20), Facebook automatically publishes it in your News Feed and adds three ways that Facebook users can interact with that content (see Figure 8-21): Like, comment, and share.

- ✔ **Like:** Users can Like the photo, which generates an action that the user's friends will see.

- ✔ **Comment:** Users can comment on the photo, which also generates an action that the user's friends will see.

- ✔ **Share:** Users can share the photo, which reposts the photo on their own News Feeds (Page admins can also choose to share photos on their Page).

Figure 8-20: Dog Bless You posts interesting photos each day.

Dog Bless You
Mr. Big's Pool Party - Pawtastic. Happy Labor Day. Lucky
Like · Comment · Share

Album: Wall Photos · 322 of 328
Posted: September 5

Figure 8-21:
Facebook users can Like, comment on, and share a photo.

Facebook users can also tag Pages and people in your photo. When a Page or a person is tagged, a notification is automatically sent to that user or admin (see Figure 8-22).

Figure 8-22:
Facebook users can tag friends or brands in photos.

In A Pickle — a local diner in Waltham, Massachusetts, uses photo tagging in a creative way on Facebook by uploading customer photos with the faces blocked out. They then post an update to the Page challenging their fans to identify themselves or a friend through tagging. (See Figure 8-23.)

Figure 8-23:
In A Pickle uses photo-tagging as a promotion strategy.

If you're looking to increase engagement on your Page with photos, those photos must be interesting enough to get Facebook users sufficiently motivated to Llike or comment on them.

Some things to keep in mind are

- ✔ Make sure your photos are in focus and easy to see.

- ✔ Make sure that the size of your photos are big enough so that the resolution isn't grainy. A recommended dimension is at least 500 x 500 pixels.

- ✔ Always include a compelling title that describes the photo.

- ✔ Always include a comment with the photo.

 ✔ Although it might be perfectly legal to post pictures of people in public spaces, it might be a good idea to check with people first — particularly if you're posting unflattering pictures. Keep in mind that you can tag any Facebook user in a photo. When you tag someone, she gets a notification to approve the tagging.

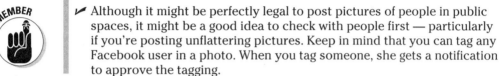

Using Webinars to Build Your Fan Base

Webinars are live online seminars or presentations conducted by companies or organizations that include audio and visual aspects. They're mostly used to educate customers or to promote products and services to prospects. In many cases, webinars are used as a way to demonstrate an organization's expertise in a specific subject matter. One really powerful way to build your Facebook Page fan base and improve your Page's EdgeRank is to use your Facebook Page as a follow-up venue to a webinar. Webinars, after all, are a way for your business to provide free information to potential customers. And as you know, sometimes free is a great motivator.

Charityhowto.com is a great example of a Page that consistently uses this strategy. A few times a month, Charityhowto.com conducts free webinars on how nonprofits can use various social media platforms. The webinars are limited to one hour, and all attendees are told that Q&A will be conducted on the Facebook Page right afterward (as shown in Figure 8-24).

Another thing that Charityhowto.com does consistently is to seek feedback about recent webinars, and potential topics for future webinars. Customers have also provided constructive feedback on the Page, or have asked questions about a recent purchase. Many times, other fans will show up to help this customer.

By using the Facebook Page for this type of interaction, Charityhowto.com saves resources on market research and customer service.

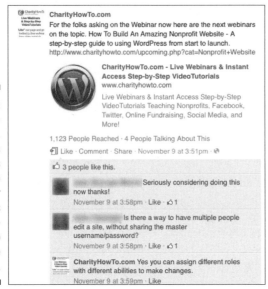

Figure 8-24:
Charity-
howto.
com uses
Facebook as
a follow-up
venue for
webinars
as a power-
ful way to
increase
fans.

Engaging with Your Fans with Your Mobile Phone

If you're like most people, you have limited time to manage Facebook and are often away from your computer. Fortunately, Facebook Page admins have the ability to post Page stories from their mobile phones.

Posting content and managing your Page Wall with mobile web browsers

You can post content and reply to Page updates and comments on sto-ries from any phone with mobile web access. To get the mobile browser URL sent to your mobile device, go to `https://www.facebook.com/mobile/?v=photos`.

Posting content and managing your Page Wall with mobile apps

Mobile devices are one of the fastest-growing ways people use to connect to Facebook. The great news for Facebook marketers is that you can also share content on your Facebook Wall from a variety of mobile devices. Facebook has developed applications for nine mobile devices, which can be accessed at `https://www.facebook.com/mobile/`. (See Figure 8-25.)

Figure 8-25:
Facebook
has devel-
oped
several
mobile appli-
cations.

Facebook for your phone

Download rich, interactive applications built for your phone. Available for:

iPhone	Nokia
Palm	Android
Sony Ericsson	Windows Phone
INQ	Sidekick
Blackberry	

Because all these platforms are inherently different, we won't go into detail about how to use each one. However, they're all very easy to use, and most of them allow you to post text updates, photos, videos, and replies to fan comments.

How to post content and manage your Facebook Wall via SMS

You can update your Facebook Page via text messaging (SMS) by setting up your Page to respond to specific texts. When you do, you can update your status, post on your Wall, send messages to friends, add friends, and much more, simply by sending SMS messages to 32665 (FBOOK).Configuring this feature can be found in your Mobile settings while in edit mode on your Facebook Page. (See Figure 8-26.)

Figure 8-26:
You can
access the
various
different
ways to use
a mobile
device for
your Page in
the Mobile
section
of your
Facebook
Page.

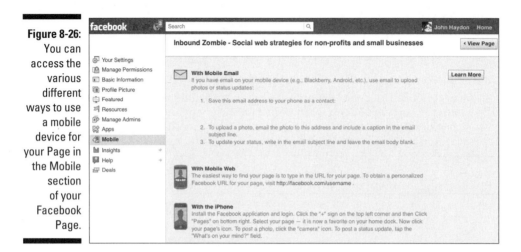

Figure 8-26:
You can access the various different ways to use a mobile device for your Page in the Mobile section of your Facebook Page.

How to post content and manage your Facebook Wall via e-mail

Finally, you can update your Facebook Page via e-mail. You can do this by sending e-mail messages to a specific e-mail address Facebook reserves for your account. This address is private, so don't share it with anyone except other admins. You obtain this address by following these steps:

1. **Log in to your Facebook Page and select Mobile in the admin panel (refer to Figure 8-26).**

2. **Click the Learn More button at the top right.**

    A new window appears. (See Figure 8-27.)

3. **Click the link Send the Upload Email for My Page to Me Now link.**

4. **Choose how you want Facebook to send you this information — to your e-mail account or to your phone.**

5. **Save this e-mail address to your mobile phone as a contact (use the name of your Page).**

When your address is secured, you can post a status update simply by sending an e-mail to that address — just enter your update into the e-mail's subject line and leave the rest of the message blank. If you want your status update to include a photo or video, attach the photo or video file to your e-mail message, and the text in your subject line will appear as the caption for your photo or video.

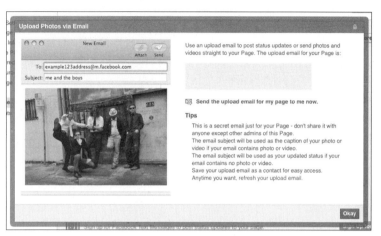

Figure 8-27:
In the Upload Photos via Email window, you can retrieve your Page's e-mail address.

Using the Facebook Subscribe Button on Your Profile

With all the amazing features that Facebook Pages have, the one thing that they've always lacked is the capability to create that personal connection that Facebook users like.

This all changed recently when Facebook released a new feature on Facebook Profiles called the Subscribe button. This feature allows Facebook users to publish content on their personal profiles (that anyone can subscribe to) without compromising any privacy.

For example, more than 45,000 people have subscribed to Sheryl Sandberg's (COO of Facebook) Profile's public updates. (See Figure 8-28.) These subscribers will receive these updates in their News Feed. Because of the Subscribe button, Sheryl can publish an update and share it with her subscribers even though they aren't Facebook friends. This allows Sheryl to engage with her subscribers without being forced to share her personal photos or her friends lists with them.

Figure 8-28:
Facebook
Profiles
now allow
people to
subscribe
to public
updates.

Sheryl Sandberg

⚐ Lives in Atherton, California
⚑ From Miami, Florida

Add Friend   Subscribe   ⚙ ▾

4 Mutual   45,256   2 ▾

About   Friends   Photos   Map   Subscribers

This ultimately means you can create a deeper, more personal experience around your business on Facebook. And after all, we have entered a consumer culture where people expect to have personal connections with the brands and businesses that they do business with.

To enable the Subscribe button on your Profile, follow these steps:

1. **Click the Subscriptions tab on your Profile and then click Allow Subscriptions.**

2. **Turn commenting on by selecting On next to Comments.**

   This allows Facebook users who aren't your friend to comment on your public updates.

3. **Choose who you want to get notifications about: Anyone, Friends of Friends, or No One.**

   Keep in mind that you can always edit these notifications.

After you activate the Subscribe button, Facebook users will be able to see the number of people who subscribe to your public updates. Kevin Rose, founder of Digg, for example, has more than 223,000 subscribers already!

As soon as you allow people to subscribe to your public updates, users who subscribe to your Profile will be able to see updates that you've published as public. Keep in mind that you'll have the choice to make updates public every time you publish an update on your Profile.

Activating the Subscribe button implies that you're sharing information that's interesting and valuable. Your content strategy should now include ways that your org leaders can optimize content for Facebook.

The Subscribe button may allow new people to see some of your content, but it doesn't change the way you and your friends connect on Facebook. Your friends have always been able to see your updates (and vice versa), so "subscribing" to each other isn't necessary.

Chapter 9

Measuring Success with Facebook Insights

In This Chapter

▶ Using Facebook Insights to gain insight into your fans

▶ Knowing which data to measure based on your goals

▶ Downloading data into spreadsheets

▶ Using third-party analytic tools

Facebook Insights is a suite of tools that helps you make informed decisions about how you should be adjusting your marketing strategy on Facebook. It helps you determine how you should spend your advertising dollars, how you should improve your content strategy, and how you can better understand the prospects and customers who are your Facebook fans. Most importantly, Insights helps you see how your marketing efforts are translated into new and returning customers.

Insights (see Figure 9-1) gives you access to standard metrics such as the number of Page visitors and fan demographics such as where they live and what type of Page stories they like. Stats are updated constantly, so you can quickly identify what's working and what's not, and then adjust your marketing strategy accordingly.

In short, Facebook Insights is the eyes and ears of your Page.

In this chapter, we show you how to use the information Facebook Insights provides to improve your Page. We explain what the different metrics are and how to use them to realize your content goals. We also offer tips on how to integrate third-party analytics into your Page.

Figure 9-1:
Insights
data show-
ing fan
acquisition
data.

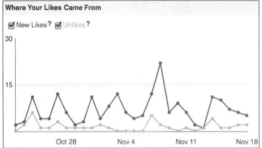

Getting Analytical with Facebook Insights

As you proceed with your Facebook marketing journey, you will begin to get a sense of what's working and what isn't working. You'll see that some of your Page updates get a lot of Likes and comments, while others get only crickets.

Based on these simple on-page observations, you'll get hunches about what kind of Page stories will work, and you might eventually get better at posting Page stories that effectively engage your fans.

Although this type of nonanalytical analysis —thinking with your gut — is an effective way for beginners to understand how fans react to your messaging, it doesn't give you insight into other important data you'll need to be truly successful as a Facebook marketer. What sorts of data? The following list includes some questions you won't be able to answer by simply observing the activity on your Wall:

- How many Facebook users view your Page each day?
- How many Facebook users (fans and nonfans) interacted with your Page this month?
- What were the top three days for post comments within a specific time period?
- How many of your fans return more than once to your Page?
- How many fans did you lose on this specific date?
- How many people liked your Page on this specific day?
- How many people liked your Page through a Like Box (one of Facebook's social plug-ins)?
- How many fans are hiding your Page stories on their News Feed?

We're not saying you shouldn't listen to your intuition, however. Following your gut can give you great information. However, *confirming* your intuition is just smart business. Additionally, with Insights you can identify trends within your Facebook Page that you would never see by scrolling down your Page Wall. For example, knowing that most of your new fans come from Like Boxes and Page Like Sponsored Story Ads is much better information than just knowing how many new fans you've gained. Knowing your top Like sources enables you to adjust your fan acquisition strategy based on what's really working instead of basing it on best guesses and random shots in the dark.

Using Facebook Insights

The next few sections show you how to access and use Facebook Insights. Keep in mind that Insights can only be accessed by Page admins.

Understanding the two types of Likes your Facebook Page receives

Before you dive into analyzing how effective your Facebook Page efforts are, you need to understand that with your Facebook Page, there are two types of Likes:

- ✔ **People your Page.** This is when they become a fan or connection of your Page. Facebook users can *Like* (become a fan by clicking the Like button) and unlike your Page.

- ✔ **People liking your content.** This is when they click Like after reading a specific post or Page story that you publish on your Wall. Facebook users can also hide a single story or all stories from your Page from appearing in their News Feed.

Accessing Page Insights

There are two ways you can access Facebook Page Insights:

- ✔ **Directly on the Page:** To access Facebook Insights, click on the Insights icon in your Page sidebar. (Note that only Page admins see this icon.)

- ✔ **From facebook.com/insights:** If you manage more than one Page, you can bookmark the webpage where all your Pages are listed for future reference (see Figure 9-2). Go to www.facebook.com/insights and select the Page you'd like to analyze.

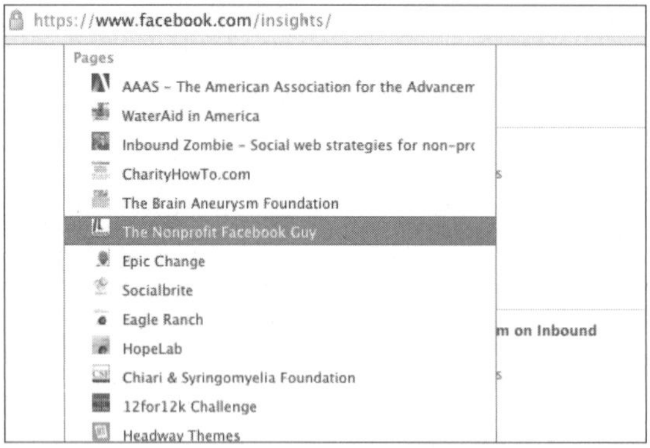

Figure 9-2:
Access
Insights at
www.
facebook.
com/
insights.

Exploring Facebook Page Insights

Facebook Insights for Pages provides critical data about activity around your Page, such as when someone Likes your Page, and activity around your Page updates, such as when users comment on or Like one of your Page stories.

Facebook breaks down its analytics into five reports:

- **The Dashboard Report:** An overview of how your Page is performing day to day.

- **The Likes Report:** A report about the Facebook users who Like your Page.

- **The Reach Report:** A report about the Facebook users who see your Page content.

- **The Talking About This Report:** A report about the Facebook users who create content about your Page.

- **The Check Ins Report:** A report about the Facebook users who checkin to your Facebook Place

In the next few sections we discuss each of these reports in greater detail:

Understanding the Dashboard Report

The Dashboard Report, the first tab you see when you click on Insights, is an overview of your Page. It shows you how your posts are being interacted with and how many people are seeing stories on your Page. You should view this report on a day-to-day basis.

At the very top of this report, you'll see the following data (see Figure 9-3):

- **Total Likes:** Total Likes is simply the number of people who Liked your Facebook Page (as of yesterday).

- **Friends of Fans:** This is the total number of friends among all your Facebook fans, taking mutual friends into account. This number is most useful if you are running a Facebook Sponsored Like Story because it represents the total number of people who could see that ad. The percent increase or decrease next to this number is a comparison with the previous seven-day period.

- **People Talking About This:** The number of people that engaged with your Page over the past seven days. This number includes the users who Liked your Page; the users who Liked, commented on, or shared a post from your Page; the users who answered a Question you asked on your Page; the users who tagged your Page in an update or in a photo; and the users who responded to an event on your Page. The percent increase or decrease next to this number is a comparison with the previous seven-day period.

- **Weekly Total Reach:** This is the number of people who have seen any content associated with your Page (including any Ads or Sponsored Stories pointing to your Page) over the past seven days. The percent increase or decrease next to this number is a comparison with the previous seven-day period.

Figure 9-3: The top of the Dashboard report.

Under these four data points, you see a graph that shows how frequently Facebook users are seeing and engaging with your Page stories (see Figure 9-4). The graph culls data from the rolling weekly numbers for "Talking About This" and "Weekly Total Reach" for the past month.

As shown in Figure 9-5, f you mouse over any point in this graph, a small window will display the timeframe that data covers. For example, in Figure 9-6 10,408 people were reached between 10/31/11 and 11/6/2011. You'll also see dots for each day that you've posted to your page (dot size indicates the number of posts for that day).

Figure 9-4:
Data at the
top of the
Dashboard
report
shows you
how much
people have
interacted
with your
Page in
the recent
week.

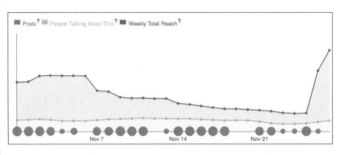

Figure 9-5:
The
Dashboard
graph
allows you
to view
more details
about each
data point.

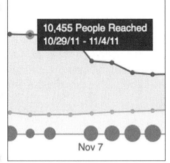

Understanding the Page Posts report

Under this graph you see a table containing information about how Facebook users engaged with your most recent Page updates (see Figure 9-6). You can sort each column in this table and even filter by post type. (Click All Post Types at the top right to filter).

The columns in this table are as follows:

- **Date:** The date that your post was published.
- **Post:** The type of post (post, photo, video, link, platform post) and excerpt.
- **Reach:** The number of people who saw that update, or the number of times that update was displayed.
- **Engaged Users:** The number of people who have clicked anywhere on your post.

✔ **Talking About This:** The number of people who have created a story from your post.

✔ **Virality:** The number of people your post reached who "talked about it" (This is calculated by dividing your Reach value by your Talking About This value.)

Figure 9-6:
In the Page Posts report you can view data on how each of your Page stories performed.

Page Posts						
All Post Types ▾						
Date ? ▾	Post ?		Reach ?	Engaged Users ?	Talking About This ?	Virality ?
11/26/11	📷	Cutting off all my hair tom...	622	11	3	0.48%
11/25/11	🔗	These guys are looking fo...	604	11	2	0.33%
11/25/11	💬	Q: What's the best YouTu...	654	7	2	0.31%
11/25/11	🔗	How to understand the R...	568	4	--	--
11/25/11	🔗	Three Simple Rules on T...	546	4	--	--
11/25/11	📷	I hope your turkey day wa...	520	91	10	1.92%
11/25/11	🔗	The difference between ...	600	11	1	0.17%

You can view more details about any data point in this table simply by clicking on that data point. For example, clicking a data point in the Engaged Users column produced the pie chart shown in Figure 9-7.

Figure 9-7:
You can view details about Page Post data by clicking on any data point in the table.

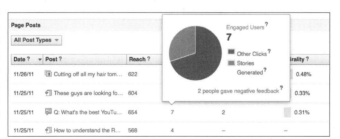

By analyzing Page Post data, you can better understand what type of content Facebook users interact with the most. You can also begin to see what type of content gets the most comments, the most likes, and the most shares. In other words, the information in this report improves your ability to engage existing fans, attract new fans, and create more awareness about your business throughout Facebook.

Understanding the Likes Report

To view the Likes report, click on Insights and then the Likes Report link. The Likes report shows you the locations from which Facebook users are Liking your Page (that is, from the NewsFeed, Likebox, or another source), as well as demographic information about your Page fans (as shown in Figure 9-8). At the top left of the tab, you can change the date range for all of the data on this tab (the range maximum is 89 days).

Figure 9-8:
The Likes report allows you to analyze the gender and age of your Facebook Page fans.

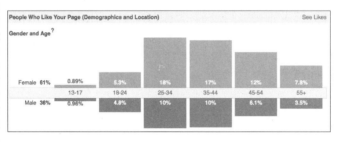

People Who Like Your Page (Demographics and Location)						See Likes
Gender and Age?						
Female 61%	0.89%	5.3%	18%	17%	12%	7.8%
	13-17	18-24	25-34	35-44	45-54	55+
Male 36%	0.96%	4.8%	10%	10%	6.1%	3.5%

Below the demographic data, you see statistics about where your fans are located and what languages they speak. Countries, cities, and languages are listed from the most fans to the least fans. Clicking on the More link below each category allows you to see all locations or languages.

While you're viewing demographic and location data, look for any trends. For example, in the demographics in Figure 9-8, notice that this Page's fanbase is fairly evenly distributed between men and women, but there are few fans under age 25. This information could be used when creating Page content or targeting ads on Facebook.

Where your likes came from

The last chart on the Likes report tab shows you how many new fans you've been acquiring and losing, as well as the sources for your new fans.

The graph shown in Figure 9-9 contains one very spiky line for New Likes and a rather flat line for Unlikes. Mousing over any data point in this graph shows you exactly how many new fans you acquired (or lost) on each day.

Figure 9-9:
The Likes report shows you fan acquisition (and attrition) and how people are Liking your Page.

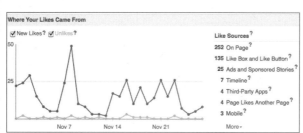

Understanding Like Sources

The right side of Figure 9-10 lists the locations from which people are Liking your Page. The top source of Likes is first, followed by the second, third, and so forth.

Facebook's platform includes many opportunities for Facebook users to Like a Page, including

- ✔ **From a New Facebook User Registration:** People who registering for Facebook can Like your Page in the registration wizard.
- ✔ **From creating a Page:** When you create a Page, Liking it is now part of the process.
- ✔ **Admin Registration:** People can Like your Page when you add them as admins.
- ✔ **Invite Friends Feature:** Admins can use the Invite Friends feature to ask their friends to Like your Page.
- ✔ **One the Page:** People who Like your Page from the Page itself.
- ✔ **Sponsored Stories:** People can Like your Page in a Sponsored Story ad.
- ✔ **Recommendation:** Someone can recommend your Page when they Like it.
- ✔ **From a Mobile Device:** People can Like your Page directly from an iPhone or any other mobile device.
- ✔ **Pages Can Like Pages:** In addition to Profiles, other Pages can Like your Page.
- ✔ **From a Profile Edit:** Facebook users can add your page to their Likes when they edit their profiles.
- ✔ **From a Facebook Search:** People who Liked your Page from Facebook's search results.

Understanding the Reach Report

To view the Reach report, click on Insights and then the Reach Report link. The Reach report shows the number of unique Facebook users who viewed your Page stories, Events related to your Page, or Sponsored Stories promoting your Page. This report includes both fans and nonfans. At the top left of the tab, you can change the date range for all of the data on this tab (the range maximum is 89 days).

Much like the Like report, the top of the Reach report displays demographic, location, and language information about the Facebook users who viewed your Page content (see Figure 9-10).

Figure 9-10: You can view demographic, location, and language of the Facebook users you've reached.

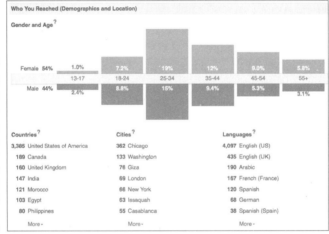

Understanding the Reach and Frequency graphs

Beneath the demographic, location, and language information are graphs describing the ways in which your content reached people. The Reach graph (on the left) shows four ways that your Facebook users saw your content on Facebook (see Figure 9-11):

- **Organic:** The number of unique Facebook users who saw content related to your Page in News Feeds, in the ticker, or on your Facebook Page.

- **Paid:** The number of unique Facebook users who saw a Facebook Ad or Sponsored Story that pointed to your Page.

✔ **Viral:** The number of unique Facebook users who saw a story about your Page that was published by a friend.

✔ **Total:** Total number of Facebook users you reached in a specific time period.

At the top left of the Reach graph is a drop-down menu that allows you to filter this data to view All Page Content, Your Posts, or Stories By Others.

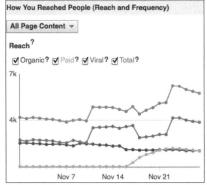

Figure 9-11: The Reach graph shows you various ways that you're reaching people.

The Unique Users by Frequency graph (on the right) shows how frequently you reached unique Facebook users in the previous seven days (see Figure 9-12). Each bar in the graph represents the number of times Facebook users saw your content. For example, in Figure 9-12, 1,771 Facebook users were reached just one time between 11/21/2011 and 11/27/2011. This report can give you a sense of how frequently you're reaching people — the number of people who repeatedly see your content during the previous week.

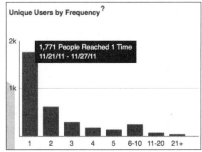

Figure 9-12: The Unique Users by Frequency shows you how frequently you reached unique Facebook users in the previous seven days.

Understanding the Visits to Your Page reports

Finally, you can see how Facebook users arrived at your Page with the following information (see Figure 9-13):

- **Page Views:** This graph shows you the number of Page views and unique Page views each day during the period specified (remember that you can change the date range for all of the data on this tab). Page views include people who have viewed your Page more than once, Unique Page views don't. For example, if John Smith visits your Facebook Page three times in one day, you'd have three Page views but only one Unique view.

- **Total Tab Views:** This lists your most visited tabs, arranged by number of visits (most visited to least visited).

- **External Referrers:** This is a list of external websites (external to Facebook.com) that send the most traffic to your website, arranged by number of visits (most visited to least visited).

Figure 9-13: The Visits to Your Page report shows you how people are visiting your Facebook Page.

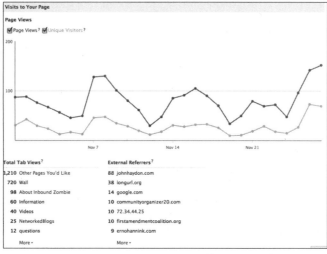

Understanding the Talking About This Report

To view the Talking About This report, click on Insights and then the Talking About This link. The Talking About This report shows you the number of unique Facebook users who have created a story about your Page on Facebook. Understanding how Facebook users talk about your Page helps you identify the kind of content that gets the most engagement. At the top left of this tab, you can change the date range for all of the data on this tab (the range maximum is 89 days).

Much like the Like and Reach reports, the Talking About This report contains demographic, location, and language information about the Facebook users who are "talking about" your Page (see Figure 9-14).

Figure 9-14:
You can view demographic, location, and language of Facebook users Talking About Your Page.

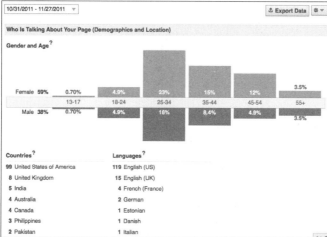

Below the demographic, location, and language information you'll see information about how Facebook users are talking about your Page (see Figure 9-15).

Figure 9-15:
Talking About This and Viral Reach graphs.

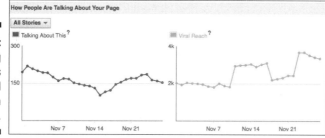

The Talking About This graph (on the left) shows the various different ways that Facebook users have been spreading the word about your Page. Each data point in this graph represents the number of unique Facebook users "talking about" your Page in the previous seven days.

At the top left of this graph is a drop-down list from which you can filter the data in the following ways:

- ✔ **Page Stories:** When Facebook users like your Page or RSVP to an event related to your Page.

- ✔ **Stories From Your Posts:** When Facebook users comment, Like, or share stories from your Page, or answered a Question you asked on your Page.

- ✔ **Mentions and Photo Tags:** When Facebook users tag your Page in a photo or a status update.

- ✔ **Posts By Others:** When Facebook users post content on your Page.

- ✔ **All Stories:** All of the above.

The Viral Reach graph (on the right of Figure 9-16) shows how awareness was created about your Page when people talked about your Page. The graph displays data according to the dataset shown in the Talking About This graph. For example, if you select Page Stories as the dataset, the Viral Reach graph displays the number of unique friends of the Facebook users who have Liked your Page or RSVP'd to an event related to your Page.

Understanding the Check Ins Report

The Check Ins report shows check-in activity for Facebook Places (Local Place or Business). Unless you have a Facebook Place, this report is unavailable to you. You can view the countries your Page fans are from and the languages they speak, as well as other demographic information. At the top left is a drop-down list from which you can change the date range for all of the data on this tab (the maximum is 89 days).

Beneath the demographic data, is a graph that represents how people have checked into your Place (via mobile or web) as shown in Figure 9-16. The How People Check In at Your Place report shows you how many people use a mobile device versus Facebook.com to check into your Facebook Place.

Figure 9-16:
The How
People
Check In at
Your Place
report.

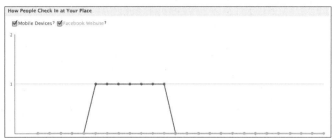

Exporting Data from Facebook Insights

Facebook has added some features to help you look at the data you collect from Insights in new ways. With these features you can

✔ **Export the data as an image file**. Just right-click the graph you want to save and select Save Image.

✔ **Export the data as an Excel or CSV file.** You can work with the data in your spreadsheet program. This way, you can view the data as one page simply by clicking the Export button on the top-right corner of the page, and selecting a date range and a format for your export (refer to Figure 9-17).

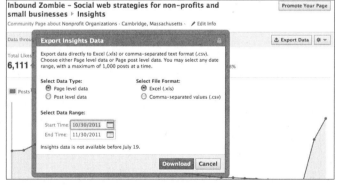

Figure 9-17:
You can
export
Insights
data as an
Excel or
CSV file.

Viewing Weekly Page Updates via E-Mail

Facebook sends a weekly e-mail to all Page admins highlighting some key metrics and providing direct links to important Page admin functions. If you're admin to more than one Page, stats for each Page are represented in the e-mail. This e-mail is a big time-saver because even a quick glance gives you some insight into your Pages' performance.

Integrating Third-Party Analytics

Although Facebook Insights is an invaluable tool to measure the most important metrics for tracking your Page activity, sometimes you may want to have additional information— such as the keywords users entered to find your Page or the average amount of time people stay on your site— at your disposal.

Facebook made its Page Insights data available to third-party analytics through its Open Graph protocol. A number of companies have already integrated this data into their existing services. Leading analytics companies, such as Webtrends and IBM Coremetrics, have begun to roll out new offerings with Facebook data alongside their existing website analytics. The following list includes several such companies:

- **Webtrends:** A very detailed analytics package that you can use via self-installation or with the Webtrends services team. This is a paid service, and you must contact Webtrends for package pricing based on your needs. See Figure 9-18. You can find more info on this product at www. webtrends.com/products/analytics/facebook/.

- **IBM Coremetrics:** In addition to traditional website analytics, Coremetrics' solutions help you track your Facebook return on investment (ROI). You can request a demo and speak with a salesperson by clicking the Request a Demo button on the top right at www.coremetrics.com/solutions/ web-analytics.php. See Figure 9-19.

- **HootSuite:** Social media-management tool that allows users to schedule posts to a variety of social media platforms (such as Facebook, Twitter, LinkedIn, and so on). This tool also includes a reporting module that allows you to select what Facebook Page Insights data you want to track. These reports are perfect for managers because they're presented in a way that's easy to understand. You can find more info about this tool at www.hootsuite.com.

Additionally, social media-management platforms from companies such as Buddy Media (www.buddymedia.com) and Involver (www.involver.com) incorporate Facebook Page Insights analytics, providing Page admins with a one-stop service for posting, monitoring, and measuring their Facebook activities.

Figure 9-18: Webtrends integrates Facebook data to track activities on a Page.

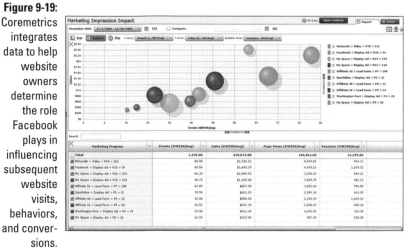

Figure 9-19: Coremetrics integrates data to help website owners determine the role Facebook plays in influencing subsequent website visits, behaviors, and conversions.

Part IV
Marketing beyond the Facebook Page

The 5th Wave   By Rich Tennant

"Has the old media been delivered yet?"

In this part . . .

*I*f you've read previous parts of this book, you've gotten some great ideas for establishing your Facebook presence, but there are strategies and tactics that can make it even stronger. In this part, we discuss a variety of strategies that help promote your business on Facebook. We show you how best to advertise on Facebook and how to set up promotions and events. There's even a chapter on marketing your business locally through Facebook.

You also find out how to cross-promote your business with Facebook and how to use social plug-ins to bring the advantages of Facebook to your website.

Chapter 10

Using Facebook Advertising to Promote Your Business

In This Chapter

▶ Planning your Facebook ad campaign

▶ Designing compelling ads

▶ Creating your ad

▶ Defining your landing page

▶ Managing and measuring your Facebook ads with Ads Manager

*W*ith more than 800 million members worldwide, Facebook ads can reach an audience six times bigger than a Super Bowl's television audience, and if you're not looking to go global (which is most likely the case), you can target Facebook ads to specific demographics (location, gender, relationship status, education, and so on).

Facebook's ad platform allows you to easily create your ad, select your target audience, set your daily budget, set a start and end date, and measure results. Ads can be purchased based on cost per impression (CPM) or cost per click (CPC). And unlike Google ads, Facebook allows advertisers to leverage Facebook's Social Graph, which displays which friends also like a particular Page, Event, or app. To help advertisers, Facebook provides an overview of how to use Facebook ads, a Facebook ad guide, and a series of case studies at `https://www.facebook.com/advertising/`. (See Figure 10-1.)

In this chapter, we show you how to use Facebook ads to your advantage. We introduce you to the different options available and how to use them. We offer tips on evaluating your advertising budget, targeting your audience, writing ad copy, uploading an effective image, and designing an ad. Finally, we help you create your landing page strategy and evaluate its effectiveness in fulfilling your marketing goals.

Figure 10-1:
Facebook's
Advertising
home page
with
resources
for
advertisers.

Introducing Facebook Ads

According to Facebook, 50 percent of its active users log on to Facebook every day. These consumers also spend more time per visit than they do on Yahoo!, MSN, and Myspace combined. For the past year and a half, Facebook has consistently surpassed Google in terms of website visitors. (See Figure 10-2.)

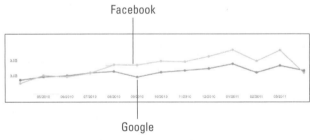

Figure 10-2:
Facebook
consis-
tently beats
Google for
visits.

Facebook Ads also allows you to form a sustained relationship with potential customers. By linking to your Facebook Page, you can keep the user engaged within the Facebook environment. And through Sponsored Stories, you can amplify that engagement with your fans to even more Facebook users, who in turn engage with your Page's content, which promotes awareness of your business to their friends. And so on, and so on.

Using Facebook Ads as part of your overall marketing mix

When advertising on Facebook, make sure you follow your overall marketing strategy, which hopefully includes other channels such as e-mail marketing, in-store promotions, or radio ads. The more you combine all channels in a cohesive ad strategy, the more results you'll get from each channel.

For example, an e-mail marketing campaign to promote your Facebook Page will be more effective if it's combined with a Facebook ad for your Page that's geographically targeted to where most of your e-mail subscribers are located. A Facebook user who isn't a Page connection (fan) but is on your e-mail list will be more likely (pun intended) than someone who isn't a newsletter subscriber to Like your Page because she gets twice the exposure to your campaign.

You can place two types of ads directly through Facebook:

- ✔ A **display ad,** which includes text and an image, as shown in Figure 10-3.
- ✔ **A Sponsored Story ad**, which allows you to leverage social connections related to a Page, Event, Group, or application. (See Figure 10-4.)

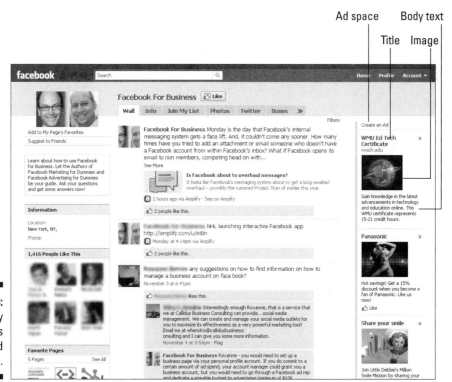

Figure 10-3:
A display ad contains text and an image.

Figure 10-4:
Facebook
Sponsored
Story Ads
allow users
to Like and
comment
on Page
stories.

Facebook ads appear in the far-right column of the user's page in the ad space. Up to four ads can appear in the ad space, but you can't control the order in which your ad appears.

The following sections go into more detail about how you can reach a specific audience with a Facebook ad and how to decide on a budget.

Understanding Facebook's targeting options

Targeting your audience is as important as the ad itself, and Facebook allows you to very specifically target only the audience you desire. In order to understand exactly who you should be targeting, start developing personas, or personality characteristics, to represent your target audience. *Personas* are simply imaginary prospects or clients with entire back stories, quirks, challenges, and needs for what you offer. The real value of personas is in how you imagine each of them reacting to your products or services. Well-developed personas can make it easier to effectively target your ads on Facebook.

For example, let's take Jane. She's a 30-year-old professional who works in downtown Boston. She doesn't have a car because she wants to lower her carbon footprint, but she loves meeting up with friends on Cape Cod to go surfboarding. She's smart and very selective about what she shares online. Jane would be a persona for Zipcar, Zappos and REI because these companies cater to customers who are environmentally conscious.

Here are some ways that you can target ads in Facebook:

✔ **Targeting by location:** Facebook allows for precise location targeting, based in part on your profile data and the IP address of the computer that users log in with, or their precise country, state/province, city, or postal code. Most cities in the United States, Canada, and the United Kingdom allow you to expand the targeting to include surrounding areas of 10, 25, and 50 miles if you target specific cities.

✔ **Targeting by interests:** Facebook lets you define your target audience using terms people have included in their Facebook Profiles. These terms may be drawn from their interests, activities, education, and job titles, Pages they like, or Groups to which they belong.

✔ **Targeting by connections:** You can target people already connected to your Facebook Page or those people who aren't already connected to your Page so that your existing fans aren't shown your ad. You can target the friends of people who are already connected to your Page, which is powerful because friends of fans are more likely to become fans themselves.

To maximize the total reach of your campaign, start by casting a wide net (broad, general targeting) and then finely tuning the targeting specifications until you reach an optimum balance between targeting specifics and the number of people targeted.

Setting your budget

Facebook employs a bidding structure for its advertising inventory based on supply and demand. If there's greater demand to reach a specific demographic, the ad typically has higher bids. The company also provides a suggested bid for you based on the approximate range of what other ads reaching this demographic have historically cost.

Facebook's ads are based on a closed bidding system; you can't see what others pay for ads, nor can they see your bid. Facebook provides a recommended bidding range when you create your ad and updates that range throughout the life of your campaign.

Start by setting your bid on the low side of the suggested range. You can monitor your campaign to see whether the ad performs at your given bid. You can also set a daily maximum budget. (For details, see "Managing Your Ad Campaigns with Ads Manager," later in this chapter.)

You don't have to follow the Facebook pricing guidelines, but if you bid too low, your ad won't appear.

Your purchase strategy should be based, in part, on your goals. Facebook allows you to purchase ads based on two types of pricing:

✔ **Cost per click (CPC):** With CPC, you pay each time a user clicks your ad. If your goal is to drive traffic to a specific page, paying based on CPC will probably be the best performer for you. Ask yourself, how much are you willing to pay per click?

✓ **Cost per impression (CPM):** With CPM, you pay based on how many users see your ad. If your objective is to get as many people within your target demographic to see the ad but not necessarily click through, ads based on a CPM basis may be your best option. Ask yourself, how much are you willing to pay per 1,000 impressions?

Test your ads on a CPC basis because using a CPC model allows you to identify the best performing ads and gives you a good idea of your cost per click.

Creating Winning Ads

Before we go into detail about how to actually create an ad on Facebook, we want tell you how to create compelling ads that drive clicks. In the following sections, we discuss ways to write effective ad copy and choose the optimal image. We also discuss the importance of knowing your audience and delivering incentives that are right for them. Finally, it's important to know the restrictions that govern Facebook ad guidelines so your ads are approved.

Copywriting tips

Given a 25-character limit on the title and a 135-character limit on the body, you can't waste a whole lot of words. Be direct, straightforward, and honest with your objective. Keep in mind that Facebook is also about building trust, and your copy must show an openness and willingness to share and connect with your audience.

Facebook ads should entertain, if the subject calls for it. Ads with a humorous message deliver higher rates of user engagement. For example, the Facebook ad in Figure 10-5 uses a funny juxtaposition between image and headline.

Figure 10-5:
This ad uses humor to attract interest.

Following are four guidelines when considering your Facebook ad copy:

✓ **Pose a question in your headline or in the body of the ad.** Don't be afraid to use a question mark where appropriate.

✔ **Reference your target audience.** By relating to your audience, you're more likely to grab their attention. Consider giving shout-outs, such as "Hey, housewives . . ."

✔ **Be direct.** Tell your target audience explicitly what you want them to do. For example, "Click here to receive your free t-shirt."

✔ **Use influencer's testimonials.** To establish credibility, consider high-lighting an endorsement, such as "Voted South Jersey's best pizza."

When using keywords of interest to target an ad campaign, it's always a good idea to include those keywords in the ad copy.

Choosing the right image

An image says a thousand words. This is why ads accompanied by images overwhelmingly perform better than text-only ads.

Preferably, use images that are easily recognizable, aren't too intricate in detail, and feature bright colors without the use of the blue that's so strongly identified with the Facebook logo and navigational color scheme.

Here are five other ideas to select the right image to get your Facebook ad noticed:

✔ **If your image includes people, they need to reflect the demographic you're targeting.** People like to see people who look like themselves.

✔ **Test different images with the same copy.** When you test a single factor, such as the ad's image, you can easily identify the stronger per-forming image.

✔ **An amateur photo style sometimes works better than stock photogra-phy.** A more personalized approach can help you stand out in the crowd.

✔ **Use a smaller image or one with a solid background color.** The maxi-mum size for an ad image is 110 x 80 pixels, but sometimes smaller images stand out among the rest of the full-size images people are used to seeing in Facebook ads. For example, using a dark background in the image makes the ad in Figure 10-6 stand apart from the rest on the page.

✔ **Make your image stand out with a decorative border.** Consider adding a branding element around the image or making the ad current. (For instance, if it's the holiday season, add a decorative holiday border.)

Figure 10-6:
The image is the most important element in your ad.

Simplifying your offer

Because you have a small amount of space from which to communicate your offer via your Facebook ad, don't waste words or overcomplicate things. Your call to action needs to be direct, clear, and easy to follow. Cleverness and wit aren't as effective as using the simplest word choice possible, as shown in the ad in Figure 10-7.

Figure 10-7:
Sometimes the simplest way to say something is the best.

Creating a Facebook Ad

The process for creating Facebook ads is very easy. Just follow these basic steps:

1. **Go to** www.facebook.com/ads.

   The Facebook Ads home page appears.

2. **Click the green Create an Ad button on the upper right of your screen.**

   The Advertise on Facebook page appears, displaying the options for designing your ad.

Facebook uses a three-step process for creating an ad: Design your ad, target your ad, and select pricing and scheduling. The following sections explain how to fill in the information for that three-step process.

Keep in mind that the available options dynamically change depending on specific choices you make while creating the ads. For example, if you select an external URL for your ad's destination, Sponsored Stories will disappear as an option. All of these variations are noted in the following sections.

Step 1: Design Your Ad

Before you create a Facebook ad, decide where you want the landing page — the page a user is taken to when he clicks your ad — to be. You can either link to an external URL, a Facebook Event, a Facebook app, or your Facebook Page. We recommend that you choose a destination within Facebook, as outlined in the following steps. (See the later section, "Devising a Landing Page Strategy for Your Ads," in this chapter, for more on choosing between an internal or external destination.)

Follow these steps to design your ad:

1. **Specify a destination for the ad in the Destination box. (See Figure 10-8.)**

   You can specify either an external URL or your Facebook Page, Event, Place, or app. In the Destination drop-down menu is a list of your Facebook Pages, Events, Places, and apps. Choose one of these, or specify an external URL by entering the URL in the field provided.

Figure 10-8:
Facebook allows you to send users to a specific tab on your Facebook Page.

Destination:	The Nonprofit Facebook Guy [?]
Type:	○ Sponsored Stories [?] ◉ Facebook Ads [?]
Destination Tab:	Default [?]

2. **For Type, select either Sponsored Stories or Facebook Ads.**

   • *Sponsored Stories:* Allows you to select one of these options: *Page Like Story* (when people Like your Page, their friends see a story about it), or *Page Post Like Story* (when fans Like your Page post, their friends see a story about it). (See Figure 10-9.)

   • *Facebook Ads:* Allows you to send traffic to specific tabs on a Facebook Page, a Facebook Event, or a Facebook app.

Sponsored Stories have been found to have a higher ROI than traditional Facebook ads. In fact, according to Inside Facebook (http://insidefacebook.com) Sponsored Story ads have a a 46 percent higher click-through rate than Facebook's standard ads. This is simply because Sponsored Stories ads leverage users' social connections inherent within the Facebook network. With traditional Facebook ads, users must go from your ad to your Page in order to Like the Page – an unnecessary additional step that some people aren't willing to make. With Sponsored Stories ads, users can Like the Page directly in the ad.

Figure 10-9:
Facebook
Sponsored
Stories
selection.

3. **If you're advertising an external URL, type a title or headline for your ad in the Title text box. (See Figure 10-10.)**

   You're limited to 25 characters and must adhere to the Facebook formatting policies.

   This step applies only to Facebook Ads posted to external URLs. If you're advertising a Page, the page title is the default title, and you can't change it. If you have chosen Sponsored Stories, no title option is available because the ad itself will be a post from your Page.

4. **In the Body text box add body copy, up to 135 characters.**

   Keep your copy concise, compelling, and focused on what's interesting to the viewer.

5. **If you're advertising a Page, Event, or app, you have the choice of selecting the avatar for your ad's image. To do so, in the Image section, click the Browse button and then navigate to the image on your computer that you want to upload and use in the ad.**

6. **Press Continue to move on to Targeting.**

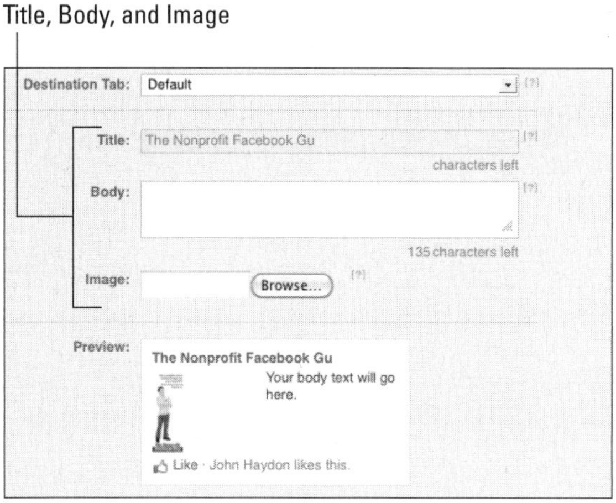

Title, Body, and Image

Figure 10-10:
Facebook
ads include
a title,
image, and
body.

Step 2: Targeting

After you design your ad, you need to target your audience by selecting the Targeting criteria, as shown in Figure 10-11. You can think of targeting in terms of an archer's bull's-eye. The closer you get to the center, the narrower the circles; the farther out you go, the wider the area. (For more information on targeting your ad, see the section, "Understanding Facebook's targeting options," earlier in this chapter.)

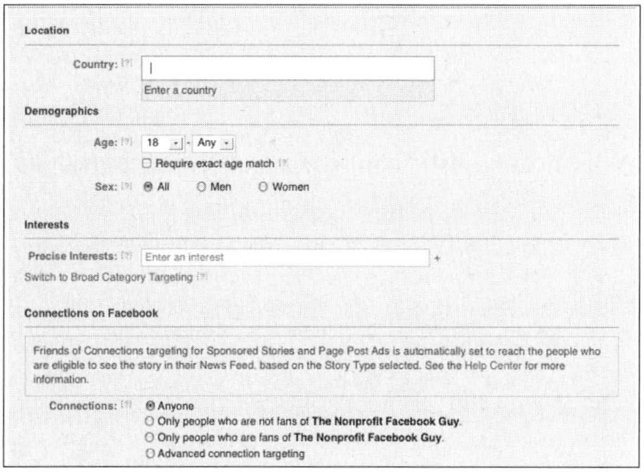

Figure 10-11:
Target your
audience's
location,
demograph-
ics, and
interests.

To the right of Facebook's Targeting section, you see a number that represents the approximate number of people who would be exposed to your ad, as shown in Figure 10-12. The audience size shown here changes as you add or remove targeting factors in the following steps.

Figure 10-12:
The estimated reach in Facebook's Ad tool provides real-time numbers.

Estimated Reach [?]
137,101,260 people
- who live in the **United States**
- age **18** and older

If you reach too small an audience, your ad might not generate any click-throughs. Widen some factors, such as age range, or add surrounding locations to your geotargeting.

Follow these steps to target a specific audience for your Facebook ad campaign:

1. **In the Country field, type the location in which you want your ad to be seen.**

   There are nearly 100 countries from which to target, and each ad can reach up to 25 countries. You can also drill down to the state/province or city level. For many cities, you can even specify up to 10, 25, or 50 miles surrounding the city.

2. **In the Age drop-down lists, choose the age range of the audience you want to see the ad.**

   If you know your audience's approximate age range, this is a great way to target them. For example, if you sell retirement homes, you can target people 55 and older. To reach the widest-possible audience, leave this at the default setting: Any. Keep in mind that Facebook doesn't allow you to target members younger than 13.

3. **Select All, Men, or Women for the gender of your audience.**

   You can target just men, just women, or both. By default, All is selected, making the ad available to the widest amount of members possible.

4. **In the Interests section, you can choose either "precise interests" or "broad interests." To choose precise interests, simply type any keywords in the Precise Interests textbox that you want to target specifically. To choose broad interests, click the Switch to Broad Category Targeting link.**

When you start typing a term in the Precise Interests textbox, Facebook displays a range of possible keywords. These keywords are derived from Facebook member profiles, specifically from members' interests, activities, education, job titles, Pages they like, or Groups to which they belong. If the keyword you enter isn't identified in enough Facebook profiles, it's not statistically large enough to target. You can enter as many keywords as are relevant.

You can target an ad to fans of a popular competitor's Facebook Page by typing that competitor's Page name into the Precise Interests text box. If you switch to broad interests, choose a category within the Broad Category box and then select the specific subcategories you'd like to target (see Figure 10-13). These subcategories include the most popular terms that Facebook users include in their Profiles.

Figure 10-13:
Facebook
allows you
to target
your ad to
specific
broad cat-
egories.

5. **In the Connections on Facebook section, select one of the following options (see Figure 10-14):**

   - *Anyone:* This allows you to target anyone on Facebook regardless of their connection to a Page, Event, Group, or application.

   - *Only People Who Are Not Fans of* Your Page: This targets users of your Application or attendees of your Event who are not fans of your Page.

   - *Only People Who Are Fans of* Your Page: This targets users of your Application or attendees of your Event who are also fans.

   - *Advanced Connection Targeting:* This allows you to select a group, app, Event, or Page for which you are an admin.

   If you're advertising an external website URL, you have the option of selecting only Anyone or Advanced Connection Targeting.

   Pay close attention to what options you're selecting to see if they align with your advertising goals. For example, targeting users who aren't fans of your Page, Event, Group, or app makes sense if your goal is to acquire new fans.

Figure 10-14:
Facebook allows you to target users who aren't fans of your Facebook Page, or who are part of a group or Page for which you are an admin.

Connections on Facebook

Connections: [?]
- ⚪ Anyone
- ⚪ Only people who are not fans of **The Nonprofit Facebook Guy.**
- ⚪ Only people who are fans of **The Nonprofit Facebook Guy.**
- ⦿ Advanced connection targeting

Target users who are connected to:

| 12for12k Challenge ✕ | [?] |

Target users who are not already connected to:

| Enter your Page, Event, or App | [?] |

Friends of Connections:
☐ Only show my ad to friends of the fans of **The Nonprofit Facebook Guy.** [?]

6. **If you're creating a Sponsored Story ad, you can target users who are friends of people connected to your specific Facebook Page, Event, Group, or application. To do so, check the Friends of Connections box in the Connections on Facebook section (refer to Figure 10-14).**

   This can be very powerful because friends of existing fans may have similar interests and may be influenced by existing fans.

7. **Select criteria for Advanced Demographics.**

   Make your selections for Interested In (Men or Women), Relationship Status (All, Single, Engaged, In a Relationship, or Married). In the Languages field, start typing the language you want to target (if there is one).

   Facebook allows you to target people by their native language. Reaching a specific culture, such as Chinese-speaking Americans or Spanish-speaking people in Florida has never been easier. If your business is particularly culture based, this is a highly effective way for you to target your audience.

   Facebook has more than 100 languages listed, and the list keeps growing.

8. **Select the desired educational level of your audience.**

   Your options are All, College Grad, In College, or In High School. You can choose to reach just college graduates, or current students at a particular school. This is a great tool for recruitment because you can target people with the right schools and degrees you're interested in hiring.

9. **Target down to the workplace.**

   As you start to type the workplace, you see a range of workplace possibilities. If the workplace you're entering isn't statistically large enough to support an ad, it remains blank.

For example, say you're a business-to-business (B2B) marketer and want to reach folks at Fortune 1000 companies. Why not just target employees at a specific company, such as IBM, with an ad and landing page just for it? It's now possible and very cost-effective via Facebook ads.

10. **Proceed to the Campaigns, Pricing, and Scheduling section, which we discuss next.**

Step 3: Campaigns, Pricing, and Scheduling

The final step to creating your ad is to set your daily ad budget, bid, and schedule (see Figure 10-15).

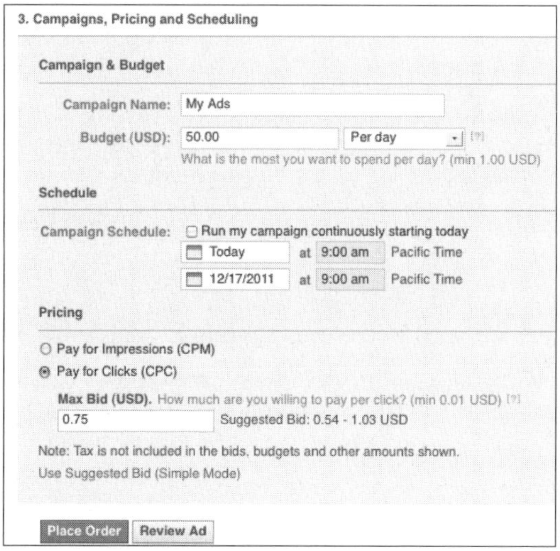

Figure 10-15: The Campaigns, Pricing, and Scheduling step.

The following steps detail how to set your Facebook ad budget:

1. **In the Campaign Name textbox, type the name of your campaign.**

   Campaign refers to a group of ads that all share the same daily budget and schedule; it can consist of many separate ads. By grouping ads under a single campaign, it's easier to manage various campaigns and determine how each group of ads performs.

2. **In the Budget text box, set your daily maximum budget.**

   You can also choose to set a lifetime budget and enter the amount you want to spend for the entire life of that campaign.

The minimum daily spending amount is $1; you can run a Facebook ad for as little as $1 a day, albeit to a very small number of people.

3. **In the Schedule section, choose from two options for when the ad runs:**

   • *If you want the campaign to start today and run indefinitely,* select the Run My Campaign Continuously Starting Today check box.

   • *If you want to choose a specific date range,* deselect the Run My Campaign Continuously Starting Today check box and enter the starting and the ending date and time.

4. **In the Pricing section, Facebook suggests a per-click bid amount. Accept or reject the suggested bid.**

   If you're satisfied with this suggested per-click bid, proceed to Step 7.

   If you prefer a different bid, click the Set a Different Bid (Advanced Mode) link.

5. **Select the radio button next to the type of pricing structure you want to go with: Pay for Impressions (CPM) or Pay for Clicks (CPC).**

   Facebook allows you to bid based either on CPM or CPC. If you select Pay for Impressions (CPM), remember your bid represents every 1,000 *impressions,* or ad views.

6. **Enter the maximum amount you're willing to pay per click or per impression.**

   The minimum allowable bid is 2cents for CPM and 1cent for CPC, although Facebook often rejects bids above this threshold that it deems too low.

   Facebook gives you a suggested bid range. As a strategy, we suggest you initially set your bid on the low side of the suggested range.

7. **Click the Review Ad button.**

   The Review Ad page appears and recaps your ad's creative elements, targeting, type of bid (CPC or CPM), bid price, daily budget, and duration of ad *flight* (the time period in which an ad runs).

8. **After you review your ad, click the Place Order button.**

   On the following Page, the following message from Facebook appears: "Your ad was created successfully. It will start running after it is approved, which can take up to 24 hours. Please check back once your ad is approved to monitor its performance. You can also edit your ad creative, or change targeting and delivery information below at any time."

9. **Once your ad is approved you will get an e-mail from Facebook notifying you of the approval with a link to the ad manager.**

Creating Multiple Campaigns

Facebook makes it easy for you to duplicate an existing ad, change a number of variables, and launch multiple multifaceted ad campaigns. An advertiser has several reasons for doing this:

- ✔ **Tailor each ad to a specific region.** Because economical, educational, and personal preferences vary from region to region, the ad copy and image may need to reflect these differences.

- ✔ **Reach multilingual audiences.** You can use Facebook's language targeting on an ad-by-ad basis.

- ✔ **Test which variables in ads perform better.** By changing variables, you can optimize the campaign to the better-performing ads.

- ✔ **Test different bids and models (CPC versus CPM).** This enables you to determine which model is more economically efficient.

Facebook makes it easy to pattern a new ad after an existing one. When designing your new ad (as we describe in the section "Step 1: Design Your Ad" earlier in the chapter), you can copy an existing ad by selecting that ad from the Select Existing Creative link, which opens a new window, as shown in Figure 10-16.

Figure 10-16:
Copy an existing ad to make multiple campaigns that target different audiences.

Facebook offers you a full range of metrics to measure success from within your Ads Manager. Because replicating an ad and creating different iterations for testing is easy, Facebook is quickly becoming the advertising platform of choice for savvy marketers.

Devising a Landing Page Strategy for Your Ads

If you're familiar with online marketing, you understand the importance of making a good first impression with your ad link. Your *landing page* (as it's known in advertising) is the page that opens when users click your ad, and it can be an internal Facebook page or an external website. All engagement begins on the landing page.

Successful landing pages provide an easy path to *conversion,* or realizing your goal. A conversion can include capturing user data via an input form, driving membership for your Page, getting people to sign a petition, or simply making a sale. Regardless of your objective, if your landing page doesn't deliver the desired result, your campaign is worthless.

Facebook allows you to create ads that link to either an internal Facebook location or an external website (URL), but only one per ad. The following sections explain how to choose a destination for your ad.

Landing on a Facebook location

As a best practice when running a Facebook ad campaign, link your ads to an internal Facebook location as opposed to an external website. For internal Facebook ads, you can link to a Facebook Page or app, Groups, or Events page.

If you're advertising a Facebook Page, you can send users to a customized landing tab within your Page. Figure 10-17 shows the Inbound Zombie landing page, which features a newsletter sign-up form.

The bottom line here is to bring visitors to your Facebook Page, where they're just one click away from becoming a fan. Because you have access to your fans' profiling data, your fanbase can become an extremely valuable marketing asset.

Figure 10-17:
The land-
ing page
for Inbound
Zombie.

Landing on a website page

Facebook also allows you to refer your ad visitors to an external web address (URL), provided it adheres to the company's advertising policies and guidelines at `https://www.facebook.com/ad_guidelines.php`. If you choose an outside website, you aren't required to prove that you're the owner of the web domain.

You might want to send visitors to your website for several reasons. Linking to an outside website offers you greater control over your landing page's content, technology, and design. You might already have finely tuned landing pages that you prefer to drive ad traffic to, regardless of where the traffic originated, and you can employ much more sophisticated web analytics on your site than are presently available on Facebook.

Because ads can be purchased on a CPC basis, you can opt to pay only when a user clicks through to your page, regardless of whether it's an internal Facebook Page or an outside website. In Figure 10-18, QualityHealth directs its Facebook ads to a landing page on its website that features the same offer that's highlighted in the ad.

Revealing content on your landing page

A new technique that's gaining a lot of favor with Facebook marketers is using a reveal tab for a landing page. A *reveal tab* is a great way to get your visitors to click the Like button and become a fan of your Page. With a reveal tab, you give visitors a reason to become fans, by showing only part of the Page they land on, as shown in the Teesey Tees example in Figure 10-19.

Figure 10-18:
Quality-
Health's
external
landing
page.

This technique, known as *fan gating,* is also effective when used with coupons and special promotions. Hide the information users need to redeem the promotion until they Like your Page.

By adding a custom reveal tab, you can significantly increase the number of fans to your Page.

Figure 10-19:
Teesey
Tees uses
a reveal
landing tab.

Managing and Measuring Your Ad Campaigns with Ads Manager

After you create an ad with Facebook, you want to keep tabs on that ad's performance. Facebook's Ads Manager is your personalized, central hub where you can view all your ad activities (see Figure 10-20) and make edits to ad campaigns. To access Ads Manager, visit www.facebook.com/ads/manage.

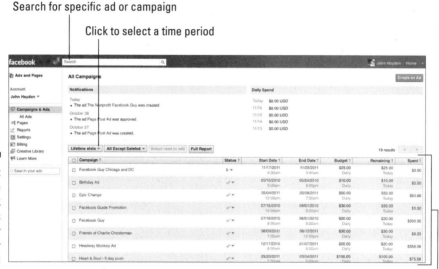

Search for specific ad or campaign

Click to select a time period

Ad management table

Figure 10-20: The Facebook Ads Manager shows your latest ad campaigns.

Viewing performance data

Facebook does a good job of balancing Ads Manager's ease-of-use with powerful digital marketing features. In the Ads Manager, you see Facebook notifications— typically messages from Facebook's advertising staff updating you on new platform developments, which come fast and furious— as well as the latest information on your most recent campaigns. You also see your daily spend for the previous five days.

The All Campaigns page includes a table (see Figure 10-21) that features the most important data on your ad's performance. At a glance, you can view the following information:

✔ **Campaign:** The name you created for your ad(s)

✔ **Status:** A checkmark indicates whether the ad is live or paused.

✔ **Start Date:** The date your campaign started.

✔ **End Date:** The date your campaign ended.

✔ **Budget:** You total budget per day or per campaign.

✔ **Remaining:** The remaining budget per day or per campaign.

✔ **Spent:** The total amount spent so far.

Figure 10-21:
The ad management table. Any of the columns can be sorted or filtered by date or status.

	Campaign ?	Status ?	Start Date ?	End Date ?	Budget ?	Remaining ?	Spent ?
☐	Birthday Ad	✓ ▾	05/10/2010 9:00am	05/24/2010 8:00pm	$10.00 Daily	$10.00 Today	$0.00
☐	Epic Change	✓ ▾	05/04/2011 12:00pm	05/08/2011 7:00pm	$50.00 Daily	$50.00 Today	$83.68
☐	Facebook Guide Promotion	✓ ▾	07/15/2010 10:06am	08/01/2010 9:00am	$30.00 Daily	$30.00 Today	$0.00
☐	Facebook Guy	✓ ▾	07/16/2010 8:00am	08/01/2010 8:00am	$20.00 Daily	$20.00 Today	$330.30

Viewing campaign details

To view campaign details, simply click on the campaign name within the ad management table. On the resulting screen, you'll see graphs and a spreadsheet with details for that campaign. (See Figure 10-22.)

Figure 10-22:
The campaign page allows you to see all the details about your ad's performance.

Audience and Response graphs

On the campaign Page at the top, you'll see two charts:

- ✔ **Audience:** The Audience graph (as shown in Figure 10-23) compares the number of people to whom your ad was displayed (Reach) to the number of people you targeted (Targeted). The Social Reach circle shows you the number of people to whom your ad was targeted if you purchased a Sponsored Story ad.

- ✔ **Response:** The Response graph shows you how many Facebook users responded to your ad (see Figure 10-24). This chart includes two types of data:

  - *Clicks:* This is the number of clicks your ads have received. This number includes Page Likes, Event RSVPs, and app installs from the ad.

  - *Connections:* This is the number of people who Liked your Facebook Page or RSVPed to your event within 24 hours of seeing your ad. (You see this information in your Response chart only when you're advertising a Page, Event, or app.) Because the Connections data tells you how many people became a fan of your Page or installed your app within 24 hours of seeing your ad—even if they didn't click on the ad itself— it shows how effective your ad is (or isn't) at getting the results you want.

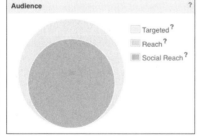

Figure 10-23:
The
Audience
graph.

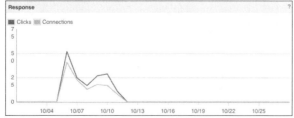

Figure 10-24:
The
Response
graph.

The default time period for these two graphs is 28 days. However, clicking the Last 28 Days button (located below the Audience graph) gives you additional view options: Today, Yesterday, Last 7 Days, or Custom (in which you enter the desired range of dates). The ROI metrics underneath the Audience and Response charts is a row of numbers in bold type that show ROI (return on investment) for your ad (see Figure 10-25).

Figure 10-25:
The ROI
of your
Facebook
ad.

Campaign Reach?	Frequency?	Social Reach?	Connections?	Clicks?	CTR?	Spent?
2,060	36.8	2,060	120	161	0.213%	$84.01

Here's what all of these numbers mean:

- **Campaign Reach:** The number of unique Facebook users who saw your ad.

- **Frequency:** The number of times that individual Facebook users you reached saw your ad.

- **Social Reach:** The number of unique Facebook users who saw an ad from your campaign with the names of their friends displayed in the ad.. This data only applies if you're advertising a Page, Event, or app.

- **Connections:** The number of people who Liked your Facebook Page or RSVPed to your Event within 24 hours of seeing the ad. You won't see this if you're not advertising a Page, Event, or app.

- **Clicks:** The number of clicks your ads have received. This also includes Page Likes, Event RSVPs, or app installs from the ad.

- **CTR:** The number of clicks on your ad divided by the number of impressions.

- **Spent:** The amount of money you've spent so far during a campaign.

Beneath this data, is a row of data in tabular form that includes many of the metrics described above, plus

- **Name:** The name of your Facebook ad campaign.

- **Status:** The status of your ad (active, paused, or deleted).

- **Bid:** The maximum amount you're willing to pay for each click (CPC) or per 1,000 impressions (CPM).

- **Price:** This is the average amount you're paying per CPC or CPM.

Ad preview and targeting summary

At the very bottom of a campaign ad page, you'll see a preview of your Facebook ad on the left and a summary of who you've targeted on the right (see Figure 10-26).

Figure 10-26:
Facebook
ad pre-
view and
targeting
summary.

You can see what your ad looks like on a Facebook Profile by clicking the View on Profile link below the ad preview. You can edit the ad or targeting information by clicking on the Edit button in the upper-right of either section. Keep in mind that you can only edit an ad during a campaign, not after it's finished.

Because typical campaigns on Facebook deliver a click-through rate of approximately 0.15 percent, keep your audience reach as large as possible to get the most out of your ad spend.

Making changes to your daily budget

When setting your campaign budget, you're wise to pay attention to your daily spend and performance results. Your *daily spend* is the maximum amount you've allocated to your campaign budget. Get some benchmarks for your campaign's performance. If you find that your CTR is greater than 1 percent, consider lowering your bid because a higher-performing ad gets preference over underperforming ones. The difference in a few cents can be significant, depending on your total spend, so constantly adjust your bids to maximize your return on investment (refer to Figure 10-25). For more information on setting a budget for your ad, see the "Setting your budget" section earlier in this chapter.

You can make changes to your campaign's daily budget from the All Campaigns view within Ads Manager in several ways:

✔ **Click the budget amount for the campaign you want to change.** A pop-up box appears that allows you to modify your daily budget (see Figure 10-27).

✓ **Select the check box to the left of any campaign you want to edit.** Click the Edit *(number)* of Rows option above the list of campaigns to change the name, status, or budget of any selected campaign.

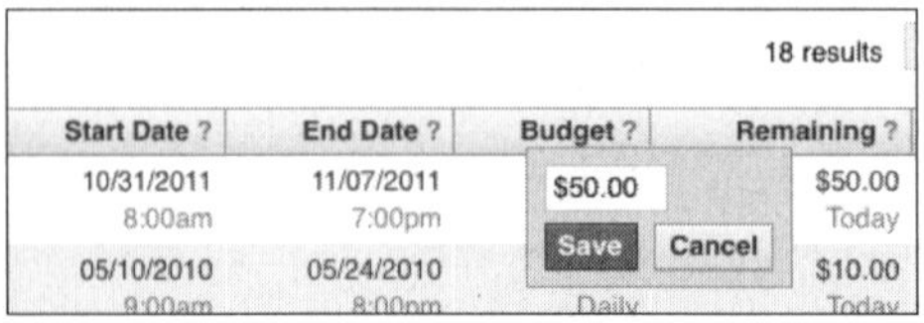

Figure 10-27:
Editing the
daily budget
from the All
Campaigns
page.

You can also change your campaign's budget and dates from the individual campaign view by clicking the Edit button next to the Budget listed at the top of the campaign details. When you do so, a new window appears (see Figure 10-28) that allows you to edit your budget and the dates the ad will run. Changes are active within a few minutes of making the change. Any ad charges already accrued for the day are included in your new budget so that your account isn't overcharged.

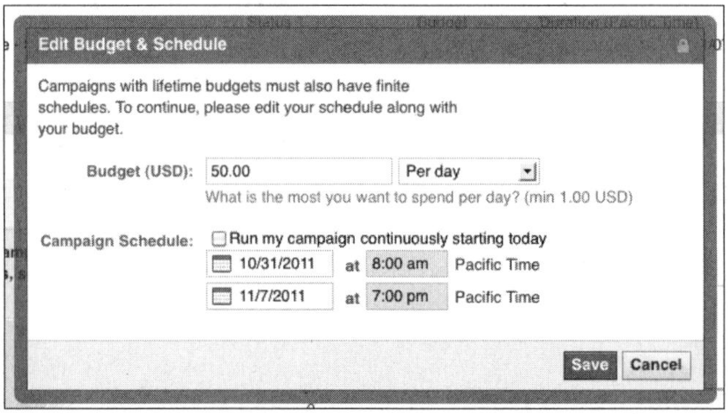

Figure 10-28:
Editing the
budget and
run dates
from an
individual
campaign
page.

Understanding Other Facebook Ad Manager Features

The Facebook Ads Manager also includes a number of features and resources to help you save time and get more out of your Facebook ads. This section provides a quick summary of these features and resources, which are found on the left sidebar of the Ad Manager (see Figure 10-29).

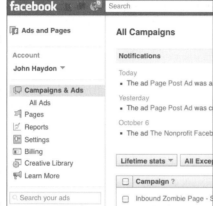

Figure 10-29:
The
Facebook
Ad Manager
includes
several
additional
resources
for
marketers.

Accessing your Facebook Page from the Ad Manager

Clicking on the Pages icon takes you to a single page listing all of your Facebook Pages (https://www.facebook.com/ads/manage/pages. php). From here, you can view Insights for your Page, view Page notifications, and login as your Page.

Creating and scheduling Facebook ad reports

You can get reports delivered by e-mail by clicking on the Reports icon and following these steps:

1. **In the Report Type drop-down list, select one of the following report types (see Figure 10-30):**

   • *Advertising Performance:* Performance info that includes impressions, clicks, CTR, and money spent.

   • *Responder Demographics:* Demographic information about users who are seeing and clicking on your ads.

   • *Conversions by Impression Time:* This report shows the number of conversions organized by time your ad was displayed (impressions).

2. **In the Summarize By drop-down list, choose the way you want your report summarized (by Ad, Campaign, or Account).**

3. **In the Filter By drop-down list, filter your report by selecting the ads or campaigns you want to include.**

Figure 10-30:
Creating
and
scheduling
reports in
Facebook's
Ad
Manager.

Report Type:	Advertising Performance ▾
Summarize By:	Campaign ▾
Filter By:	No Filter ▾
Time Summary:	Daily ▾
Date Range:	10/21/2011 ▤ to 10/29/2011 ▤
Format:	Webpage (.html) ▾
	☐ Include Deleted Ads/Campaigns
	Generate Report

4. **Select your time summary and date range in the Time Summary and Date Range fields.**

5. **In the Format drop-down list, choose the format for which you'd like your report delivered.**

   You can choose HTML or Excel (CSV).

6. **Click Generate Report.**

On the following page you can export the report by clicking on the Export Report link at the top-right of this page. You can also schedule the report to be delivered by clicking on the Schedule This Report link at the top-right of the page: Just enter your e-mail address in the pop-up window and click Save.

Adding other users to your Facebook ad account

Click the Settings icon and you can change your address, set e-mail notifications, and tell Facebook how you use ads (Business or Personal). Also, you can give other Facebook users access to your Facebook ad account. Additional users can have general access to the account or have only the ability to view reports. Added users will not have access to your personal Facebook Profile, or to any other ad account.

If you have more than one person in charge of marketing at your business, or if you work with a marketing consultant, consider adding them as a user on your Facebook Ad.

To add another user on your account, click Settings and then click the Add a User button on the right (see Figure 10-31).

Figure 10-31:
Here you
can add
other users
to your
Facebook
ad account.

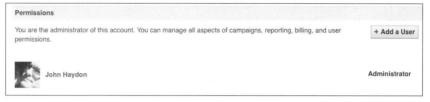

Tracking payment transactions

Click the Billing icon to view details about your payment transactions for each of your campaigns. (See Figure 10-32.) You can also change your funding source by clicking Funding Source in the left sidebar.

Figure 10-32:
Facebook
Ad
Manager's
Billing sec-
tion.

Managing ad creatives

Click the Creative Library icon to edit, view, and preview past ad creatives. (See Figure 10-33.) To the right of each creative are three buttons:

Figure 10-33:
Facebook
Ad
Manager's
Creative
Library
section.

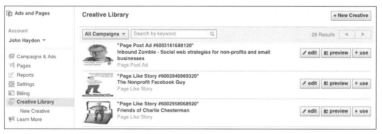

✔ **Edit:** This button allows you to edit the name of the ad creative. Click the Edit button and edit the name of your ad creative in the resulting pop-up window (see Figure 10-34).

✔ **Preview:** This button allows you to view the way your ad will appear on your profile. Click the Preview button and your ad will appear on your Profile in the right sidebar (where ads normally appear).

✔ **Use:** This button allows you to reuse an ad creative. When you select this option, you are redirected to the Facebook Ad tool, where you'll find your ad loaded and ready for you to create a new campaign.

Figure 10-34:
Edit the name of an ad creative here.

Learning about your business resources

Click the Learn More icon takes you to an overview of all Facebook's resources available to businesses — Pages, Ads, Sponsored Stories, and Developer Platform. (See Figure 10-35.)

Figure 10-35:
Facebook allows advertisers to learn about all business resources.

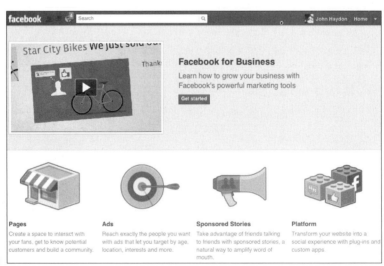

Chapter 11

Facebook Marketing for Local Businesses

In This Chapter

▶ Introducing Facebook Places for your business

▶ Comparing Facebook Places to other location-based marketing services

▶ Creating and using a Facebook Place page to market your business

Social media is more than just a set of online tools and networks. Social media — and Facebook in particular — represents an epic cultural shift in how people share their lives with each other. Nowhere else has this shift been more recently apparent than with the arrival of location-based services.

Location-based services are mobile phone applications allow people to *check in* to physical places they visit (retail stores, restaurants, nightclubs, and so on), letting friends know where they are. Location-based services also allow users to easily see if any friends have checked in at that location or somewhere nearby.

For example, Jane can visit her local coffee shop to meet a friend. Upon arriving, she can *check in* (announce online her current location) to the coffee shop's location using an application on her iPhone, which allows her to easily tell her Facebook friends where she is and what she's doing. She can also see the most recent check-ins from her friends, and know who is close by.

In August 2010, Facebook launched its own location-based service, Facebook Places, which allows users to "discover moments when you and your friends are at the same place at the same time," as Facebook describes it.

In this chapter, we explain what Facebook Places is, how Facebook users share their offline activities with their friends, and whether a Facebook Places Page is right for your business. We also show you how to create a Facebook Places Page and a Facebook Deal as well as how to manage both.

The Basics of Facebook Places

Facebook Places, a specific type of Facebook Page, is accessed through an application on a smartphone (such as an iPhone or one of the many devices on the Android platform) or through Facebook's mobile site (`touch.facebook.com`). The specific places displayed are determined by the GPS coordinates (physical location) of the phone; see Figure 11-1.

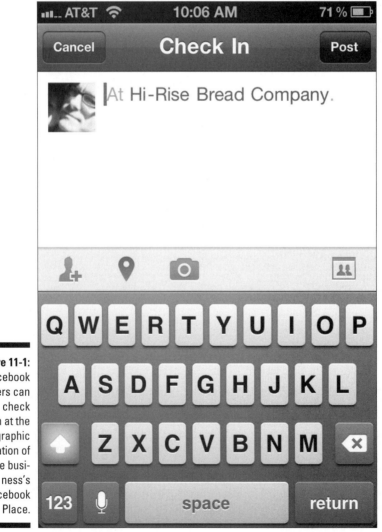

Figure 11-1:
Facebook
users can
check
in at the
geographic
location of
the busi-
ness's
Facebook
Place.

Facebook users can also check in to a Facebook Place from their desktop computer, allowing them share content associated with a Facebook Place before and after they've physically visited it. (See Figure 11-2.) For example, say that after Jane visits with her friends at the local coffee shop, she goes back home and uploads photos she took during that visit to her Facebook Page. She can tag the coffee shop in the update and then share it.

Figure 11-2:
Facebook users can check in or tag a Facebook Places Page in an update from their desktop computer.

To illustrate another example of people can use Facebook Places, say that Julie and Andy plan on meeting a few friends at a Bon Jovi concert. When they arrive at the concert, Julie uses her smartphone to check into the concert hall's Facebook Place and tags Andy, announcing online that he's also attending the concert. She can also see that several of their friends have checked in and posted comments on the concert hall's Facebook Place's Wall. Julie and Andy have used Facebook Places to easily locate their friends so that they can all have a great time at the concert with their friends. The next morning, Andy and Julie can upload pictures from the concert to their Facebook Profiles and tag the concert venue. See Figure 11-3.

As you can imagine, this can be a powerful way for local businesses and non-profits to increase awareness about their brands through both offline and online activities of their customers.

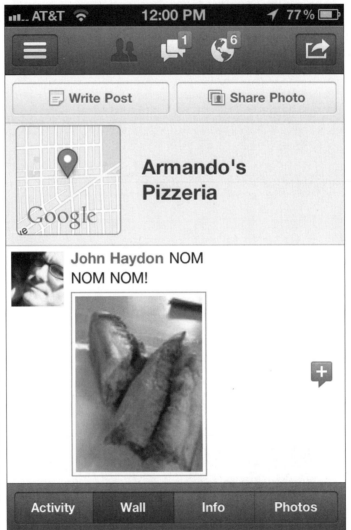

Figure 11-3:
Facebook
users can
upload
pictures to
a Facebook
Place from
a mobile
device.

Understanding the Role of Location in Your Marketing Plan

Depending on the type of business you're marketing, its geographic location will play a critical role in your marketing — or no role at all. For example, an online gaming software company doesn't sell its games at a cash register in the lobby of the company headquarters. Instead, the company deals with its customers completely online where the company's physical location is of little concern. Comparatively, a pizza shop's location is a huge factor in its success or failure, so it makes it an ideal business for a Facebook Place. Customers can check in when they stop by for lunch or dinner.

To help you decide whether a Facebook Place is right for your business, take a moment to think about how customers currently interact with you:

✔ Do my customers and prospects physically visit my place of business?

✔ Does affiliating with my business have a positive effect on how customers appear to their friends?

✔ Do my customers and prospects bring their friends and family to my place of business?

✔ Does offering discounts or other promotions increase new or repeat business?

If you answer "Yes" to one or more of these questions, Facebook Places is right for your business.

Here are some examples of businesses that are a perfect fit for Facebook Places:

✔ Museums

✔ Nail salons

✔ Concert halls

✔ Rock-climbing gyms

✔ Movie theaters

✔ Boutique clothing stores

All these examples have two things in common:

✔ Their customers physically visit them to do business.

✔ Their customers look cool (or hope they do) to their friends when they visit these places.

Knowing why your customers use location-based services

Understanding how Facebook Places works isn't as important as knowing why people use it. The short answer is that they use tools like Facebook Places and Foursquare because they get value from them. Here are at least three reasons why people use these tools:

 ✔ They like getting discounts or rewards from the venues that offer them.

 ✔ They like the coolness factor that comes with being an early adopter of the latest social medium.

 ✔ They're simply curious about technology in general.

By now, you're probably understanding that marketing with Facebook Places is about more than just your business's physical location. It's also about how visiting your business makes your customers feel. There's a reason why you don't see people checking into Botox treatment centers.

Finally, because Facebook Places is a location-based application, an admin must input the organization's geographic location when creating the Place. (Facebook Pages don't require any location information in order to create the Page.) See Figure 11-4. You can read how to create a place in "Getting Started with Facebook Places," later in this chapter.

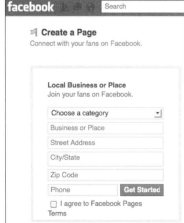

Figure 11-4: A requirement for creating a Facebook Place is the location of the business.

Other location-based services

The main difference between Facebook Places and other location-based services is the number of potential users. Facebook Places — although not widely adopted yet by Facebook users — has a tremendous potential to be the most commonly used service in the marketplace.

The reason for this is simple. Facebook currently has more than 750 million active users. These users have adopted Facebook not only as a social media tool, but as a core way to connect with friends. Because of its ubiquitous nature, Facebook will put an increased focus on the utilization of Facebook Places.

The other huge advantage that Facebook has over other location-based services is that Facebook users can tag events and places before and/or after they visit them. In our example, Julie and Andy were able to share photos from the Bon Jovi concert with their friends *after* their visit. This cannot be done with Foursquare or Gowalla. Again, Facebook realizes that consumers like to share a variety of ways in which they connect with brands and businesses.

Facebook Places versus Foursquare

Foursquare (see Figure 11-5) and Facebook Places are both location-based applications that allow users to check in to physical locations. Both allow marketers to offer deals and other specials to increase new and repeat business.

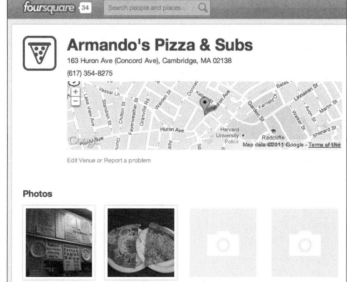

Figure 11-5: A Foursquare venue in a browser.

Foursquare was first to market and has a large and active user base: more than 750,000,000 check-ins as of November 2011, according to Foursquare.

Foursquare also has more types of specials than Facebook Places:

- ✔ **Flash specials:** These can be time restricted to the first users who check in.
- ✔ **Friends specials:** Users can unlock deals by checking in with several friends at once.
- ✔ **Swarm specials:** Users are rewarded when a minimum number of users checks in within a three-hour window. This special can only be unlocked once per day per location.

✔ **Newbie specials:** This rewards users for first-time check-ins.

✔ **Loyalty specials:** Users who frequent a venue can unlock a reward.

✔ **Mayor specials:** Users can claim the number one fan spot by visiting a venue the most within 60 days.

✔ **Check in specials:** The business can set the terms of this most basic check in to reward frequent users.

Foursquare also allows users to collect *badges*, which are graphics representing the achievement of specific milestones, such as exceeding 1,000 check-ins or for visiting a specific number of airports, Starbucks, or high-rated restaurants, and so on. (See Figure 11-6.) The standard Foursquare badges are only for bragging rights and have no real value, but marketers can still use them to offer incentives for the people who collect them.

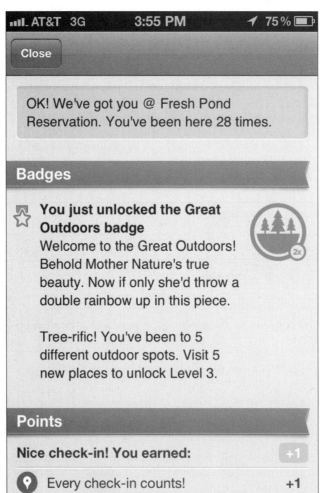

Figure 11-6: Foursquare's Great Outdoors badge.

Finally, Foursquare has many more case studies and success stories for businesses than Facebook Places. For example, RadioShack was able to double its Foursquare check-ins by offering Newbie and Loyalty deals.

Facebook Places versus Gowalla

Gowalla (see Figure 11-7) and Facebook Places both allow marketers to offer deals and other specials to increase new and repeat business.

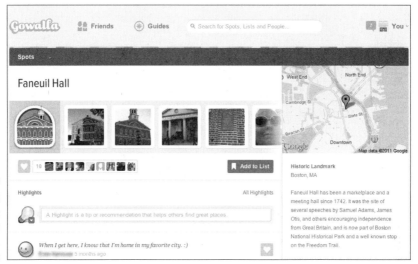

Figure 11-7:
A Gowalla
venue in a
browser.

The big advantage that Gowalla has over Facebook Places is the rich number of features for marketers. Marketers can use their logo as a badge that users can earn — much like Foursquare's badges. Gowalla also allows users to enter trips as challenges for other users. After users complete a trip, they earn the badge associated with that trip.

Gowalla has also been reported to be the most accurate with respect to GPS coordinates.

The downside with Gowalla is that it's not used nearly as much as Foursquare in the United States.

Getting Started with Facebook Places

The next few pages show you step-by-step how to create a Facebook Place. It's best if you read this section first in its entirety, and then go through the process of creating a Facebook Places. In other words, take your time.

Before you create a Facebook Place from scratch, search Facebook to see whether it already exists. This will avoid creating a duplicate Place.

If you decide to use a Facebook Page for your business, you should still claim your Place for several reasons:

- ✔ You'll have admin rights for the Place.
- ✔ You can change the address, hours, and other critical information on the Place.
- ✔ You can choose which Profile picture your Place will have.
- ✔ You can delete the Page after it's claimed.

Claiming your Facebook Place

To claim your business's Facebook Place, you have to be the owner or official representative of that venue.

To claim a Facebook Place, follow these steps:

1. **Log into Facebook.com and enter the name of your place in the search field at the top of Facebook.**

2. **Instead of pressing Enter to search, click See More Results.**

3. **Filter those results by selecting Pages to the left of the search results.**

4. **When you find your business or venue, select it and then click the Is This Your Business? link in the left sidebar.**

5. **Confirm that you are authorized to claim the business.**

6. **Complete the form on the following screen by entering your business's address, phone, website, Yelp listing, and your relationship to the place.**

7. **Authenticate your business by choosing between two methods of verification:**

   - An official company e-mail address
   - Uploading a JPG or PNG image of a legal business certificate or utility bill with the name of your business

8. **Confirm that you are an authorized representative of the business.**

   At this point, you see a notification window confirming your submission. Now you just have to wait for Facebook to review your application, which usually takes between two and seven days.

Creating a Facebook Place

A Facebook Place is a type of Facebook Page. When checking into a venue on a mobile device, that venue is referred to as a Place, whereas on a browser, it is simply called a Page. The difference between these two lies in how the Facebook user interacts with the Page. Are they physically checking in? Or are they engaging with the Page's stories on their laptop?

Any Facebook user who has the Facebook Places feature on his smartphone or mobile browser can create a Facebook Place. You can create Facebook Places with a browser and a laptop, in much the same manner you create a Facebook Page. In this section, we create a Facebook Place using a browser.

If you searched for your business as described earlier and still didn't find it, you can create a Facebook Place from scratch.

The steps for creating a Facebook Place are as follows:

1. **Go to** `http://facebook.com/pages/create.php` **and select Local Business or Place.**

   The Create a Page page appears. (See Figure 11-8.)

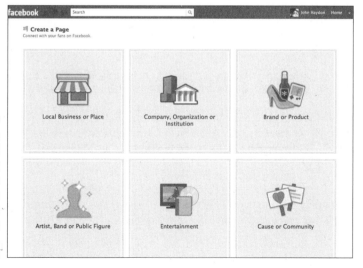

Figure 11-8: Initial Page on Facebook where you will create a Facebook Place.

2. **Choose a category from the Choose a Category drop-down menu. (See Figure 11-9.)**

   Some categories are very similar, like Arts/Entertainment/Nightlife, and Clubs. Select the one that best matches how your customers think about your business. Although you can change your category at anytime in the future, select a category that you'll stick with.

Figure 11-9: Category selection and location fields for a Facebook Place.

3. **Enter the address and phone number of your business in the fields provided. All of these are required fields.**

4. **Read and agree to the Facebook Pages Terms and Conditions.**

   Don't give into temptation and skip reading these terms and conditions for Facebook Pages. We recommend that you take time to familiarize yourself with them. The last thing you want to do is invest time and money marketing your business on Facebook, only to have your account deactivated because you unknowingly violated these Terms and Conditions.

From here, you can upload a Profile photo, get fans, and enter your business's basic information the same way you would for a Facebook Page. For the specifics of this process, see Chapter 4.

Promoting Your Business with Deals

Like traditional coupons or loyalty programs, Facebook deals can help you increase brand awareness, store traffic, and customer loyalty. With Facebook deals, you can enhance your Facebook Place's marketing power so that you can get more in-store traffic, increase tried and true word-of-mouth marketing, and encourage customer loyalty.

In this chapter, we help you understand the strategies and tactics for using Facebook deals as a marketing tool for your business. We help you understand the four types of Facebook deals and how you could use each for your business.

Understanding Facebook Deals

There are more than 250 million active Facebook mobile users who are just like you and me. They go to restaurants, buy clothes, attend church events, and take their families on much-needed summer vacations. For many of these mobile users, a natural part of these activities includes checking in on Facebook Places.

When they check in on their mobile phones, they see all the various Facebook Places that happen to be nearby and the Facebook deals offered by these local businesses. They also see where their friends have checked in and whether they've taken advantage of a specific Facebook deal.

Facebook Deals is a promotional marketing feature within Facebook Places that allows you to reward your customers when they check in on Facebook. When Facebook users check in to your Facebook Place on their mobile device, they can unlock and claim your deal to receive whatever promotion you've offered.

For example, a coffee shop can set up a deal that offers a free cup of coffee when a Facebook user has checked in ten times. On her tenth check in, the user automatically unlocks the deal to receive a free cup of coffee. (See Figure 11-10.)

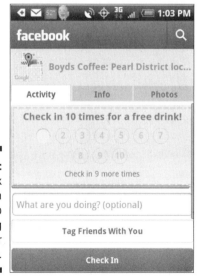

Figure 11-10:
A Facebook deal at a coffee shop encouraging customer loyalty.

The four types of deals currently available are

- ✓ **Individual Deal:** This rewards customers when they check in at your business. The strategy behind this kind of deal is to encourage people to simply visit your place of business. The best offer for this deal is a discount or a gift with a purchase.

- ✓ **Friend Deal:** This rewards groups of customers when they check in together. The business strategy behind this deal is to leverage word-of-mouth advertising to increase your business to help spread the word about your business more rapidly. Because you're asking customers to go beyond the call of duty and invite a group of their friends to your business, the best use for this deal is a deep discount or an attractive gift (not tied to a purchase).

- ✓ **Loyalty Deal:** This rewards customers for visiting your business a certain number of times within a limited timeframe. The business strategy behind this deal is to encourage repeat business. The best offer for this is something that would tie together previous purchases in a way that made sense. For example, a liquor store could offer a free wine rack after a certain amount of check-ins.

- ✓ **Charity Deal:** This is a pledge (from you) to donate to a charity of your choice when customers check in at your business. The business strategy behind this deal is to attract new customers (most likely supporters of the charity) and enhance the goodwill of your brand. In many cases, the check is written in advance, and the pledge has a cap on it. For example, "We will donate $10 for every check-in up to $5,000."

Word of mouth is still the most powerful way of marketing your business. Facebook Places leverages word of mouth instantly by allowing friends to receive recommendations from the people they know and trust.

Here are three ways how Facebook users are automatically notified of Deals:

- ✓ They see your deal on their mobile device as they check into a nearby Facebook Place.

- ✓ They're notified of your deal in their News Feed after you post it on your Facebook Places Wall. (Users must Like your Page before they see any updates in their News Feeds, however.)

- ✓ They see a mention of your deal in their News Feed when one friend checks into your Facebook Place. (This feature may be disabled. Its availablility depends on the friend's privacy settings.)

Creating a Facebook Deal

To create a Facebook deal, start by visiting your Facebook Place at on Facebook. Then follow these steps:

1. **Click Edit Page in the top-right corner, and then click the Deals link. See Figure 11-11.**

Figure 11-11: Deals link within the admin panel of a Facebook Page.

2. **Select the Facebook Deal type by selecting the deal type (on the Deal tab) you'd like to use for your promotion.**

   The choices you have (shown in Figure 11-12) are

   - Individual Deal: Rewards customers when they check in at your business.

   - Friend Deal: Rewards groups of customers when they check in together. (Only for groups up to eight people.)

   - Loyalty Deal: Rewards customers for visiting your business a certain number of times within a limited timeframe. (No fewer than two check-ins, and no more than twenty.)

   - Charity Deal: Pledges a donation (from you) to a charity of your choice when customers check in at your business.

Figure 11-12: Facebook Places offers four different deal types.

3. **In the space below the four deal types, define your offer. See Figure 11-13.**

   - Deal Summary field: Create a message promoting the offer, and be as concise as possible —you only have 50 characters.

• How to Claim field: Provide specific instructions for redeeming the deal. Typically, this involves showing the unlocked deal to a cashier or salesperson (limited to 100 characters).

Figure 11-13:
Facebook
Deals
allows you
to create a
deal sum-
mary as
instructions
on claiming
the deal
after it's
unlocked.

> **Define your offer:**
>
> Deal Summary: `50% off any dinner special (Limit 1 per customer)`
> Maximum 50 characters.
>
> How to Claim: `Present this screen to cashier`
> Maximum 100 characters.
>
> **Add details and restrictions:**
>
> Starting: `12/3/2011` 📅 `11:00 am` ▾
>
> Ending: `12/10/2011` 📅 `11:00 am` ▾
>
> Max Redemptions: ⦿ `100`
> ○ Unlimited
>
> Repeat Claims: ⦿ Claimable once every 24 hours per user
> ○ Claimable once per user
>
> **Create Deal** | Cancel
>
> By clicking the "Create Deal" button, I agree to the Facebook Statement of Rights and Responsibilities and all other Facebook policies, including the Facebook Advertising Guidelines.
>
> Have feedback? Please send us your feedback.

4. Set the date range and restrictions for your Facebook Deal, selecting the start and end dates of your promotion; see Figure 11-13.

Create your deal at least 48 hours in advance because all deals are subject to review.

If you're just starting out with a deal, we recommend using a period of two weeks. This is long enough to get a result, but short enough for you to regroup and reflect on your strategy. Remember that getting the most out of Facebook requires trying a few different strategies to see what works for your business.

As of this writing, Facebook Deals time allows you to set the number of maximum redemptions (the number of times the deal can be claimed) to 100 or Unlimited. You can also allow users to claim a deal once every 24 hours, or just once. (Loyalty deals don't allow for this option, though.)

5. Submit your deal for approval by clicking Create Deal.

Once you click Create Deal, the Deal Summary screen appears (see Figure 11-14). Note that the status on the right side of this screen says "Pending Review," which means that Facebook has to approve the Deal before you can start promoting it.

Facebook generally takes 24 to 48 hours to approve or deny a deal.

Getting the Most from Your Deal

Using Facebook Deals as an effective part of your marketing strategy obviously requires more than simply knowing how to create deals. As with any other promotional strategy, the message and the offer are that things that really determine whether a deal is successful or not. Otherwise, store coupons would be a marketing hit simply because the store owner chose the right paper to print the coupons on.

With that in mind, here are ten tips to get more out of Facebook Deals:

- ✔ **Offer something remarkable.** Offering real value will make customers happy, but offering remarkable value will inspire those happy customers to tell their friends. Think about what makes you tell your friends about your favorite restaurant. It's not that the host seated you on time — it's that he remembered your name, your kid's name, and the table you sat at last week. Again, give them something they will make remarks about (remark-able).

- ✔ **Pick the best words.** Write a deal summary that inspires people to claim it. Make sure you use simple language that's concise and easy to understand. For example, "Get a free coffee after 10 check-ins," or "Check in with a friend and get a free appetizer."

- ✔ **Be clear about restrictions.** Mention any time limits or other restrictions. Otherwise, you'll end up spending too much time explaining the offer to confused and disappointed customers.

- ✔ **Be clear about claiming the deal.** Don't leave them guessing what to do next after they unlock the deal. Clearly tell them what they need to do next: for example, "Show your phone to the salesperson."

- ✔ **Keep the deals fresh.** If you run a deal too long, people will lose interest. Remember that you want to make them happy, and you want them to tell their friends.

- ✔ **Don't run too many concurrent offers.** This will only cause confusion among your customers and your employees.

✔ **Prepare your employees.** Make sure all of your employees understand the terms of the deal, how people will claim them, and what the customers get when they claim the deal. Also, be clear about how to handle customers asking about the deal after it expires. Do you want to offer the deal to people who don't use Facebook Places but heard about it from their friends who do?

✔ **Stock the warehouse.** Make sure you have enough of what you're offering to honor all deals during the run.

✔ **Be cheerful.** Make sure your customers are treated in a cheerful manner when they claim a deal. The last thing you want is for a customer to feel like the sales staff was reluctant about honoring the deal. Be cheerful. We could say this three times, and it wouldn't be too much.

Promoting Your Deal

After you create your deal, stock appropriate quantities of product to honor the deal, and prepare your employees, you can then start making people aware of your deal by promoting it.

Promoting your deal on your Facebook Page

Many of your potential customers will be exposed to your business through their friends on Facebook. Here's how that works: One of your fans comments or Likes a post on your Page, which then is shared on News Feeds of their friends. In the same way, you can create awareness about your deal by posting stories about it on your Page Wall.

Here are effective ways you can use your Wall to promote your deal:

✔ **Announce the deal a couple of times on your Wall.** If there's a product associated with the deal, upload a photo as well. In this update, ask an engaging question like, "Who's hungry for a free appetizer?"

✔ **Create conversations about your deal when appropriate.** For example, when someone claims the deal, mention it on your Wall: "Jane just claimed the Shrimp Cocktail! Who likes shrimp?" This invites fans and their friends to comment on your Wall, creating more awareness around your deal.

These are just a few examples to get you started. Keep in mind that using your Facebook Page as a marketing tool is limited only by your creativity.

Some promotional activities are prohibited on Facebook. Make sure you review the Facebook Page TOC before promoting your deal at `https://www.facebook.com/terms_pages.php`.

Promoting your deal with Facebook Ads

Another way to promote your deal is to use highly targeted Facebook ads. You can select a specific geographic criteria as well as demographic information when you create your ad. Your criteria should be based on your knowledge about your target market, and who would be your idea customer located in the vicinity of your business. With Facebook ads, you can geotarget as specifically as a city. (Read more about this in Chapter 10.)

Promoting your deal with other marketing channels

In addition to using your Facebook Places Page, you want to use your other marketing channels to promote your deal. Many of your customers may not be very active Facebook users but would still be interested in connecting with your business on Facebook and taking advantage of your offer.

E-mail marketing

Many businesses have an e-mail list. Send out an e-mail announcement of your deal with these tips in mind:

- **Write a compelling headline that gets the reader's attention.** Ideally, this could simply be your deal Summary.

- **Keep the body of the e-mail short and concise.** You have only a few seconds after someone opens your e-mail to grab her attention. Communicate the essence of your deal with as few words as possible.

- **Include an image.** Keeping the previous point in mind, remember that a picture says a thousand words. Use a picture of the product or service offering.

- **Ask the reader to click.** In the middle of your e-mail and at the end, clearly state what you want the reader to do, such as "Click here to become a fan of our Facebook Place." This way, you can continue to remind readers of the deal.

In-store promotion

In addition to using e-mail and your Facebook Places Page, you also want to promote your deal in the store with posters, mentions at the cash register, and other traditional in-store promotional methods.

Why promote an offer that's intended to encourage in-store traffic to people in your store? The critical thing to remember about using Facebook Places and Facebook deals is that in addition to encouraging foot traffic, you also create awareness about your business as people check in and claim deals.

Remember the earlier example with the coffee shop using a Loyalty Deal? When customers unlock that deal, many of their Facebook friends are exposed to the coffee shop. Some of them will become a new Facebook fan, and some of them will show up at the coffee shop to check in with Facebook Places.

Chapter 12

Setting Up Groups, Promotions, and Events

In This Chapter

▶ Working with Facebook Groups

▶ Creating your own Group

▶ Launching a promotion

▶ Hosting an event

*F*acebook Pages are the designated tool meant to be the central place of customer and prospect engagement. Facebook Pages keep Facebook users interested in your business, and Facebook ads spread awareness about your products and services. But to successfully market your business on Facebook, you should go further — to Facebook Groups, and to promotions and events.

This chapter discusses how you can use Groups, promotions, and events to motivate and grow your audience by promoting brand awareness and building community. We show you how to create your own Group on a topic that engages potential business clients, and also how to promote the Group to attract members and prospective customers. Plus, we show you how to launch a promotion on Facebook. Finally, we discuss creating an event, promoting it to your fans, listing it, managing it, and following up.

Discovering Facebook Groups

Groups are different from Pages or Profiles because groups are less about the business or person, and more about a shared interest or cause. Groups can be a more personal option for marketing your business because you relate to an audience around a cause or local issue that your business cares about; therefore, people are more inclined to get involved.

You might have several reasons why you want to join a Facebook Group to help promote your business; conversely, you might even want to have your own Facebook Group as a stand-alone to discuss a topic outside your business interests or to coexist with a Facebook Page for your business.

For example, Figure 12-1 shows the Facebook Fan Page Owners Group, which was created to give marketing professionals a place to share ideas on how to use Facebook as a marketing medium. This is a great Group to join to meet fellow business owners and marketing professionals, gain more insight into Facebook marketing, and trade tips for marketing success.

Figure 12-1: A Facebook Group provides members with an online hub to share opinions about a topic.

A good place to start marketing your business is with a Page, but a more advanced marketing tactic is to start, join, and be active in Groups that match your business in some way.

The following sections go into more detail about the differences between Groups and Pages as well as how to find, join, and participate in Groups to help market your business. (For the lowdown on starting a group, check out the section "Creating Your Own Facebook Group," later in this chapter.)

Distinguishing Facebook Groups from Pages

Only an official representative of a business, public figure, nonprofit organization, artist, or public personality can create a Facebook Page and serve as its administrator (admin). Pages are designed to provide basic information about a business, feature community-building blocks (such as discussions and comments), upload user-generated content, and post reviews.

By contrast, any Facebook member can create a Facebook Group about any topic. Groups serve as a central hub for members to share opinions and discussions about a topic.

When an admin updates a Group's page, the News Feed story includes the name of the Group's admin. Pages, however, attribute updates to the Page and never reveal the admin's name. Groups even allow you to post updates via the status update box. And just like with Pages, you can post links, videos, and photos and even set up an event directly from the status update box.

The following are some key differences between Facebook Groups and Facebook Pages:

- ✔ **As the admin of a Facebook Group, you can dictate how open you want your Group's membership to be.** Group admins can restrict membership access by requiring a member approval process, whereas Pages can restrict members only from becoming a fan based on age and location requirements. You can make your Group

  - *Open* to all Facebook members

  - *Closed* so that only Facebook members approved by the Group's admin can see it

  - *Secret* so that it's invitation-only and not visible in a Facebook Groups search

- ✔ **You can't add apps to a Group like you can to a Page.** Whereas Pages allows for a high degree of interaction and rich media with the addition of applications (apps), Facebook Groups don't allow for the addition of apps.

- ✔ **Your friends can easily send an invite to all their friends to join your Group simply by clicking the Id Friends to Group field underneath the Froup members' pictures on the right side.** This lets you invite your existing friends by clicking their pictures as well as invite people via an e-mail message.

Consider a Facebook Group if you want to have a serious discussion around a cause. For example, you may choose to start a Group if you have strong feelings and opinions regarding Facebook privacy issues and any changes, and you want to have an ongoing discussion with fellow marketers on the topic.

The key is to keep the discussion flowing with the Group members. Join a few Groups to see how it's done before jumping in to create your own.

In the next section, we discuss how to find Groups that might be relevant to your business.

Finding a Group

Finding a Group isn't difficult; just follow these steps to use the search box:

1. **In the search box at the top of your screen, type a name or title that interests you and then click See More Results For at the bottom of the list.**

   For example, if your business designs custom t-shirts, you can search for a Group related to fashion. Use the search terms *fashion, designer clothes,* or *trends* to yield some Groups that you might want to join and be part of.

2. **Click the Groups tab on the left side of the search results page so that you look only at Groups.**

   For example, the typical Facebook search for *t-shirt* displays the results shown in Figure 12-2.

Figure 12-2:
Results of
a search
for t-shirt
groups.

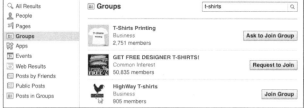

3. **Search the results until you find a Group you want to visit, and then click the image or the Group name's link.**

   In the search results, be sure to note the number of members, the type of Group, as well as any recent activity so that you have some indication of how active the Group is.

   On the Group's landing page, note the recent activity (updates, photos or videos) on the Wall. Some Groups provide a description at the top right side under the member photos.

   The most important part of Groups is the Wall – it's really where the action is.

   Join a Group to get a sense of how active that Group is and whether you want to contribute. See the following section, "Joining a Group."

Joining a Group

After you identify a Group that matches your interest and has an activity level that matches your objectives, join the Group and interact with the other members.

All you need to do is navigate to the Group's page you wish to join and click the Ask to Join Group button to the right of the Group name at the top, as shown in Figure 12-3. (See "Finding a Group," earlier in this chapter, for the lowdown on finding a group.)

Figure 12-3:
Joining a
Facebook
Group is
as easy as
clicking
Ask to Join
Group.

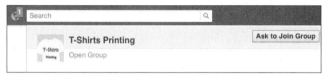

Accessing Groups you joined

Your most recently visited Groups will always be listed on your News Feed page.

To access Groups that don't immediately appear on your News Feed page, follow these steps:

1. **Hover your mouse over the word "Groups" in the left sidebar of Facebook and you see the More link. Click this link.**

   You need to be logged in.

   This takes you to the Groups page (see Figure 12-4) where you have access to all the Groups you've joined.

2. **Click the Group's name link.**

Figure 12-4:
Access
the Groups
you've
joined.

facebook

Search

John Haydon

Groups   + Create Group

FAVORITES
News Feed
Messages   13
Events   8

PAGES
Inbound Zombie - Social
The Nonprofit Facebook
The Brain Aneurysr 20+

EpicChangeX   Used today

Facebook Fan Page Owners   Used today

Fresh Pond Chapter - District and Ct   Used today

Inspiring Generosity Blogger   Used today

Nonprofit Consultants - Creating the   Used today

Participating in a Group

One of the Golden Rules of social networks and other forms of social media is to spend some time observing and listening to the conversation. Get a feeling for the rhythm of the Group's conversations before you barge in and change things.

You'll find that only a portion of the Group actively participates; many members just lurk. That's okay, and don't let that discourage you from participating. If you truly want to know more about Groups, take the first step and jump into the conversation. That really is the best (and only) way to figure out how social networks operate.

A good place to start is to find a topic that you know a lot about and offer answers to any questions. This is not only an easy, casual way to get started in Group participation, but it also goes a long way to establishing yourself as a helpful member of the Group, and an expert on particular subjects.

Do not try to sell your goods and services directly. Nobody appreciates a hard sell in this arena, and you may even be labeled as a spammer.

You might find that in some of the larger Groups, people try to hijack the conversation by posting links to their own Groups or related Web sites. Don't try this tactic. Technically, this is spam, and Facebook members have a very low tolerance for spammers. Any member who is considered a spammer can and will have his profile shut down by Facebook. Although the rules on spamming aren't published anywhere on the site, it's widely considered taboo by the members of the Group, the Group admin and, of course, Facebook.

Creating Your Own Facebook Group

When you get the hang of how a Group works, you might want to start your own Group to support your business. Creating a Group is actually quite simple, and a Group contains elements that are similar to those on a Facebook Page.

Securing your Group's name

Before jumping in and creating your Group, search for the name of the Group you want to start so you can see whether any existing Groups or Pages have that same name. (See the earlier section "Finding a Group," in this chapter, for details.) Having a name that's never been used on Facebook isn't required, but a unique name does help you distinguish yourself. Also, Facebook doesn't let you own a name in the same way as when you reserve a website address (URL). Other people can use a name that's similar to or even identical with other names on Facebook.

Setting up your Group

After you choose a Group name that you want to use, create your Group:

1. **From your Groups Page (**www.facebook.com/bookmarks/groups**), click the Create Group button at the top right.**

   The Create Group dialog box appears, as shown in Figure 12-5.

Figure 12-5:
The Create Group dialog box.

2. **Provide the basic information about your group.**

   This information is as follows:

   - *Group Name:* Because you did the research in the earlier section, "Securing your Group's name," go ahead and plug in the name you chose.

   - *Group Icon:* These optional icons are found in the drop-down list next to the Group name and can help specify the type of Group you have. For example, if you had an animal-related Group, you may want to select the paw print or the dog bone icon.

- *Members:* Here is where you invite your friends to become members of your Group. Just start typing a name into the box, and Facebook brings up your friend's name that matches.

- *Privacy:* Your Group can be Open, Closed, or Secret.

Some notes about your privacy settings:

> *Open Groups* can be found by anyone on Facebook when doing a search. Anyone can join the Group and anyone can see the Wall.

> *Closed Groups* require approval by the Group admin to join them. Anyone can see the basic Group description information, but only members can see the Wall.

> *Secret Groups* can't be found in a search or even in member profiles; they truly are secret. Membership is by invitation only; therefore, only members can see the Wall.

All members can post comments, photos, videos, links, events, and documents, which is essentially a group's version of creating a note. Keep this in mind when setting your privacy levels.

Depending on your need or the development of your group, you might want to keep the group Secret until you're fully ready to launch.

3. Click the Create button.

Congratulations! You created your first group! The last step you need to take before posting content to your group's Wall is to set up your group's custom e-mail address. Any messages sent to this address are sent to the entire group.

To set up the e-mail address

1. Click the Edit Group button on the top-right side of the page (in the drop-down menu that looks like a gear.).

You may recognize that this is the basic information you provided earlier, but this time, you can set up a group e-mail address.

2. Click the Set Up Group Email button.

Here you can choose a personalized e-mail address. All group e-mail address end in @groups.facebook.com. Say your group name is East Coast T-Shirt Designers; you want a similar e-mail address, so maybe you'd choose t-shirtsdesigners@groups.facebook.com.

You have only 50 characters to work with, so choose wisely!

3. After choosing an address, click the Create Email Address button.

You return to the Basic Information page.

4. Click the Save button to finish.

Deleting a Group

Facebook no longer allows admins the ability to delete Groups. However, Facebook automatically deletes Groups after they have no members. If you created the Group, you can delete the Group by removing all members and then yourself. To remove members, click See All in the Members section on the right side of the Group and then click the X next to each member's name.

Creating a Facebook Promotion

Promotions (sometimes referred to as "contests") and giveaways have traditionally played a vital role in consumer marketing. From cereal companies to fashion retailers, to automobile dealers, and so on, the promise of winning something of value for free is a tremendous lure. Whether backed by a media campaign, promoted on a product's packaging, or announced at an employee sales meeting, promotions have the power to motivate and drive engagement.

And the same incentives that served marketers before Facebook, such as raffles and drawings, still apply on Facebook. Promotions with high-value prizes tend to be more active. Celebrity appeal and limited edition offerings always help, too. Even if you don't have access to costly prizes, you can still offer an appropriate reward. (Even we've filled out a form for the chance to win a t-shirt if it's really cool.)

The best part about marketing on Facebook is that you don't have to be a major brand to host a successful promotion (although it doesn't hurt). And you don't have to have a boatload of money to pull off a successful promotion (although that doesn't hurt, either). Anyone with a Facebook Page can create and promote a promotion. Although Facebook doesn't offer a promotion application, you can check out some of the third-party promotion applications (apps) to find a solution that works best for your promotion. You can either search Facebook's own app directory for *promotions,* which turns up results like the Sweepstakes app, or you can do an Internet search for *promotion applications that integrate with Facebook.* Read more about adding apps in Chapter 6.

Understanding Facebook rules for promotions

The Facebook Promotions Guidelines page spells out the rules surrounding the use of promotions within the Facebook platform. In an effort to eliminate spam from promotions, the guidelines serve to protect the user's profile data from being used by brands for their own benefit. Facebook also limits the way companies can use the Facebook brand name and logo in association with the promotion.

If you employ promotions on your Facebook Page regularly, stay up to date with Facebook's guidelines. You can find the most updated guidelines at `www.facebook.com/promotions_guidelines.php`. Keep the following in mind when running a promotion and using Facebook's name in it. You have to use special wording that you can find at the link we just cited. Facebook clearly states that you must include the exact wording right next to any place on your promotion entry form where personal information is requested. You must tell the entrant exactly how her personal information will be used, for example, that you're collecting her e-mail address for marketing purposes. Finally, the person entering your promotion must know that the promotion isn't run or endorsed by Facebook.

Facebook marketers can no longer do the following:

- ✔ Have photo promotions that require entrants to make changes to their Profile in any way, such as upload a photo
- ✔ Have status update promotions that require posting status updates for entry
- ✔ Automatically enter people in a promotion after they become a fan

After you're established with a Facebook representative, that person ensures that your company creates promotions on the Facebook platform and through a certified application. Some examples of popular apps are Wildfire Interactive, Fan Appz, and Vitrue. For more on those, see the upcoming section, "Using third-party promotion apps."

Of course, you can always link from your Facebook Page to a promotion hosted on your own website, outside the Facebook guidelines. However, you still need to be mindful of how you use the Facebook name, and it's probably best not to use the Facebook name at all in association with your promotion if not on Facebook.

Setting up a promotion

Facebook offers a compelling environment from which to host a promotion or giveaway on your Page. You can use your Page as a starting point with a link to your website for promotion entry details or have the entire promotion contained within the Facebook community.

Promotions can be very creative and challenging, or can simply require a simple yes/no answer. They can motivate users to upload a video or simply complete a contact form. Some promotions require a panel of esteemed judges to determine the winner; others select winners randomly. Still other promotions allow the users to vote for the outcome.

Although promotions are as unique as the companies that host them, we offer some tips that can improve your chances of success. Here are some best practices for creating Facebook promotions and giveaways:

- ✔ **Offer an attractive prize.** The more attractive the prize, the more response you'll get. A box of Cracker Jack isn't going to garner much interest. For a prize to be attractive, though, it doesn't necessarily have to cost a lot. The best prizes tend to be those that money can't buy, such as a chance to meet a celebrity, to participate in a TV commercial, or to attend a product's prerelease party. There's no better way to get people to try your products or services than by offering them as prizes, too!

- ✔ **Use your existing customers and contacts to start the ball rolling.** Getting those initial entries is always the toughest part of running a Facebook promotion. This is when you need to reach into your network of family and friends. Reach out to your mailing list of customers with a friendly invitation. Promote the promotion on Twitter, LinkedIn, Myspace, and (of course) your Facebook Page. Wherever you have contacts, use whatever social network, e-mail exchange, or instant messenger you have to get them to participate.

- ✔ **Cross-promote via your website.** You need to promote your Facebook promotion across all your channels to gain maximum participation. That includes your website. Adding a promotional banner with a link to your Facebook Page is a good start, but you can do so much more to promote your promotion. For example, issue a press release via one of the many news wire services. Add a message to your phone answering system. The possibilities are endless.

- ✔ **Keep the promotion simple.** This goes for all aspects of a promotion: Don't make the rules too complicated. The fewer the questions on a form, the higher the rate of completion. Keep first prize a single, valuable item and then have several smaller second-place prizes.

  The fewer the clicks to enter the promotion, the better.

- ✔ **Don't set the bar too high.** If you ask the participants for an original creation, keep the requirements to a minimum. For example, don't place a minimum word count on an essay promotion. Or don't require a video for the first round of submissions because videos are a lot of work.

> ✔ **Run promotions for at least one month.** Things like word of mouth marketing require time. The more time you spend promoting the promotion, the more entries you get. The more you build up the excitement by keeping the promotion in front of your fans, the more often they take note of it and look forward to the big day when the winner is announced!
>
> ✔ **Integrate your promotion with a media campaign.** Facebook ads are an ideal complement to any promotion. By combining a Facebook ad campaign with a promotion, you maximize the viral effect and amplify the number of engagements. (See Chapter 10 for more on Facebook advertising.)
>
> ✔ **Make your promotion fun, interesting, and uniquely you.** The main thing to keep in mind when planning a Facebook promotion is that members want to be entertained. Promotions should offer an outlet to self-expression, engage members, encourage them to share with friends, and communicate something unique about your brand.

Using third-party promotion apps

Although Facebook doesn't offer a promotion application, several third-party promotion applications are available. Some are free, but some cost money to power more sophisticated promotions and sweepstakes.

Wildfire Interactive is a Facebook promotion app available for less than a dollar per day; it provides a direct solution for marketers looking to offer a promotion or giveaway on their Facebook Page. This is another way that viral marketing comes into play. When a fan enters your promotion, she's given the opportunity to share the promotion with her friends, potentially bringing in even more fans and promotion entries. The app provides everything you need to create and host a promotion on your Facebook Page. Head to its website `http://wildfireapp.com` to find out more and sign up (see Figure 12-6).

Another option when you're searching for a promotion app for your Page is Fan Appz (`http://fanappz.com`). In addition to being able to run promotions via Fan Appz, you can also create quizzes and polls that can then be posted on your fan's Wall so their all their friends can see . . . and possibly take your quiz (or poll), too! What a great way to drive traffic to your Page! Finally, there's Vitrue (`www.vitrue.com`). Its suite of applications offers options for promotions but also other apps for fan engagement. It's like a one-stop shop for all your Facebook marketing needs!

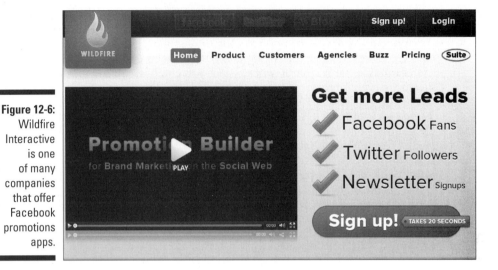

Hosting a Facebook Event

On Facebook an *event* is a way for members to spread the word about upcoming social gatherings — such as parties, trips, conventions, or other similar events — in their community. Facebook Events is a great way to get people together virtually or in person to support your business, brand, or product. Events is also an economical way of getting the word out beyond your normal in-house marketing list by inviting fans of your Facebook Page or members of your Facebook Group. Fans can also help you promote your Facebook event by sharing the event with a Group of their friends when it's valuable.

When you create a Facebook event, it lives on forever, long after the actual physical (or online) event ends. Facebook Events allows you to stay in touch with those who attended, and even the ones who didn't, by posting a steady stream of photos, videos, and updates recapping the event. By encouraging attendees to post their own pictures, videos, and comments, you make it a much more interactive and richer experience for all those on your guest list.

Creating an event

Facebook Events helps you with the fine points of creating and throwing your own event. Events can be offline, as in the case of a fundraising walk or a conference, or can be online, as in the case of a webinar or live-streaming event.

Generally, Pages should list any event you'd normally post to your business website. If it's good enough for your corporate website, post it to Facebook. First, decide what the purpose of your event should be. A good place to start is with networking events to get people introduced and interacting with each other outside the Facebook world. After you establish yourself as a great business event creator, you can branch out to other marketing-related events like a new product or service launch party or a welcome gathering if you've hired new employees to your sales team. This serves the double purpose of promoting your brand and giving these new employees a chance to network with current and potential customers.

After you create an event a few times, you can create events quickly and easily. If you want to throw an event for your Page, go to your Page and then follow these steps to create the event:

1. **Click the Events tab in the left sidebar of your Page.**

   If this is your first event, you may need to add the tab through the Apps section of your Page's admin panel. (Read more about this in Chapter 4.)

2. **Click the Create Event button in the upper-right corner to display the Create an Event page, as shown in Figure 12-7.**

Figure 12-7: Enter the details about your event.

3. **Fill in the following details about your event:**

   - *When?:* The date and time of the event.
   - *What Are You Planning?:* The purpose or reason for the event.
   - *Where?:* Where the event will be held.
   - *More Info?:* Any additional details you want to provide.
   - *Who's Invited?:* You can choose to display the guest list on the Event, and allow guests to write on the Wall. This is recommended if you want to leverage the power of Facebook's social graph.

Use as many rich keywords in the What Are You Planning? and More Info? boxes because Facebook events are indexed by search engines, which could mean extra traffic for your event.

4. **Click the Select Guests button to invite guests to your event.**

   Inviting friends to the event isn't mandatory; you can simply publish your event and hope for the best. However, Facebook makes inviting friends to your event so easy that it's hard not to. Plus, it's a good idea to get the ball rolling because you're holding an event to promote your business in some way. So why would you not invite people to get the word out to promote your event?

5. **In the Invite Friends dialog box that appears, as shown in Figure 12-8, invite friends in any of the following ways:**

Figure 12-8: Sending your first batch of invites.

• Select friends directly from the filter list.

• Search for friends with the search box on top of the list.

• Invite an entire Friends List, or *Smart List*, which is a Friends List that is automatically created based on Profile data you and your friends have in common — like your work, school, family, and city.

• Invite non-Facebook members to the event by typing their e-mail addresses (separated by commas) into the Invite by E-Mail Address box.

After your event posts to your Page's Wall, your fans can sign up right then and there!

You can also post future updates about your event to your Facebook fans (not guests) by posting a link to the event on your Wall. You can further target this Wall update to a subset of your fans by clicking on the Public drop-down menu in the status update field. Here you have the option to target the update by location or language, which can allow you to publish the update only to Facebook users located near the event.

Inviting non-Facebook members to an event means they need to register with Facebook before responding to your request, so be judicious about using this option. If you think some non-Facebook users who you have invited will be hesitant to sign up for an account just for this purpose, make sure to include an alternate way for them to contact you to RSVP.

After you publish your event, it appears on both the Wall and the Events tab of your Page. You can message guests by clicking the Message Guests link, which you can access by clicking on the gear-icon drop-down menu at the top right of your event page. Here you're given the option to send the update to all guests or to guests based on their RSVP status (Attending, Not Attending, Not Yet Replied).

If you created the event as a Page (and not through your personal Profile) you cannot update/message your guests, unless it's to cancel the event.

Also, once your event has reached 5,000 guests, you can no longer message fans. You can, however, post updates to the Event Wall and your Facebook Page Wall.

6. **Click the Add a Personal Message link to add a quick (optional) message to the invitee; click the Save and Close button.**

   In the Add a Personal Message box, provide something compelling for the reader and make sure the value that invitees can derive by coming to your event is front and center in your message. You can invite your first 100 people with this invite method.

Facebook allows you to invite an unlimited number of attendees to an event in increments of 100, with no more than 300 outstanding invitations at a time.

   You return to the Create an Event page.

7. **On the Create an Event page, select or deselect the remaining two options:**

   - *Show the Guest List on the Event Page:* Allows the guest list to be seen. By selecting this check box, your guest list is visible on the event's page.

   - *Non-Admins Can Write on the Wall:* Allows invitees to write on the Wall. By selecting this check box, your guests can add their own content on the Wall.

Next, you want to liven up your event's page with an image that can get some attention. If no image is chosen, a question mark displays.

8. **Click the Add Event Photo button on the left side of the Create an Event page.**

   The Add Event Photo dialog box opens, as shown in Figure 12-9.

Figure 12-9: Uploading a picture for your event.

9. **Click the Choose File button to search your computer for a graphic file, select the picture that you want to use, and then click the Close button.**

   Add a photo that best describes your event. Logos can be boring, so take the time to find an image that visually represents your event in a way that makes people want to attend. The file size needs to be less than 4MB.

   With all images on Facebook, be sure you have the right to distribute the image. The Internet offers plenty of sources for royalty-free images, such as Fotolia (www.fotolia.com), so be sure to use one if you don't have a proprietary image from your business.

   You're taken to the event page where you or your fans can dress up the event even more by adding comments photos, videos, and links to the event's status update box.

10. **After you enter all the pertinent details about your event, click the Create Event button.**

   Your event appears on your Wall.

Editing your event

Making changes to your event's page is easy. Simply click the event's name and then click the Edit Event link found under the event's name. Here you can change nearly everything about the event, including the location. You can also notify attendees of any changes by posting a message on your Wall or by sending a message via the Message Guests link at the top right of the event page. (To access the Message Guests link, click on the gear icon as shown in Figure 12-10.)

Figure 12-10:
You can edit your event, message guests, and export the event here.

Exporting your event

Choose Export Event from the gear icon menu shown in Figure 12-10 and Facebook allows you to export your event to a calendar on your desktop or to a web-based calendar. (See Figure 12-11.)

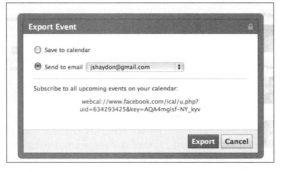

Figure 12-11:
Facebook allows you to export your event to a calendar.

Following up after an event

Wise marketers use Facebook Events after the event occurs to build a post-event community and extend the value of that event. If you had a very healthy debate with lots of questions, you could post a transcript in your Notes section for attendees or even nonattendees. If some questions weren't answered because of time constraints, you could write the answers and send them to the attendees, too.

At the very least, a short thank you note either via e-mail or Facebook mail to those who attended is just good form. As well, sending a "Sorry you couldn't make it" note to those who didn't attend, perhaps with a recap, is also good form. Taking several photos of the event and posting them is the single best way to reach out. By taking photos, tagging them with the attendee's name(s), and posting them, you can leverage the viral power of the Facebook platform. (See Chapter 6 for the lowdown on adding and tagging photos.)

Chapter 13

Cross-Promoting Your Page

In This Chapter

▶ Working Facebook into your marketing plans

▶ Using other online communication to drive fans to your Facebook Page

▶ Promoting your Facebook Page via offline marketing

▶ Making your Facebook Page search engine friendly

The best kind of Facebook promotion takes advantage of existing marketing activities to cross-promote your Facebook Page. Driving users to your Facebook Page from other marketing vehicles allows you to take advantage of all your other awesome marketing efforts in addition to Facebook.

Many marketers drive visitors from their websites to their Facebook Pages to take advantage of Facebook's capability to create an instant community around their brand at virtually no infrastructure cost. Cross-promoting your Facebook Page via your company website also helps improve your search engine optimization (SEO), which affects the ranking of your site in search engines. By creating more relevant links from your Facebook Page to your website, you allow users to find both more easily if they use search engines.

In this chapter, we cover the strategies that you can use to promote your Facebook Page outside Facebook. Consider how best to integrate your Facebook Page into your existing marketing programs. We examine how companies are adding Facebook to their e-mail marketing campaigns, websites, and blogs; we also discuss search engine marketing tricks and tips.

Making Facebook Part of Your Marketing Mix

After you set up your Facebook Page, you need to start promoting it to your existing customers so that you can build your Facebook fan community. For marketing purposes, Facebook lets you create a network that you can leverage when you have something to share. You can create brand awareness for your business by sharing or publishing a steady stream of informative, relevant, and engaging content that keeps your fans coming back, which can eventually lead to sales, subscriptions, or other calls to action.

Encourage your customers to interact with and like your Facebook Page. When a user *Likes,* or becomes a fan of your Facebook Page, she opts in to receive information about your business, sort of like if she asks to be included in your e-mail list. Additionally, the more fans who interact with your Page, the more stories your Page generates and distributes to your fans' News Feeds, which their friends see on their own News Feeds, resulting in a viral effect.

The following sections give you the lowdown on how to get started cross-promoting your Page.

Choosing a custom Facebook username

Before you start promoting the very long and abstract URL that Facebook has assigned to your Page, consider creating a custom (vanity) username for your Page. This name appears after `facebook.com` when someone views your Page. For example, the username for the Apple iTunes Page is simply `itunes`:

```
facebook.com/itunes
```

Originally, Facebook required a Page to have more than 1,000 *fans* (people who Like the Page) to qualify for a custom username or vanity URL, but Facebook has eliminated that requirement. Also, Facebook allows Page admins to use `fb.com` as a domain, so the iTunes Facebook Page URL could also be `fb.com/itunes`. This makes it even easier for your fans to remember and find your Page faster:

```
fb.com/itunes
```

You must register to have a username for your profile before getting one for your business Page. You also have to be an admin of the Page you'd like to create a custom username for.

You can create a custom username very easily by visiting the Username page described in the following steps.

1. **Log into Facebook and go to the Username page at** `facebook.com/username`**.**

   A page similar to Figure 13-1 appears.

Figure 13-1:
Set a vanity
URL for your
Facebook
Page.

2. **From the Page Name drop-down list, select the Page (if you're an admin for multiple Pages) for which you want to create a username.**

3. **In the empty text box to the right of the Page Name, enter a username that makes sense for your brand and to your fans, and then click the Check Availability button.**

Choose your name carefully. After you choose a customized username for your Facebook Page, *you can't change it under any circumstances*, so make sure you choose a name that best describes your business or organization. The best option is, of course, the name of your business, but if that's not available, consider trying an industry-related keyword.

Facebook may take a minute or so to check the availability of the name.

4. **If you see a message that your name is available, click the Confirm button to claim that name.**

If you get a notification that your Page isn't eligible, maybe you still need to create a username for your profile, or someone else has already taken your selected username.

If you did everything right, you see a Success dialog box, similar to the one shown in Figure 13-2. Now, you can let the world know about your Facebook Page URL, as described in the next section.

Figure 13-2:
Getting con-
firmation on
a username
for your
Facebook
Page.

Cross-promoting your Page

Your Facebook URL, or web address, is a new touch point for your customers. If no one knows where to find you on Facebook, though, your Facebook marketing efforts can't help your business. That's why you need to plaster your Facebook URL everywhere, online and off: on your website, on your printed marketing materials, in your store window, on your drum set (if you're a musician) — basically, wherever people look, you should promote your Facebook address.

Social media can really boost your company's visibility and brand awareness, but it does have a downside: Many businesses end up with fragmented media. Therefore, you need to establish a strong policy of cross-promoting these sites, which you can do in a variety of ways.

Be sure to cover at least the basics when it comes to letting everyone know about your various sites. Here are some ways you can get the word out:

- ✔ In your e-mail signature and on your website home page, list all the ways that the reader can connect with you.

- ✔ On your blog, list your Page in a special Social Links section or with the Facebook Like Box plug-in, which can pull updates to your blog directly from your Page (covered in Chapter 14).

The preceding options are ideas on how to cross-promote your Facebook Page by getting users to discover your various sites, which then pulls them back to your Facebook Page. Facebook also provides a variety of applications that can plug your blog feed, Twitter feed, Delicious bookmarks, and RSS (really simple syndication) feeds into your Page.

Facebook also allows you to use Facebook social plug-ins on your website, adding many of the same capabilities that have made Facebook so popular, such as commenting, the Like button (discussed in detail in Chapter 16), and the ability for visitors to log in by using their Facebook ID and password. Read Chapter 16 for more information on Facebook plug-ins.

Leveraging Your Facebook Presence via Your E-Mail, Website, and Blog

Most likely, more than half the people you e-mail for your business have Facebook accounts. Because all Facebook Pages have their own URLs, you can copy and paste your Page's URL into your corporate e-mail, inviting customers and prospects in your database to sign up as fans.

Better yet, you can add a Facebook badge or Like button to an HTML e-mail, as well as on your website or blog, as described in the following sections. A badge is simply a Facebook logo that links directly to your Page.

A number of third-party apps, such as WiseStamp, help you inject a little Facebook into your e-mail signature by automatically adding your latest Facebook status update to the bottom of your e-mail messages. This creates an opportunity to automatically engage e-mail recipients who might find your latest Facebook Page update interesting. Find the instructions on how to do this here:

```
http://wisestamp.com/goodies/how-to/create-your-personal-
              facebook-signature/
```

You get to decide what you want to include in your online communications, but explain the value of checking out your Facebook Page to fans by encouraging them to make use of these social features. The more ways you allow your fans to share and consume content, the more content they will consume and share. Integrating Facebook into your e-mail and website marketing offers you a viral distribution channel like no other.

We recommend using a Like Box instead of a badge for your website because visitors can like your Page directly from your website, and you can track how many people have liked your Page via your Page Insights. See Chapter 9 for more information on this topic.

Creating a Facebook badge for your website or e-mail newsletter

Facebook badges allow you to embed a snippet of code on a web page or blog, or even in e-mail, and the badges appear in the format you choose, along with your Page's profile image. This allows anyone visiting your website or reading an e-mail message from you to click the badge and become a fan of your Page. You can create a Facebook badge for either your profile or Page.

To create a badge for your Page, follow these steps:

1. **Go to** www.facebook.com/badges/page.php **and click the Edit This Badge link (on the right-hand side).**

   Note that you will see badge options for every Page you admin.

2. **Choose what information to include on your badge, as shown in Figure 13-3.**

Figure 13-3:
Start here to
get badges
for your
page.

You can adjust the following badge settings:

- *Layout:* Vertical, Horizontal, and 2 Columns
- *Items:* Name (the name of your Page), Status (the current status on your Page), Picture (your Page's picture), and Fans (the number of fans your Page has)

3. **Click Save.**

   The original Page Badges page reappears, displaying a message that the badge was successfully updated.

4. **Choose what platform you'd like to add your badge to.**

5. **Embed this badge into an HTML e-mail, a newsletter, or a web page:**

   a. Click the Other button (as shown in Figure 13-4).

   b. Copy the code that appears in the text box below the button.

   c. Paste it into the location where you want it to appear in your e-mail, e-newsletter, or web page.

Figure 13-4:
Getting
the HTML
embed-
dable code
for your
customized
Facebook
badge.

Adding a Facebook Like Box to your website

Here are three reasons why using a Facebook Page Like Box is one of the most effective ways of converting website visitors into Facebook fans:

- ✔ **You can convert more fans.** Website visitors can Like your Page directly from the Like Box, which avoids any drop-off that might occur as they click through to Facebook.

- ✔ **You can leverage social proof.** When visitors see your Like Box, they'll notice the faces of their friends who have already liked your Page. This social "authority" makes it more like-ly (pun intended) that they'll join as well.

- ✔ **You can measure it.** Facebook Insights shows you exactly how many people have Liked your Page through a Like Box. Links or buttons from your site show up only as Unknown. (Read more about using Facebook Insights in Chapter 9.)

Adding a Like Box to your website is as easy as adding a badge, as in the preceding section:

1. **Go to** http://developers.facebook.com/docs/reference/plugins/like-box.

2. **Enter your Facebook Page URL into the Facebook Page URL field; see Figure 13-5.**

Figure 13-5:
Create a customized Like Box.

A preview of your Like Box appears on the right side.

3. **Adjust the following Like Box settings:**

   - *Width:* This sets the width of your Like Box in pixels.

   - *Color Scheme:* Your choices are Light or Dark.

   - *Show Faces:* Selecting this displays a limited number of fans in your Like Box.

   - *Border Color:* You can customize the border color (based on hexa-decimal colors).

   - *Show Stream:* Select this to display your latest Page stories.

   - *Show Header:* Selecting this will display `Find us on Facebook`.

4. **Click Get Code.**

   Your choices are HTML5, XFBML, or iframe. Get help from your webmaster if you don't know what these mean.

Promoting Your Facebook Presence Offline

Companies invest a lot of their marketing budget in offline activities, such as events, direct marketing, and outdoor advertising. Increasingly, offline efforts are driving online results. Do all that you can to promote your Facebook Page in the real world, such as including your Facebook Page URL in your offline communications.

Everyone, from politicians to celebrities to small businesses to the Fortune 500, is leveraging the offline world to promote their Facebook presence for a simple reason: Facebook's social features make it a great place to interact and build relationships with consumers in unprecedented ways. The viral aspects of the Facebook Platform are also ideal for spreading a message beyond the original point of contact.

Although this chapter discusses many great online strategies to enhance your Facebook presence, you can also promote your Page in offline ways, which may be more in line with your traditional marketing efforts, not to mention more effective for many of the small businesses, stores, restaurants, and local community groups that are marketing on Facebook. Closing the loop between marketing online and offline can be as simple as hanging a sign in your store window saying you're on Facebook and giving your Page name.

Some businesses go to great lengths to promote their Facebook Page offline. Check out Figure 13-6 and Figure 13-7 for some ideas.

Figure 13-6:
Crandon,
Wisconsin's
Chamber of
Commerce
promotes its
Facebook
Page by
using an
oversized
billboard.

Figure 13-7:
Skittles
promotes its
Page on all
its product
packaging.

Networking offline

Grow your network in the real world, as well as online: Join business networking groups, attend conferences and trade shows for your industry,
and get involved in local organizations that hold frequent events. By joining
professional organizations and attending industry events, you can establish
your credibility in your particular niche. You can also connect to the other

influencers and industry movers and shakers. Always network, whether through professional events or casual get-togethers. After all, what better opportunity is there to be able to hand out your business cards that include your Facebook Page URL?

If people want to find out more about your business, direct them to your Facebook Page. Let them know about all your business's social-media outposts, not just Facebook, but Twitter, LinkedIn, YouTube, Flickr, SlideShare, and so on. Invite your real-world social network to connect with you online.

Placing the Facebook logo on signs and in store windows

If you own a restaurant, retail store, or professional office, put up a decal in your window or a sandwich board on the checkout counter that asks your customers to visit your Facebook Page. Make sure that anyone who visits your establishment can see the sign. Let your customers know that you offer them something of value on your Page. Encourage them to Like your Page and become a fan.

Tell your customers that you plan to reward them for visiting your Page. Give them a discount, a coupon, or special content (for example, recipes if you're a restaurant). Often, the people with whom you engage offline everyday are your best potential Facebook supporters. Invite your real-world customers to connect with you on Facebook and don't forget to reach out and connect to them by rewarding them for their continued support.

Referencing your Page in all ads and product literature

Spread the love and your Facebook Page URL wherever you can. Put your Facebook Page address on all company-printed materials. Display the Facebook logo and your Page link on your business cards; letterhead; direct-marketing campaigns; print, radio, and TV ads; catalogs; product one-sheets; customer case studies; press releases; newsletters; and coffee mugs, umbrellas, T-shirts, mouse pads, and holiday gifts. Basically, wherever eyes might look, you want to place your Facebook URL.

Don't forget to get employees involved in spreading the word about your Facebook presence. Make sure you inform the people who work for your business about your Facebook Page because they can become your biggest brand ambassadors.

Optimizing Your Page

It's very important to optimize your Page so that it shows up at the top of Facebook's internal search results as well as on Google. A poorly indexed Page can result in a lot of missed opportunities because visitors just can't find your Page.

Facebook search results now include a member's friends (and Pages that she's a fan of) status updates; photos, links, videos, and notes that match your search query; along with Profile, Page, Group, and application results.

If other users have chosen to make their content available to everyone, members also can search for their status updates, links, and notes, regardless of whether they're friends. Search results continue to include people's Profiles as well as pertinent Facebook Pages, Groups, and applications. Users can filter the results so that they see only friends' News Feeds or News Feeds for everybody who has made their privacy settings accessible to all. For example, Figure 13-8 shows the results of a Posts by Everyone search for the phrase *Facebook Marketing*.

Figure 13-8: Facebook's internal search displays search-related public posts.

Using search engine optimization to drive traffic

Pages hosted by Facebook tend to rank well when searched for and then displayed in other search engines, including Yahoo! and Google, particularly when users search for businesses or people. In addition to making your content easy to find on Facebook's internal search, consider making your content easy for Google and the others to find and index.

Here are some practices to help you optimize your Facebook Page across all search engines:

- ✔ **Play the name game.** Choose your Page name and username wisely. For example, a pizza shop named Pete's Pizza is going to get buried far down in search results. However, naming your page something like Pete's Pizza-Minneapolis will bump you to the top of the search results for people looking for pizza in Minneapolis. (For details on how to acquire your username, see "Choosing a custom Facebook username," earlier in this chapter.)

- ✔ **Anticipate keywords in text.** When you write your description and the overview section of your Page's Info tab, use descriptive keywords that people are likely to search for. For example, to go along with the preceding pizza example, make sure you mention what your restaurant is known for, so maybe go with something like

    We have the best New York-style pizza, the hottest wings, and the coolest staff in all the Twin Cities! Stop by one of our three metro locations: St. Paul, Minneapolis, or our newest shop near the Mall of America in Bloomington.

- ✔ **Use custom content.** Use iframes or HTML. Include relevant keywords that complement your description and Info sections. Include relevant links in the code.

- ✔ **Anticipate keywords in titles.** When adding content such as photos, discussion topics, and status updates, use appropriate keywords in the titles. For example, if your pizza shop recently donated food to a local school, post pictures of the kids enjoying the special treat with a caption like this:

    Pete's Pizza staff enjoying some pizza with the kids at Main Street Elementary School.

- ✔ **Exploit plug-ins.** Add one or more of Facebook's social plug-ins (see Chapter 14) to your website or blog. Integrate Facebook buttons, Share buttons, and Like buttons to increase the number of links to your

Facebook Page. (See "Leveraging Your Facebook Presence via Your E-Mail, Website, and Blog," earlier in this chapter, for details on how to create these buttons.)

✔ **Get topical:** Whenever you create an update on Facebook, such as a discussion topic on a Page, choose topics that your intended audience is likely to search for. For example, if you want to know whether your fans would be interested in a whole-wheat pizza crust option, post that question on the discussion board and point out some of the health benefits of using whole-wheat crust (think fiber).

If you take the time to optimize your content, you see the benefits in your Page traffic and fan engagement. If people can quickly and easily find you in search results because you've posted interesting, engaging information, they're more likely to return to your Page in the future. Future visits mean interested fans and fun interaction!

Using Facebook Questions

Facebook has recently released *Facebook Questions,* a way to harness members' social graphs to ask and answer questions. Facebook Questions offers marketers an excellent opportunity to boost their presence by either asking or answering a question. Keep in mind that the more Likes you get for your Facebook Question, the more likely it will show in search results, so make it likeable by using descriptive works, look at ways to encourage interactivity, and promote it throughout your network. At the time of this writing, this feature is still in beta. However, you can find out more information at www.facebook.com/questions/.

Driving more likes to your Page

Are you doing all you can to encourage people to like your Facebook Page? Okay, you're not CNN or Lady Gaga, but you can think like a marketer and increase the number of fans and level of engagement and interaction by employing some best practices in fan building.

Here are five ways for attracting more fans to your Facebook Page:

✔ Use the Facebook Like Box social plug-in on your website.

✔ Create a customized landing page that encourages visitors to click your Page's Like button.

- ✔ Run promotions on your Page by using a customized tab. For example, if you're a photography studio, use a third-party app like Promotion Builder from Wildfire Interactive. (See Chapter 12.)

- ✔ Integrate Facebook's Activity Feed and Recommendations plug-ins on your website to engage your visitors more effectively by keeping your content in front of them in multiple formats. If you have regular events, add Facebook's Live Stream plug-in to your website and webcast the event for all to see and become a fan of. (See Chapter 14 for details.)

- ✔ Review your Page's Insights on a regular basis to understand how your visitors are engaging with your content, and to keep track of what's resonating and what's not. (See Chapter 9 for more on Insights.)

Stories posted in the early morning or just before bed have higher engagement rates because people typically check their Facebook feeds when they get up, get to work, or are winding down for the night.

Chapter 14

Understanding and Using
Facebook Social Plug-ins

In This Chapter

▶ Using Facebook social plug-ins

▶ Getting Facebook friends' recommendations and comments

▶ Connecting with the Login button, Activity Feed, and Like Box plug-ins

▶ Showing visitors' Facebook Profile pictures with Facepile

▶ Using Live Stream to engage your users during a live event

*F*acebook offers ten different ways of bridging Facebook's social activities with your website, each with its own take on the Open Graph data that your Page generates. These *social plug-ins* allow you to set up your website so that whenever a reader interacts with your site, such as by leaving a comment on a blog post, a story about that action appears on that person's News Feed.

Social plug-ins can do lots of things: They can personalize the content that your visitors see, display the names of Facebook friends who have visited the site, or allow visitors to engage with their Facebook friends, all without having to log in to your website. By integrating these plug-ins with your website, you essentially give your website the same capability that your Facebook Page has to build a fan base, engage Facebook users, and increase brand awareness.

In this chapter, you find out about the different social plug-ins available and which ones you can implement to meet your marketing objectives. We show you how to turn your site into a more personalized experience for your users by adding the Login button plug-in and how to leverage a user's social graph with the Recommendations plug-in. We introduce the Activity Feed and Comments plug-ins, which bring your Facebook Page's activity to your website, and the Live Stream plug-in, which allows you to interact in real time with your visitors. And finally, we show you how to use the Registration plug-in to build a community on your site, and how to use the Send button to allow visitors to send messages to Facebook friends about content from your website.

Extending the Facebook Experience with Social Plug-ins

Social plug-ins allow visitors to your website to view content that their Facebook friends have Liked, commented on, or shared. If visitors to your site are logged in to their Facebook accounts, they can help your website content *go viral* (become very popular very quickly through sharing on the Internet) on Facebook without ever leaving your site.

Facebook has created a special section within its developer site (at `https://developers.facebook.com/plugins`) that explains the different plug-ins, provides tools for generating the code needed to embed each within your site, and showcases superior implementations on real-world websites. (See Figure 14-1.) The plug-ins are free for anyone to use and allow you to add an interactive layer to your site that complements your Facebook marketing strategy. You can use these plug-ins individually or in tandem, extending to your site many of the same features that people have become familiar with inside Facebook.

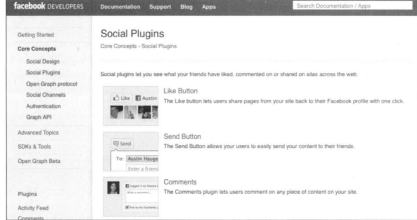

Figure 14-1:
Facebook's Social Plugins developer page.

Deciding which plug-in (or combination of plug-ins) to integrate into your site can be a bit daunting because some of their capabilities overlap. To help you decide which plug-in is right for your needs, here are brief descriptions and examples of each:

✔ **Like button:** This simple one-button design allows anyone who's signed into Facebook to show approval of your content. Figure 14-2 shows how Moviefone integrates the Like button for movies. The Like count (which appears to the right of the button in Figure 14-2) increases as more people click it.

Figure 14-2:
Moviefone integrates the Like button for every movie.

When a user clicks the Like button, a news story publishes to his News Feed, and this story includes a link back to the content on your site. If your site offers a lot of content that users can Like individually (such as in a catalog, blog, media site, or product description), the Like button is a good way to establish more opportunities to connect with users. If you're more interested in generating Likes for your company or website (rather than for a specific piece of content), the Like Box plug-in (described later in this list) may be a better option for you.

✔ **Send button:** Allows Facebook users to send your website's content to specific friends or Facebook groups. This plug-in also gives website visitors the option to e-mail your website content. You can also integrate the Send button with the Like button by adding `send=true` as an attribute to the XFBML version of the Like button (or `data-send="true"` to the HTML5 version). This displays the Like and Send buttons next to each other on your web pages. (See Figure 14-3.)

✔ **Comments:** Allows you to add a comment box to your website so that Facebook users can enter their comments, as shown in Figure 14-4. The plug-in gives users the option to have their comments published to their Facebook News Feeds, and these republished comments include a link back to the comments on your site. For content that isn't appropriate for people to comment on, such as product information, don't use this plug-in. However, for blogs or more opinionated content, the added exposure through the News Feed can provide you with a good source of traffic.

Figure 14-3:
John Haydon's blog allows readers to either Like or send blog posts.

THE DIFFERENCE BETWEEN MINUTES AND MOMENTS

6 retweet   Like   Send

Comments here...

👍 Like ⬛ 1,012 people like this. Be the first of your friends.

Add a comment...

Sep 22
excellent :)
Message – Delete

Sep 18
nice
Message – Delete

Sep 16
Great! Very nice
Message – Delete

Sep 13
Love it! Nice page...
Message – Delete

vidiyan Sep 8
jkhkjhkj
Message – Delete

Sep 2
I got this from Sherri – "Success is not a destination, it is a journey". I know she didn't write but I like to believe that! LOL ♥
Message – Delete

Figure 14-4:
The Comments plug-in allows visitors to add a comment to your website.

You do have options to delete or report negative comments, but you have to manually manage the process.

✔ **Activity Feed:** Shows recent Facebook-related activity around your site as a stream, which includes how many people have Liked or shared your content. The plug-in shows activity from the visitors' Facebook friends, as shown in the CNN example in Figure 14-5, but if it can't find enough friend-only content, it includes more general recent activity from Facebook users that the visitor doesn't know. This plug-in can really up your site's exposure if it has an active Facebook following and regularly updated content, such as a blog.

The Activity Feed is a powerful plug-in that keeps your visitors up to date on your site's topics. It also overlaps slightly with the Recommendations plug-in (described earlier in this list), so make sure you review your options before you decide which plug-in to implement.

✔ **Recommendations:** The Recommendations plug-in displays to visitors of your site a personalized list of the content on your website that their Facebook friends have recommended. For a logged-in Facebook user, the plug-in gives preference to friends with whom the visitor has inter-acted the most (as shown in Figure 14-6). This plug-in is different than the Activity Feed plug-in, which displays all activity that Facebook users have taken around your site's content (shares, comments, Likes, and so on) instead of just recommendations.

Figure 14-5:
CNN's Activity Feed plug-in shows the visitors' Facebook friends' interactions with the site.

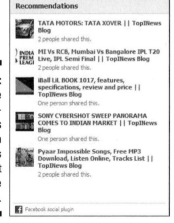

Figure 14-6:
The Recommendations plug-in highlights content that people like the most.

✔ **Like Box:** Similar to the Like button, the Like Box plug-in (as shown in the Mashable example in Figure 14-7) provides a one-click button, but the Like relates to your Facebook Page, rather than to the content on your website. It also publishes a story about Liking your Facebook Page directly to users' News Feeds. When customizing the Like Box for your site, you can include Profile pictures of Facebook users who have already liked your site and show the Wall stream for your Facebook

Page. This plug-in can be extremely helpful if you want to build your fan-base on your Facebook Page by creating a bridge between your website and Page. With the Like Box, the option to Like your page is right in front of your readers. They don't have to search for your Page directly on Facebook to Like it.

✔ **Login button:** Allows visitors to log in to your website by using their Facebook user IDs and passwords. This plug-in also displays the Facebook Profile pictures of a user's friends who have signed up, as shown in Figure 14-8. If you want to increase user registration on your website, this option is a good choice: By showing a user which friends are already logging in to your site, it helps you encourage engagement. You can resize the plug-in to best fit your site design, and it dynamically resizes depending on the number of friends already signed in. As with most social plug-ins, the user is asked to give Facebook permission to access his Profile information when he logs in.

✔ **Registration:** Allows Facebook users to register on your website with their Facebook account. When logged into Facebook, users see a form that's already filled in with their Facebook information. This plug-in gives you the flexibility to ask for additional information, such as the visitor's favorite band or movvie. Even visitors who don't use Facebook can use this plug-in to register for your website.

✔ **Facepile:** Shows your visitors the Profile pictures of their friends who are already site members without requiring them to be logged into Facebook or to their already-established account within your site. If none of a visitor's friends have previously signed up, no Profile pictures appear. When combined with Facebook's Login button, this plug-in can dramatically increase user registrations to your site because users who see that their friends have registered, as shown in Figure 14-9, are more likely to register with your site.

If your site offers a service that requires a separate login process, the Facepile plug-in is a nice way to highlight the visitors' Facebook friends who have already signed up. Just like the Login Button plug-in (described earlier in this list), the Facepile plug-in dynamically resizes its height depending on how many friends of the user have already signed up.

Figure 14-7:
Mashable
wants you
to Like
its Page.

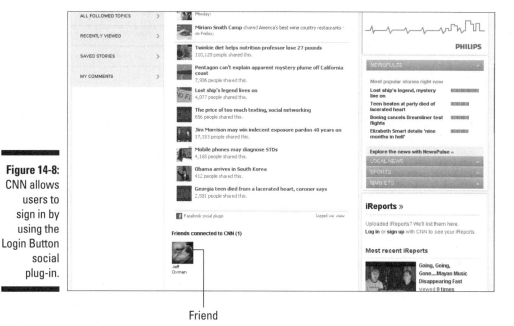

Figure 14-8:
CNN allows users to sign in by using the Login Button social plug-in.

Friend

Figure 14-9:
The Facepile plug-in shows Profile pictures.

✔ **Live Stream:** Allows Facebook users to comment on your website in real time, as shown in Figure 14-10. This plug-in is a good option if your website streams a live event, such as a video broadcast, and you want to offer visitors a real-time chat experience to go along with the live content being streamed. The Live Stream plug-in is used specifically for live activities that will end eventually, and not for written content, such as blog posts, which can exist indefinitely, along with the comments made on them. If you want to include comments for your static content, the Comments plug-in (described earlier in this list) is a better choice.

Although these social plug-ins may allow your site to display visitors' personal Facebook data, they won't actually pass that data to your site —that is, you can't track that data, manipulate it, or store it in a database — and visitors' Profile pictures and comments are visible only if they're logged into Facebook.

Adding the Code

Adding a social plug-in to your site is as simple as embedding a single line of code into your website's HTML, in much the same manner as adding a YouTube video. Most of the sections in the rest of this chapter explain how to generate the code needed to embed most of these plug-ins within your site. After you have the code, you follow these general steps to incorporate it into your website. (*Note:* You must have access to your website's source files. If you don't know where these are located, get your website developer to point you in the right direction.)

1. **Open the HTML file for your web page using whatever editor (Adobe Dreamweaver, Microsoft Word, or a Unix editor like vi) you normally use to make changes to your files.**

2. **Go to the spot in the HTML file where you want the social plug-in to appear.**

3. **Input the lines of code generated on the Facebook Developers site into the HTML file.**

4. **Save the HTML file and, if necessary, upload the new HTML file to your website.**

5. **Using a web browser, go to that web page (refresh your browser, if necessary) and make sure that the plug-in appears in the correct location.**

In most cases, installing another plug-in is just a matter of using a different line (or lines) of code in Step 3. Refer to the Facebook Developers page for each plug-in for the specific code you need.

Integrating Facebook Insights into Your Social Plugins

One great thing about using social plug-ins is their capability to measure how those plug-ins are being used, and to determine who's using them with demographics data.

Facebook allows you to use Facebook Insights to see how visitors to your website interact with the Facebook social plug-ins you've installed on your website. For example, when a user shares a link to your site on Facebook using the Recommendations plug-in, that action can be tracked in a Facebook Insights report about your website.

The next few sections show you how to do this.

Setting up your website as a Facebook application

In order to access Insights data for your website you must first create a Facebook application. Creating a Facebook application allows you to associate an application ID for each social plug-in on your site, which enables Facebook to track the ways Facebook users interact with the plug-in. Creating an app gives you the ability to access Insights for each of your plug-ins.

To create an application, follow these steps:

1. **Visit** `https://developers.facebook.com/apps` **or click the Create a New App button on the right side of the Page.**

   If this is your first time creating an application, you must first grant Facebook permission to access your basic information.

2. **Enter the requested information (as shown in Figure 14-11):**

   • *App Display Name:* This is a unique name for the application you are creating. Because only you will see this info, you can simply use the name of your website or the social plug-in you are creating the app for.

   • *App Namespace:* This field doesn't apply for our purposes, and for now you can leave it blank.

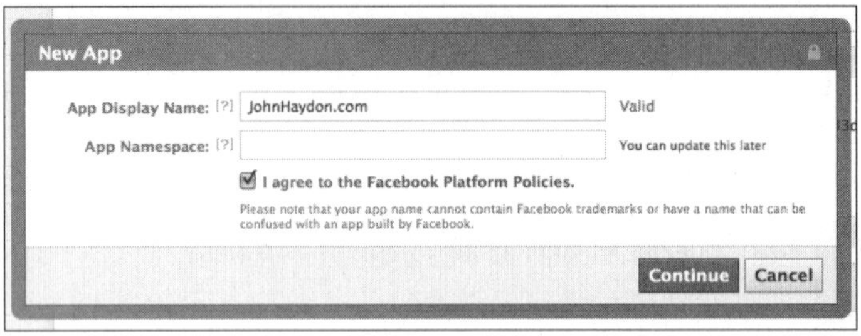

Figure 14-11:
The applica-
tion creation
window.

3. **Agree to Facebook's platform policies by checking the I Agree to the Facebook Platform Policies check box.**

   Read more about the policies at `https://developers.facebook.com/policy/`.

4. **Click Continue.**

5. **On the next screen, enter the CAPTCHA as you see it and then click Submit.**

   The Basic screen appears. In this screen are many fields, some of which are already filled in. (See Figure 14-12.) For our purposes here, we walk you through only the fields necessary to obtain a Facebook App ID for your website:

   • *App Display Name:* This is the name you created in Step 2.

   • *App Namespace:* This is the name you created, if any, in Step 2.

   • *Contact Email:* This is your default e-mail address, but you can change it to any e-mail address you prefer Facebook to use.

   • *App Domain:* Enter your website's domain URL.

   • *Category:* (Optional) Select a category from the drop-down list.

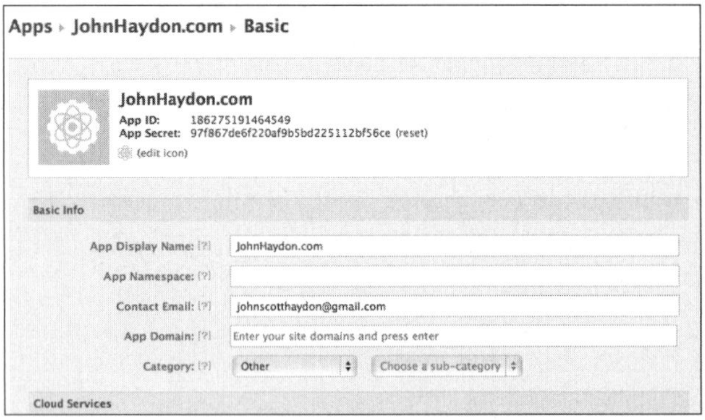

Figure 14-12:
The top of
the Basic
screen of a
Facebook
App.

6. **In the Select How Your App Integrates with Facebook section, enter your website's URL in the Site URL field, as shown in Figure 14-13.**

Select how your app integrates with Facebook	
✓ **Website**	
Site URL: [?]	http://johnhaydon.com
✓ **App on Facebook**	I want to build an app on Facebook.com.
✓ **Mobile Web**	I have a mobile web app.
✓ **Native iOS App**	I have a native iOS app.
✓ **Native Android App**	I have a native Android app.
✓ **Page Tab**	I want to build a custom tab for Facebook Pages.
	Save Changes

Figure 14-13: The bottom of the Basic screen of a Facebook App.

7. **Click Save Changes.**

You are finished creating your Facebook app! Now you must edit the HTML in your website to integrate with your application — and particularly your app ID.

The goal here is to allow Facebook's platform to collect information about the way people interact with the social plug-ins on your website. Your application ID, then, allows Facebook and your website to "talk" to each other.

Integrating the Facebook's software into your website

The last step requires you to have access to your website's HTML. If you don't know how to do that, consult a professional to help you.

To allow Facebook the capability to integrate with your app, you need to include the JavaScript SDK for the social plug-in on your webpage, right after the opening <body> tag.

After you create your application, it will appear in the Get Code window for each social plug-in (see Figure 14-14). The Javascript SDK that you must add after the <body> tag begins with <div id="fb-root">. When the SDK has been added, the plug-in is now active on your site!

Figure 14-14:
The Get
Code
window for
each social
plug-in
includes the
Javascript
SDK for your
website.

Getting More Visibility with the Like Button

The Like button lets visitors share your website content with their Facebook friends. When the user clicks a Like button on your site, a story appears in the user's friends' News Feed with a link back to your website. To integrate Facebook's Login Button with your site, follow these steps:

1. **Visit** `https://developers.facebook.com/plugins` **and click the Like Button link.**

2. **Fill in the requested information to customize your button (see Figure 14-15), as follows:**

   • *URL to Like:* Enter the exact URL you want visitors to Like.

   • *Send Button (XFBML Only):* Check this button to add the Send Button features to the XFBML code.

   • *Layout Style:* Choose from three different options (Standard, Button Count, Box Count), each of which can be viewed in the preview to the right.

   • *Width:* Enter the desired width of the Like button in pixels.

   • *Show Faces:* Checking this box sets the Like button to display the faces of users who have clicked the Like button.

   • *Verb to Display:* Choose *Like* or *Recommend.*

   • *Color Scheme:* Choose light or dark.

   • *Font:* Select any font from the drop-down menu.

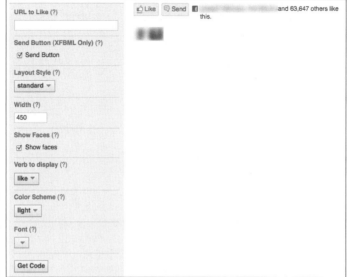

Figure 14-15:
Customizing
a Like
button.

3. Click Get Code.

Copy the code and paste it into your HTML at the location you want the plug-in to appear. If you are not familiar with HTML, or if you don't have access to your website's HTML, please get a professional to help you. If you want to have the ability to measure how people are using this plug-in, you must first create a Facebook application for your website. See the section, "Integrating Facebook Insights into your Social Plug-ins," earlier in this chapter for instructions.

Allowing for Private Sharing with the Send Button

The Send button lets visitors to your website send your content to friends. They can send a link and short note as a Facebook message, Facebook Group post, or an e-mail message. This is different from the Like button, which allows users to share content with their friends by publishing that content to their Profiles or News Feeds.

You can incorporate the Send button's features into a Like button by adding `send=true` as an attribute to the XFBML version of the Like button (or by adding `data-send="true"` to the HTML5 version).

To integrate Facebook's Send button with your site, follow these steps:

1. **Visit** `https://developers.facebook.com/plugins` **and click the Send Button link.**

2. **Fill in the requested information to customize your button (see Figure 14-16):**

   • *URL to Send:* Enter the exact URL you want visitors to share.

   • *Font:* Select any font from the drop-down menu.

   • *Color Scheme:* Choose light or dark.

3. **Click Get Code.**

   Copy the code and paste it into your HTML at the location you want the plug-in to appear. If you are not familiar with HTML or if you don't have access to your website's HTML, please get a professional to help you. If you want to have the ability to measure how people are using this plug-in, you first must create a Facebook application for your website. See the section, "Integrating Facebook Insights into your Social Plug-ins," earlier in this chapter for instructions.

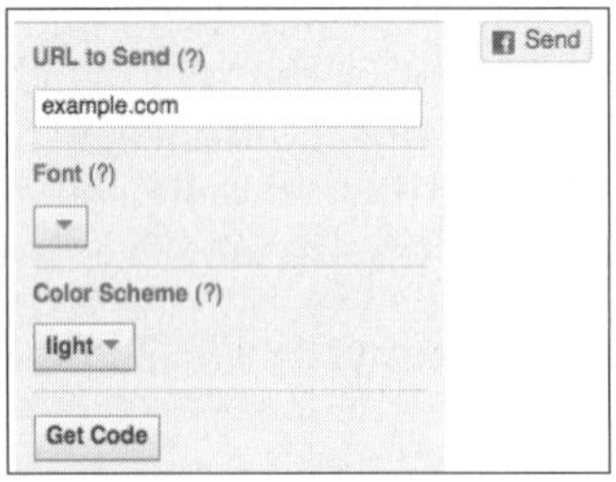

Figure 14-16:
Customizing
a Send
button.

Leveraging Popular Content with the Recommendations Plug-In

When you use the Recommendations plug-in on your site, visitors who are logged into their Facebook account see a list of the content that generated the most Likes across your site, making your site more relevant to visitors. For example, visitors to CNN.com can immediately see articles that people recommend and share with their friends in real time, as shown in Figure 14-17.

You can think of the Recommendations plug-in as a Facebook-powered version of most-popular lists, as chosen by a user's friends and other Facebook members. When you integrate this plug-in with your website, visitors see these recommendations in real time, so the recommendations most likely change every time users visit the site.

Figure 14-17: CNN shows visitors the site's most popular content.

To generate code for the Recommendations plug-in, follow these steps:

1. **Visit** `https://developers.facebook.com/plugins` **and click the Recommendations link.**

2. **Fill in the requested information to customize your plug-in (see Figure 14-18):**

   • *Domain:* Enter the domain (URL) where you want to place the plug-in.

   • *Width:* Enter the width, in pixels, for the plug-in.

   • *Height:* Enter the height, in pixels, for the plug-in.

   • *Header:* Select the Show Header check box if you want a header to appear in the plug-in.

   • *Color Scheme:* Select either Light or Dark for the color scheme that you want to use in the plug-in.

   • *Link Target:* Select how you'd like the link to open. By default all links open in a new browser window (`_blank`). However, if you want the content links to open in the same browser window, select `_top` or `_parent`.

   • *Border Color:* Enter the border color for the plug-in, such as red or blue.

   • *Font:* Select the font type you'd like to display in the plug-in.

Figure 14-18:
Enter the
attributes
to generate
code for the
Recommen-
dations
plug-in.

3. **Click Get Code.**

Copy the code and paste it into your HTML at the location you want the plug-in to appear. If you are not familiar with HTML or if you don't have access to your website's HTML, please get a professional to help you. If you want to have the ability to measure how people are using this plug-in, you first must create a Facebook application for your website. See the section, "Integrating Facebook Insights into your Social Plug-ins," earlier in this chapter for instructions.

Place the Recommendations plug-in on your website's home page so that you can immediately make a connection with your website visitors and provide a more personalized experience for them.

Integrating Facebook's Login Button

The Facebook Login button enables visitors to sign in to your site with their Facebook login information and displays Profile pictures of any of the user's friends who are already signed up for your site (refer to Figure 14-8). When you add the plug-in to your site, you can customize the maximum length and width settings for the box that will appear, which determines the number of friend Profiles that can be displayed in each line and row. However, if you specify that you want it to display four rows of pictures and the user has only two rows of friends who have signed up for your site, the plug-in dynamically adjusts to the two rows.

To integrate Facebook's Login button with your site, follow these steps:

1. **Visit** `https://developers.facebook.com/plugins` **and click the Login Button link.**

2. **Fill in the requested information to customize your button (see Figure 14-19):**

   • *Show Faces:* Select this check box if you want to show Profile pictures.

   • *Width:* Enter the width, in pixels, of the plug-in.

   • *Max Rows:* Enter the number of rows of Profile photos that you want to display. This number depends on the amount of space you want to allocate on your website for this plug-in.

3. **Click Get Code.**

   Copy the code and paste it into your HTML at the location you want the plug-in to appear. If you are not familiar with HTML or if you don't have access to your website's HTML, please get a professional to help you. If you want to have the ability to measure how people are using this plug-in, you first must create a Facebook application for your website. See the section, "Integrating Facebook Insights into your Social Plug-ins," earlier in this chapter for instructions.

Figure 14-19: You can easily create your own version of Facebook's Login button.

Consider combining the Login button plug-in with the Activity Feed plug-in (described later in this chapter) for maximum exposure.

Adding Comments to Your Website

The Comments plug-in enables you to add a comments thread to any page on your website that allows visitors already logged in to Facebook to add comments (see Figure 14-20). Users have the option to have their comments also posted to their Facebook Profiles; those comments then show up in those users' News Feeds, viewable by all their friends. By installing this plug-in, you allow users to leave comments and interact with you, and because their friends see that activity, you can drive more traffic back to your website.

Figure 14-20:
Add a
Comments
plug-in to
get users
engaged
with the
content
on your
website.

To add the Comments plug-in to your site, follow these steps:

1. **Visit** http://developers.facebook.com/plugins **and click the Comments link.**

2. **Enter the requested information to customize the plug-in (see Figure 14-21):**

   - *URL to be commented on:* This is the unique ID number associated with the Comments plug-in. Typically, you can leave this field blank, and the value will be generated by the web page when the box is being drawn.

   - *Number of Posts:* Enter the number of posts you want displayed. The default is two, but the actual amount you display depends on any space constraints on your site.

   - *Width:* Enter the width, in pixels, of the plug-in.

   - *Color Scheme:* Select either Light or Dark for the color scheme that you want to use in the plug-in.

3. **Click Get Code to generate the code.**

   Copy the code and paste it into your HTML at the location you want the plug-in to appear. If you are not familiar with HTML or if you don't have access to your website's HTML, please get a professional to help you. If you want to have the ability to measure how people are using this plug-in, you first must create a Facebook application for your website. See the section, "Integrating Facebook Insights into your Social Plug-ins," earlier in this chapter, for instructions.

Figure 14-21: Create the code for your very own Comments plug-in.

 You can add a Comments plug-in to any piece of content from which you want to solicit user feedback. Consider integrating it with product review pages or your blog, or you can use it to gauge user interest on website- related things like a new layout.

 If you integrate the Comments plug-in within your site, you need to monitor the comments closely and delete spam and malicious or overtly negative remarks.

Showing User Activities with the Activity Feed Plug-In

When a visitor to your site is logged in to Facebook, the Activity Feed plug-in is personalized with content from that user's friends. It shows the content within your site that the visitor's friends are sharing, recommending, and commenting on (refer to Figure 14-5). If they aren't logged in, however, it shows general recommendations from your site, not personalized ones.

To add the Activity Feed plug-in, follow these steps:

1. **Visit** `http://developers.facebook.com/plugins` **and click the Activity Feed link.**

2. **Enter the requested information to customize your plug-in (see Figure 14-22):**

   • *Domain:* Enter the domain of the page where you plan to put the plug-in.

   • *Width:* Enter the width, in pixels, of the plug-in.

- *Height:* Enter the height, in pixels, of the plug-in.

- *Header:* Select the Show Header check box if you want to include the Recent Activity header on the plug-in.

- *Color Scheme:* Select your color scheme (you can choose between Light and Dark).

- *Link Target:* Select how you'd like the link to open. By default, links open in a new browser window (_blank). However, if you want the content links to open in the same browser window, select _top or _parent.

- *Border Color:* Type a color, such as red or blue.

- *Font:* Select the font that you want to display within the plug-in.

- *Recommendations:* If you select the Recommendations check box, the plug-in displays recommendations in the bottom half of the plug-in when you don't have enough activity to fill the entire box. If the box isn't selected, no recommendations are shown. We suggest you always select the check box so it looks like your page is active, even when you may be experiencing a slow activity period.

Figure 14-22: Enter the requested information to create the Activity Feed plug-in.

3. **Click Get Code to generate the code.**

   Copy the code and paste it into your HTML at the location you want the plug-in to appear. If you are not familiar with HTML or if you don't have access to your website's HTML, please get a professional to help you. If you want to have the ability to measure how people are using this plugin, you first must create a Facebook application for your website. See the section, "Integrating Facebook Insights into your Social Plugins," later in this chapter, for instructions.

Liking the Like Box

If you want to acquire more fans for your Facebook Page, consider integrating the Like Box social plug-in on your website (see Figure 14-23). With one click, users can Like your Facebook Page without leaving your website. The Like Box also provides a current count of how many Likes your Facebook Page has accumulated and which of the visitor's friends Like it, too. The Like Box plug-in can also display recent updates you've posted on your Facebook Page.

Figure 14-23:
Use the Like Box to get more people to Like your Page.

To add the Like Box plug-in to your website, follow these steps:

1. **Visit** `https://developers.facebook.com/plugins` **and click the Like Box link.**

2. **Fill in the requested information to customize your Like Box plug-in (see Figure 14-24):**

   - *Facebook Page URL:* Enter the Facebook Page URL that you want your visitors to Like.

   - *Width:* Enter the width, in pixels, of the plug-in.

- *Height:* Enter the height, in pixels, of the plug-in.

- *Color Scheme:* You can choose between having a light or a dark background.

- *Show Faces:* Select the Show Faces check box if you want the faces of some of your fans displayed in the Like Box. This is a very powerful feature because it shows the friends of the viewer who have already liked your Facebook Page.

- *Border Color:* Enter the border color for the plug-in, such as red or blue.

- *Stream:* Select the Show Stream check box if you want to show the most recent stream of updates you've posted on your Facebook Page.

- *Header:* Select the Show Header check box to include the Find Us on Facebook header at the top of the plug-in.

3. **Click Get Code to generate the code.**

   Copy the code and paste it into your HTML at the location you want the plug-in to appear. If you are not familiar with HTML, or if you don't have access to your website's HTML, please get a professional to help you. If you want to have the ability to measure how people are using this plug-in, you first must create a Facebook application for your website. See the section, "Integrating Facebook Insights into your Social Plugins," earlier in this chapter for instructions.

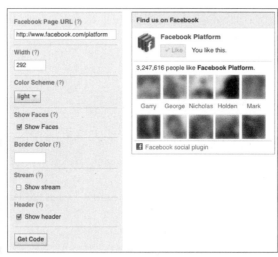

Figure 14-24:
Generating code for the Facebook Like Box plug-in.

Making Registration Painless with the Registration Plug-in

The Registration plug-in lets people register for your website with their Facebook account. When implemented, the form appears to Facebook users prefilled with their Facebook information. You can also set up the form to ask for additional information, such as shirt size (if, say, you're giving away a t-shirt for each new registrant). Additionally, the registration plug-in allows people who don't have a Facebook account to register, which is great because it eliminates the need to have two separate forms on your website.

Unlike the other plug-ins, the Registration plug-in requires intermediate knowledge of HTML and access to your website's files. We recommend that you get a professional to help you install this plug-in. Installation instructions (and code) are located at `https://developers.facebook.com/docs/plugins/registration/`.

Personalizing a Site with the Facepile Plug-In

Similar to the Login button (described earlier in the chapter), Facepile allows you to personalize the user's experience with your website by displaying the user's friends who have also registered on your site. The Facepile plug-in differs from the Login button in that Facepile dynamically resizes its height based on how many of the user's friends are displayed and doesn't show up at all if no friends have signed up with your site (or if the user isn't logged into Facebook).

The Facepile plug-in, which you can add to the header or top area of your website's home page or its key landing pages, encourages users to explore your site further by showing them which of their friends are also signed onto the site.

To generate the Facepile plug-in code that you need to embed on your website, follow these steps:

1. **Visit** `https://developers.facebook.com/plugins` **and click the Facepile link.**

2. **Enter the requested information to customize your plug-in (see Figure 14-25):**

   • *URL:* Enter the URL of the domain of the page where you plan to put the plug-in.

- *Size:* Choose the size of the images and social content you want to display.

- *Width:* Enter the width, in pixels, of the plug-in.

- *Num Rows:* Enter the number of rows of Profile pictures that you want to display. Don't worry about adding too many rows. If there aren't enough pictures to fill all the rows, the box is resized to fit.

- *Color Scheme:* Select your color scheme (you can choose between Light and Dark).

Figure 14-25:
Generate
code for the
Facepile
plug-in.

3. **Click Get Code to generate the code.**

   Copy the code and paste it into your HTML at the location you want the plug-in to appear. If you are not familiar with HTML or if you don't have access to your website's HTML, please get a professional to help you. If you want to have the ability to measure how people are using this plug-in, you first must create a Facebook application for your website. See the section, "Integrating Facebook Insights into your Social Plugins," earlier in this chapter for instructions.

Engaging in Real Time with Live Stream

If you integrate the Live Stream plug-in with your website, visitors can view and post comments in real time. You can use this tool to add a real-time chat stream to accompany live content that you're offering on your site, such as a live video webcast, webinar, conference, and so on. This plug-in allows visitors to filter the chat stream by everyone watching or just their friends.

To create the Live Stream plug-in code for your website, follow these steps:

1. **Visit** `https://developers.facebook.com/plugins` **and click the Live Stream link.**

2. **Enter the requested information to customize your plug-in (see Figure 14-26):**

   - *App ID:* Enter your App ID number in this text box. To find out how to generate a unique App ID, see the preceding section.

   - *Width:* Enter the width, in pixels, of the plug-in.

   - *Height:* Enter the height, in pixels, of the plug-in.

   - *XID:* If you want your site to include more than one Live Stream plug-in, enter an *XID number,* which is a unique ID, to help you identify the stream. You can choose any combination of letters or numbers.

   - *Via Attribution URL:* This is the URL that users are taken to when they click the app's name in the status update. This is optional because Live Stream can be used for websites and applications.

   - *Always Post to Friends:* If you check this check box, everything a user posts will show up on their Facebook Profile. If you don't check this check box, then users will have the choice to share it on their Facebook profile or not.

3. **Click Get Code to generate the code.**

   Copy the code and paste it into your HTML at the location you want the plug-in to appear. If you are not familiar with HTML or if you don't have access to your website's HTML, please get a professional to help you. If you want to have the ability to measure how people are using this plug-in, you first must create a Facebook application for your website. See the section, "Integrating Facebook Insights into your Social Plugins," earlier in this chapter for instructions.

Checking your plug-ins with Debugger

Facebook provides the Debugger tool for you to check your plug-ins after you add them to your website. Visit `https://developers.facebook.com/tools/debug`, enter the URL of the web page you want to review to make sure the plug-ins are installed properly, and click the Debug button. If you have a plug-in that isn't working, a warning message returns, letting you know where the issue is so you can return to your HTML code and fix the problem.

Live Stream isn't a good option for static sites or sites that offer live events that have a very small audience because there isn't enough activity to keep it interesting and the audience engaged.

Figure 14-26:
The Live Stream plug-in can help you engage users with live content on your website.

App ID (?)

186275191464549

Width (?)

400

Height (?)

500

XID (?)

Via Attribution URL (?)

Always post to friends (?)

☐ Always post to friends

Get Code

facebook   Privacy   Log Out

Discuss this event

Post to Facebook ☑ Share

Be the first to share your thoughts on this event

Part V
The Part of Tens

In this part . . .

The three chapters in this part are packed with quick ideas and recommendations to help you get more out of Facebook. Chapter 15 tells you how to avoid the biggest Facebook marketing mistakes. In Chapter 16, we explain the rules and etiquette for conducting yourself on the social network. And in Chapter 17, we reveal the secrets of long-term Facebook marketing success.

Chapter 15

Ten Common Facebook Marketing Mistakes (And How to Avoid Them)

In This Chapter

▶ Using a Profile or Group to market your business

▶ Making posting errors

▶ Selling too much or too little

▶ Ignoring fans

*J*ust because you've created a Facebook Page for your business doesn't mean that you won't make mistakes. Of course mistakes aren't necessarily bad if you can learn from them, but it's always good to avoid mistakes in the first place! Many common mistakes have to do with understanding how people use Facebook. For example, you shouldn't use a Facebook Profile to market your business — Profiles are for people. Other mistakes involve unwittingly making a bad impression — such as being too pushy.

In this chapter, we discuss ten of the most common mistakes that you should avoid on Facebook.

Using a Profile to Market Your Business

We don't recommend that you use a Facebook Profile to market your business on Facebook, and here are at least three reasons why:

> ✔ **Facebook Profiles don't have any analytics tools,** which show you how fans engage with your content. Without these analytics in your information toolbox, you have no way of knowing what strategies are working on Facebook.

✔ **Sending a friend request is very different from asking someone to like your Page.** If you're sending friend requests as a Profile, you're essentially asking the user if you can see her photos, friend list, address, phone number, and perhaps relationship status. This crosses the unspoken social boundaries that most people have between their personal life and the brands they do business with. For example, it's perfectly acceptable for you to like a pizza shop, but creepy if a pizza shop likes you. On the other hand, Pages allow Facebook users to like Pages without compromising privacy.

✔ **Using a Facebook Profile to market your business could end up violating Facebook's Terms of Service.** This means that after spending a lot of resources of building up a large amount of friends — say 5,000 — Facebook can simply delete the profile.

Using a Group to Market Your Business

Another very common mistake that businesses make on Facebook is to use a Group to market their business. The problem with this is that Groups are solely intended for Facebook users to connect with each other around common interests and goals — not a single brand. Group members all have an equal say about what's discussed in the Group as well as what's appropriate (or not). Groups with a single person controlling topics generally aren't successful. Plus, Facebook didn't create Groups to be used for the purposes of marketing: That's what Facebook Pages are for!

Setting an Ineffective Default Tab

One feature that all Facebook Pages have is the capability to set a default tab for nonfans. Many times, businesses don't even know that this feature exists, and unknowingly send first-time visitors to either the Info tab or the Wall. The problem with this is that neither of these tabs convert as well as a custom welcome tab because both tabs require first-time visitors to spend a considerable amount of time trying to determine whether they should Like the Page. According to BrandGlue (www.facebook.com/BrandGlue), a custom welcome tab with a simple and clear call to action converts nonfans into fans at a 25 percent higher rate than not having a custom tab. In Chapter 6, we discuss several ways to add a custom welcome tab to your Facebook Page.

Posting Shortened URLs

Along with the surging trends in social media marketing, many third-party tools designed to manage multiple platforms have become available. Many of these, like HootSuite and TweetDeck, use URL shorteners to make long URLs fit within the character constraints of sites like Twitter. Although these tools also offer the capability to post links on Facebook, they don't offer the flexibility of posting a long URL when there aren't such character constraints, as with Facebook.

Buddy Media (`www.facebook.com/buddymedia`) conducted a study in 2011 that revealed that full-length URLs get three times as many clicks as URLs that have been shortened. In other words, using shortened URLs on Facebook actually has a negative impact on your ability to create awareness about your business! Instead of using shortened URLs, post content directly on Facebook, or use a third-party tool like Post Planner (`www.postplanner.com`), which is made specifically for Facebook marketers to schedule and post various different types of content to a Facebook Page.

Winging It

Another common mistake that Facebook marketers make is that they treat their Facebook Page with the same relaxed approach that they treat their Profile. People using Facebook Profiles rarely (and should never) have a primary business agenda. For the most part, using Facebook Profiles is a completely social activity that's relaxed and fun. Pages are very different.

Sure, having a relaxed demeanor on your Facebook Page is important, but so is having a well thought-out strategy that includes understanding your fanbase, presenting a unique message, and measuring results. In other words, don't just "wing it."

Posting During Bad Times

Facebook Page marketers generally work 9-to-5 jobs like everyone else. And as part of their job, they update their Facebook Page with useful content that hopefully has been well planned. However, what they fail to realize is that most of their Facebook fans also have 9-to-5 jobs and don't have time or aren't permitted to use Facebook during the day. Posting during the workday is generally not as effective as posting in the early morning or early evening, or any other time when users are on Facebook. The reason for this is that the News Feed flies by very quickly, so posting an update during the times when users are present increases the likelihood that you'll be at the top of their News Feed right when they're checking it.

Selling Too Much

Selling too much is probably the most common mistake by Facebook marketers. Say a Facebook marketer sets up a Page and starts posting content that's all about her business or products. The problem is that Facebook users don't care about her products and services, but they do care about things related to those products or services. For example, hikers want to discuss great places to go hiking, or share photos from a recent adventure. A sporting goods store that only promotes the latest hiking gear through a discount keeps its fans interested only as long as the Facebook Page discount lasts.

Selling Too Little

Conversely, selling too little is probably less common, but it's still a potential mistake. Imagine that our friends at the sporting goods store have learned their lesson about selling too much and start focusing on what their fans are interested in. Their fans start engaging, which is great, but sales don't increase as a result because the Page isn't posting any promotions or any calls to action. Facebook users love to converse about the things they care about, but they also love a good deal!

Posting Lengthy Updates

Another study by Buddy Media found that status updates of less than 80 characters received a 27 percent higher reaction than longer updates. This makes sense when you think about how you use Facebook and when you think about how fast the News Feed flies by.

Posting lengthy paragraphs as a status update is like giving your Facebook fans homework. (And when was the last time you celebrated getting homework?) On the other hand, short updates such as questions and short polls get a higher reaction simply because the barrier to participation is very low.

We know that it might be very tempting to cram as much information as possible about your new product or service into a status update, but in the long run, this practice will have a negative impact on your EdgeRank. Read more about EdgeRank in Chapter 8.

Ignoring Comments

Facebook fans are people, like you (and us). If they make the effort to leave a comment or reply within a thread on your Facebook Page, they want to know that you're listening. Pages that consistently ignore posts by fans aren't as successful as Pages that participate in comment threads. Fans are less likely to return if they don't feel heard.

The other reason why you want to reply to posts from fans is that Facebook sends that fan a notification, bringing him back to your Page! So, in addition to showing fans that they are heard, you also get them to continue posting on your Page.

Chapter 16

Ten Business Etiquette Tips for Facebook

In This Chapter

▶ Keeping it clean

▶ Maintaining a professional demeanor

▶ Understanding when not to reply

▶ Keeping your info private

As Facebook grows, so do the surprising number of embarrassing faux pas committed by individuals and companies alike. The occasional slips of the tongue, the odd photos, and, of course, everyone's favorite: the embarrassing tags in notes, photos, or videos.

You can and must protect your brand's reputation on Facebook, as well as maintain the utmost respect for the Facebook community. The downside is steep; you can lose your Page, your profile, or both. After you're banned from Facebook, it's hard to get back in, and by that time, the audience that you worked so hard to build is gone. Therefore, it's a good idea to abide by the tips and warnings we outline in this chapter.

Don't Drink and Facebook

This should go without saying, but sometimes our ability to communicate is impaired by drinking. Naturally, drinking and e-mailing or social networking just don't go together. You're better off not logging in. It takes only one bad or off-color Wall post to get you reported in Facebook. Members tend to be vigilant about things that they find offensive, so just say no to drinking and Facebooking.

Keep It Clean and Civilized

Here's another no-no: sending threatening, harassing, or sexually explicit messages to Facebook members. Also, unsolicited messages selling a product or service aren't tolerated. You should refrain from any of this behavior because the downside is that your account could receive a warning, be banned, and eventually be disabled. What's worse, Facebook won't provide you with a description or copy of the content that was found to be offensive. Facebook doesn't provide any specifics on the rules it enforces. Err on the side of caution if you aren't sure.

Avoid Overdoing It

You can overindulge in Facebook in several ways, so watch out for these traps because they're very easy to fall into. First, don't randomly add people to your personal profile in the hopes of converting them to become fans of your Page. Befriending random people is considered poor form and may make you look like a stalker. Also, avoid poking. If the member has poking activated, a Poke *Name* link appears under his profile picture. This allows one member to send another a gentle notice that you're thinking of him. However, this is an impersonal form of communication. Poking a friend can be fun, but poking a stranger is poor form — so avoid being a joke, and don't poke.

Dress Up Your Page with Applications

Independent developers have written an endless sea of apps for Facebook. One or more of those could make a great fit for your business, so find an app or two (but no more) that you can use to make your Page more engaging. The nice thing is that apps are easy to install and don't require any knowledge of how to build or modify them. Each tab has a unique URL, so consider creating individual tabs for each application. You can even send out an e-mail to your customer base asking people to engage with your new application (for example, a survey application). But be careful not to overdo it. (We discuss applications in more detail in Chapter 12.)

Respect the Wall

Your Wall is one of the most important places on your Page. It's where your fans can leave messages and start a discussion on a topic. All messages on your Wall are visible to everyone who's a fan of your business or anyone who visits your Page. Think of your Wall as a place of public record, so make sure you're professional and courteous to anyone posting. Thank fans for posting and make it fun for them and others.

Be Careful When Talking to Strangers

Sometimes written communication can seem flat and impersonal, so choose your words carefully — and be sure to reread your responses before you post them, especially if the situation is getting heated. Better yet, if you think the conversation is getting too heated, feel free to take it off Facebook and address the person via e-mail.

Don't Be Afraid to Ignore a Fan

Many people feel compelled to respond to every message in their e-mail inbox. Similarly, in Facebook people feel the need to respond to every comment or posting. Sometimes fans can overuse the various communication features in Facebook. New fans sometimes binge on the information you present. We suggest that you always welcome new fans and respond to comments and posts on your Wall within 24 hours, but try to know when to respond and when to let the conversation rest. For example, if the same fan leaves several comments on a single post, replying once should be enough. If a fan is irate, that's another thing; ignoring the fan can often work against you. See the following section for more.

Deal with Your Irate Fans

Irate fans pose one of the biggest challenges that this new medium has to offer. You have several ways to deal with an irate fan:

- **Honestly consider his point and try to find something (anything) to agree with.** Finding and establishing common ground is a great way to get the conversation back on track.

- **Correct factual inaccuracies in a very tactful and pleasant way.** The fan may not have all the data, which could be causing him to be irate.

- **If you don't know the solution to a particular situation, don't bluff your way out of it**. Be honest, commit to finding out more, and give the fan a date when you'll get back to him.

- **Don't forget that you can always take your conversation offline.**

Don't Forget Birthday Greetings

With the power of Facebook, you can never forget a birthday of any of your friends. Then why not make it a point each day to see whether fans of your Page are having a birthday? Just visit their profile and leave a birthday greeting on their Wall or send a Facebook e-mail to their inbox (you can only see birthdays of fans if their settings are set so they share that information). And if that isn't enough, you may want to offer them something unique that only you can provide for their birthday. For example, fans might be open to getting a happy birthday greeting from a local restaurant with an offer to come in that week for a free dessert or drink.

The power of this platform is there — and surprisingly few companies are taking advantage of this personalized happy birthday greeting opportunity.

Maintain Your Privacy

For some business owners, privacy is of paramount concern. If you're a local business owner — say, a local jewelry store owner — you might not want to list any personal information such as an address or phone number on the Info tab of your personal profile. Make sure that your profile settings are set to Private (which is no longer the default) rather than Public, which makes your personal information, including your home address, available to Internet search engines for all prying eyes to see. Also, be careful what groups you join. If someone you know in business sees controversial political, sexual, or religious activist groups on your profile, they might stop shopping at your store. Often, the less revealed the better.

Chapter 17

Ten (Okay, Eight) Factors for Long-Term Facebook Marketing Success

In This Chapter

▶ Understanding why Facebook users share

▶ Building trust with Facebook fans

▶ Understanding why you should measure your results

▶ Being creative and fearless

*E*very marketer wants her Facebook campaign to succeed, but not everyone can be so lucky. What are the best approaches to ensure success? This chapter lists the most time-tested ways to make sure your campaign makes the most of Facebook.

Learn the Language, Eat the Food

One of the best ways to ensure long-term marketing success on Facebook is to use it for personal use. Sure, you can read books and the latest research about why people use Facebook and why it continues to have amazing growth even after exceeding 800 million users worldwide. However, no book can take the place of the Facebook experience.

By signing up and using Facebook to connect with old high school friends, share photographs with family, discover new music, and comment within threads about various topics, you will begin to understand how to better connect with your customers. It's like the old adage with the apple: I can try and describe to you what it tastes like, but until you take a bite yourself, you'll never really understand.

Understand Why People Share

Obviously, one of the most important things you want your Facebook fans to do is to share content that you post on your Facebook Page. Understanding the psychology of sharing enables you to optimize your content for specific "sharing personas." (Find out more about personas in Chapter 2.)

Some people share to promote their careers, keeping everything they share professional and "safe for work." These folks are generally well educated, use LinkedIn, and keep their Facebook profile privacy settings very closed. Other people share because they want to look cool in front of their friends. They will share new music, breaking tech news, the latest threadless t-shirt they bought, and will most likely have very open privacy settings. A good person to follow to understand more about what motivates people to share is Dan Zarrella (`http://danzarrella.com`).

Be Useful and Helpful

One of the most powerful social laws that functions across cultures and languages is the law of reciprocity. Helping others is at the very core of our evolution as a species. If I help you shovel your driveway after a major snowstorm, you're much more willing to help me out in the future. Take this example, multiply it by 1,000, and you get Facebook.

When you make consistent efforts to promote other like-minded businesses on your Facebook Page, they promote yours in return. John believes this so much that he's created a custom welcome tab on the Inbound Zombie Facebook Page called Other Pages You'll Like. You can also be helpful by joining relevant Facebook groups and keeping an eye out for questions you can answer.

Listen to Your Fans

One of the biggest reasons why people use social media in the first place is to be heard. And the brands that do really well listen to their Facebook Page connections.

One example is FanPageEngine (`www.facebook.com/FanPageEngine`). When customers post technical questions on its Wall, they always get a quick and helpful answer. Make sure that the moderation settings on your Facebook Page are configured so that Page connections can post updates on your Page. Also make sure that you can be notified quickly when someone comments on your Wall (which can be configured by clicking on the "Edit Page" button on your Page and selecting the "Your Settings" tab. It's not as much work as it seems, and the positive effect on your brand in the long run will more than pay for the effort.

Your Facebook Page is essentially a platform where you can have conversations with your customers and prospects. You can ask them for feedback on products and services, which will enable you to give them more of what they really want. And even if you can't give them what they want, you can at least show them you care by replying. For example, "We're sorry we don't offer that, but here's what we do have." The fact that they've been heard leaves them with a positive feeling about your business, even if you don't have exactly what they want.

Consistently Participate

One of the biggest reasons why you're using Facebook for your business is to better connect with your customers and prospects. You want to make them aware of your business, get them interested in buying from you, and motivate them to take action. Every single step that they take along this path requires trust. Nothing obliterates trust more than being inconsistent. After you begin to use your Facebook Page as a platform for conversation — meaning that you quickly reply to questions and share interesting and useful content — your Facebook Page connections will naturally expect a certain consistency. For example, if during the first month on Facebook you post three times daily and quickly respond to questions, but then disappear in the following months, fans begin to question not only your commitment on Facebook but also your ability to provide good products and services.

Appreciate and Recognize Your Fans

If you want to stand apart from the crowd on Facebook, make a concerted effort to recognize and appreciate your Facebook fans. Being recognized and appreciated is a basic desire that all people share, immediately making them feel valued and inspiring them to appreciate others in return. The positive feeling that starts with you causes them to more likely share your business with their friends, and even give you money!

One way you can express appreciation is to state it simply: "We have the best Facebook fans on the planet!" (Notice how many comments you get after that update.) You could also do what Diapers.com does — it highlights specific parents in its Facebook avatar (see www.facebook.com/diapersdotcom). When you highlight a specific fan on your Facebook Page, you make all fans feel appreciated. They think to themselves, "Wow, look at how this business treats its fans, which includes me!"

Measure and Monitor

Chances are that you're a business owner. And if you've been in business long enough, you know the value of measuring return on investment (ROI). What you're measuring on Facebook is the response from your efforts. What topics get people excited? Which fan acquisition strategies are working best? When fans click to your website, how many of them end up a customer?

If you can't answer these questions, you'll never know whether you're using Facebook effectively. In today's economy, you can't afford to wing it. Think about measuring your Facebook efforts as a compass that tells you how far away you are from your destination, when you have arrived, and how to change direction if needed.

Be Fearless and Creative

Right now, millions of businesses are competing for attention on Facebook. Many of them are pleading for the attention of your current Facebook fans. They're using video, photos, conversation strategies, and highly interactive custom tabs to achieve this goal. The good news is that you can be just as innovative and have the same or even better ability to attract and retain.

To stay creative, keep reading books like this, attend webinars on Facebook marketing, and watch what other brands are doing. Still, all this knowledge won't mean a thing if you don't take action. Your competition isn't waiting for the perfect idea, and you shouldn't, either. View everything that you do on Facebook as a draft — a never-ending beta. That way, you get both a real education about what actually works on Facebook, and more business in the process.

Index

• A •

account
  creating, 34, 56–58, 103–104, 153
  deletion by Facebook, 53, 70, 206, 281–282
  e-mail address, 142
  Facebook Ad, 192–193
  involving individuals without Facebook, 230, 252, 269
Activity Feed plug-in
  adding, 265–267
  combining with Login button plug-in, 263
  described, 246–247, 250–251
administrators, 68–69, 153
Ads. *See also* advertising
  described, 15, 173–174, 215
  display, 167
  on Page, 32
  Page Likes, 117
  Page post, 117
  Page post Likes, 117
  payment strategies, 15
  promoting deals on, 213
  with promotions, 226
  Sponsored Story ads compared, 174
Ads Manager
  accessing, 185
  accessing Page from, 190
  adding users, 192–193
  budget changes, 189–190
  campaign information, 186–189
  creative library management, 193–194
  described, 185
  learning resources, 194
  payments, tracking, 193
  performance data, 185–186
  reports, 191–192
  as research tool, 24–25
  scheduling changes, 190

advertising. *See also* Ads Manager; marketing, Facebook
  advantages, 166
  application tools, 83
  approval process, 180
  classified, 46
  combining with other marketing, 167
  copywriting, 170–172
  costs, 169–170, 179–180, 189–190
  creating, 172–175
  destination, 173, 182–183, 245
  home page, 166
  images, 171–172, 174
  including offer in, 40
  limitations, 170–171, 174
  location on display, 168
  metrics, 188–189
  previewing, 189
  promotions, 242
  purchase strategies, 15, 165, 169–170, 180, 183
  reach, 165
  reports, 191
  resources for learning, 165, 194
  results, measuring, 182
  scheduling, 180
  strategies, 36
  targeting, 165, 168–169, 175–179
  title, 174
  tools for, 165
  traditional campaigns, adapting, 46
  types, 167–168, 173
Advertising Performance report, 191
advocacy stage of customer behavior, 20–21
advocates, 20
age factor in target audience selection, 22, 25
aggregating content, 81
albums, photo, 105, 126

Ann Taylor, promotions, 32
Appbistro online marketplace, 89
applications (apps)
  adding to Page, 55, 66, 83, 87–88
  advantages, 83
  as advertising/branding tools, 83
  blog sharing, 83, 85–86
  configuring, 93–94
  contest, 16, 83, 86
  core, 94
  costs, 47
  coupon, 86
  creating, 255–257
  customer-service, 85
  customizing Page with, 83
  described, 16, 84
  e-commerce, 9, 90–92
  Facebook platform for, 83
  finding, 65–66
  goals, integrating with, 87
  group deals, 86
  Groups, limitations on, 217
  iLike, 31
  installing, 92–93
  lead-generation, 85
  marketing-related, 85–87
  number of, 83
  overuse, 282
  permissions, granting, 92–93
  petition, 83
  photo tagging, 138
  photo upload, 102–103
  poll, 82, 135
  promotional, 16, 85, 224, 226–227, 236, 246
  removing, 94
  searching for, 87–89
  shopping cart, 84, 91
  slide presentation, 83
  tabs, 84, 87, 95
  trying out, 87
  types, 16, 85
  user participation, 85
  YouTube Video, 85
appreciation, fan, 287

approval process
  for Facebook advertising, 180
  for Facebook Places deals, 210
apps. *See* applications
Artist Page type, 56
audience, marketing
  content creation, effect on, 77
  defining, 19, 21–22
  described, 19
  factors for, 22, 25–26, 168–169
  gathering information on, 31, 187–188
  motivations, 31–33
  personas to understand, 23–24, 168
  researching, 24–25
  understanding, 22–24, 30–31
Audience graph, 187–188
awareness stage of customer behavior, 20

• *B* •

badges, Facebook, 237–238
badges, Foursquare, 202
Band Page type, 56
behavioral variables, 31
benchmarks to gauge progress of
    marketing, 43
birthday greetings, 284
BlendTec, 115–116
blogs
  applications for sharing, 83, 85–86
  costs, 47
  marketing on, 28
  plugging into Page, 236
  promoting Page via, 114
Brain Aneurysm Foundation Page, 80,
    102–103
Brand Page type, 56
branding
  applications, 83
  Facebook tools, 9
  history, 34
  monitoring, 38–39, 45
  strategies, 13, 34–35

Buddy Media
  use of Facebook analytics, 160
  user participation applications, 85
budget, marketing
  advertising, 169–170, 179–180, 189–190
  calculator, online, 47
  changes, 189–190
  cost-per-click ad payments, 15, 165, 169, 180, 183
  cost-per-impression ad payments, 15, 165, 170, 180
  costs by method, 47
  traditional, 47
business goals, met via Facebook, 9–10, 13
"business is personal" paradigm, 14
buyers, customers as, 22

• *C* •

calendar for posting, 78
call to action, 77, 79, 172, 276
Campaign Reach (advertising metric), 188
campaigns, Facebook marketing. *See* marketing, Facebook
category, Page, 57–58
Cause Page type, 56–57
charity deals, 208–209
CharityHowTo, 114–115, 139–140
Check in specials, Foursquare, 202
Check Ins Report, 148, 158–159
classified advertising, 46
clicks
  monitoring, 44
  paying by, 15, 165, 170, 180
Clicks (advertising metric), 188
click-through rate of typical Facebook advertising (CTR), 188–189
closed groups, 217, 222
CNN website use of Recommendations plug-in, 260–261
comments
  effect of, 17
  ignoring, 279
  monitoring, 44

photos, 137–139
responding to, importance, 135–136, 279
viewing details, 104, 121–125, 148–149, 151, 157–158
Comments plug-in, 247, 249–250, 253, 263–265
commercial use, unauthorized, 53
Community Page type, 56–57
Company Page type, 56
complaints, responding to, 135–136, 283
connections. *See also* fans
  among users, 14
  described, 51, 53
  expectations of, 287
  targeting, 26, 169, 177–178
  tracking, 187–188
  using existing, 108, 113–114
Connections (advertising metric), 188
consideration stage of customer behavior, 20–21
consistent participation, value, 287
content. *See also* Wall
  audience, creating for, 77
  consistent message, 78
  costs, 47
  creating, 47, 76–77
  goals, defining, 78–79
  guidelines, Facebook, 70
  repurposing, 77
  sharing location, 73
  viewing, 72
content strategy
  communication strategy, 41
  defining by communication channel, 39
  delivery format, 40
  described, 71
  developing, 29, 39–40
  importance, 71
contests. *See also* promotions
  applications, 16, 83, 86
  example, 43
  motivators for, 46
  photo, 55

conversion stage of customer behavior,
    20–21
conversions
  described, 182
  increasing number, 104, 182
  monitoring, 45, 161, 191
  reasons for, 77
Conversions by Impression Time report, 191
converting Profile to Page, 54
copywriters, web, 47
Coremetrics analytics, IBM, 160–161
cost-per-click (CPC) ad payments, 15, 165,
    169, 180, 183
cost-per-impression (CPM) ad payments,
    15, 165, 170, 180
coupons, 13, 86, 184
Creative Library management, 193–194
creativity, importance, 288
criticism, dealing with, 125
CTR (click-through rate of typical
    Facebook advertising), 188–189
custom tabs, 89–90, 93, 94–98
custom URLs
  advantages, 114
  choosing, 234, 244
  creating, 116, 234–235
  described, 234
customer behavior, stages, 20–21
customer research, strategies, 13
customer service
  advantages of Facebook for, 10
  applications, 85
  example, 80–81
  Facebook tools, 9
  monitoring Facebook for, 21
customers
  analyzing current, 21
  as buyers, 22
  engagement, 121
  getting repeat, 17
  research on, 13
  types, 20
  as users, 22
customer-service applications, 85

• D •

daily spend, 189
Dashboard Report, 42, 148–150
Deals
  approval process for, 210
  creating, 208–211
  described, 207–209
  maximizing benefit, 211–212
  notification of, 208
  promoting, 212–214
  uses, 206
Debugger tool, 271
Delicious bookmarks, plugging into Page, 236
demographic variables, 31
description of business, adding to Page, 60
Diapers.com fan appreciation, 287
discounts
  adapting for Facebook, 46
  Ads, integrating with, 226
  advertising, 242
  applications for, 16, 85, 224, 226–227,
    236, 246
  best practices, 225–226
  call to action, translating into, 77, 79,
    172, 276
  described, 223, 225
  to develop content strategy, 39–40
  environment for, 224
  Facebook rules, 223–224
  Fan of the Month, 80
  to obtain photos, 112
  promoting, 225–226
  requiring user to Like, 32, 43, 54, 86, 184
  in-store example, 116–117
display ads, 167
Dog Bless You, 137
downloads, monitoring, 44

• E •

e-commerce applications, 9, 90–92
Ecwid shopping cart app, 91

EdgeRank value, 75–76, 124, 139, 279
education, importance, 288
education factor in target audience
    selection, 26
educational resources for marketing,
    69–70, 165, 194
e-mail
  account setting, 142
  advertising reports via, 191–192
  Group settings, 222
  Page updates, 142–143
  photo uploading, 143
  promoting deals on, 213
  promoting Page, 110–111, 113–114, 236–237
  using Facebook via, 142–143
  using signature to promote Page, 113
  video uploading, 143
  weekly metrics updates via, 159–160
Engaged Users, 150
engagement
  actions showing, 79
  asking questions, 134
  described, 79, 120
  Events, creating with, 134
  of fans, 81–82, 102–104, 134, 137, 139–140
  importance, 119–120
  measuring, 104, 121–122
  methods for achieving, 79–82
  motivations for, 79
  photos, 137
  questions, 134
  quizzes, 81–82, 134
  reasons for, 121
  research on, 133
  responding to comments, 135–136
  via mobile phone, 140–142
  via webinar, 114–115, 139–140
  videos, 137
engagement posts, 39
Entertainment Page type, 56
Epic Change, 55, 85
errors, marketing
  applications, overuse, 282
  appropriateness, violations of, 282–283
  birthdays, ignoring, 284
  comments, ignoring, 279
  drinking, 281
  failure to plan, 277
  ineffective default tab, 276
  lengthy updates, 278–279
  privacy options, not using, 284
  responding to every message, 283
  selling too much/too little, 278
  shortened URLs, 277
  timing posts, 277–278
  using Groups for marketing, 276
  using Profile for marketing, 275–277
  Wall, inappropriate posts on, 282–283
etiquette, violations of, 281–284
evangelists, 20
Events
  contacting participants, 230–231
  creating, 227–231
  described, 14, 227
  to drive sales, 37
  editing, 231–232
  engagement, creating, 134
  exporting, 232
  following up, 232
  inviting participants, 229–230
  posting photos, 222, 227, 231–232
  promoting, 46, 228, 230
  RSVPing, 122
External Referrers, 156

• F •

Facebook
  growth, 9, 10–11, 14
  history, 1, 10–11
  Terms and Conditions, 70, 206, 213, 276
  user activity, 166
Facebook Ads. *See also* advertising
  described, 15, 173–174, 215
  display, 167
  on Page, 32
  Page Likes, 117
  Page post, 117

Facebook Ads *(continued)*
  Page post Likes, 117
  payment strategies, 15
  promoting deals on, 213
  with promotions, 226
  Sponsored Story ads compared, 174
Facebook Ads Manager
  accessing, 185
  accessing Page from, 190
  adding users, 192–193
  budget changes, 189–190
  campaign information, 186–189
  creative library management, 193–194
  described, 185
  learning resources, 194
  payments, tracking, 193
  performance data, 185–186
  reports, 191–192
  as research tool, 24–25
  scheduling changes, 190
Facebook Deals
  approval process for, 210
  creating, 208–211
  described, 207–209
  maximizing benefit, 211–212
  notification of, 208
  promoting, 212–214
  uses, 206
Facebook Events
  contacting participants, 230–231
  creating, 227–231
  described, 14, 227
  to drive sales, 37
  editing, 231–232
  engagement, creating, 134
  exporting, 232
  following up, 232
  inviting participants, 229–230
  posting photos, 222, 227, 231–232
  promoting, 46, 228, 230
  RSVPing, 122
Facebook Groups
  accessing, 219–220
  closed, 217, 222
  commercial use, 55
  common interests, 37

creating, 217, 220–222
deleting, 223
described, 14, 37, 52, 215–217
e-mail settings, 222
finding, 218, 221
frequency of contact, 37
hierarchy, lack of, 56
inviting friends to join, 217
joining, 219
landing page, 218
limitations, 217
for marketers, 88–89
for marketing, 276
member feedback, 38
membership requirement, 217
naming, 221
open, 217, 222
Pages compared, 55–56, 216–217
participation, 220–221
precautions when using, 220
privacy options, 222
searching discussions, unavailability, 38
secret, 217, 222
sharing activities on Wall, lack of, 56
social cause-related, 37–38
user behavior, 55
Facebook Insights
  accessing, 122, 147–148
  Advertising Performance, 191
  availability, 53
  Check Ins, 148, 158–159
  Conversions by Impression Time, 191
  Dashboard, 42, 148–150
  data available to third-party analytics, 160–161
  described, 145
  e-mail updates, 159–160
  engagement, measuring, 104, 121–122
  exporting data, 159
  fan acquisition information, 118, 146, 237, 239, 246
  How People Check In at Your Place, 158–159
  information available, 30, 41–42, 44, 146–147, 148
  integrating social plug-ins, 255–258

Likes, 148, 152–153
  overview, 130–131
  Page overview report, 123
  Page Posts, 150–151
  post-level report, 123–124
  Reach, 148, 150, 154–156
  Responder Demographics, 191
  Sponsored Stories, fans acquired
    through, 118
  Talking About This, 104, 121–125, 148–149,
    151, 157–158
  tracking by time period, 124
  using to create relevant content, 76
  Viral Reach graph, 104, 122–123, 157–158
Facebook Marketing for Dummies (Haydon),
  1–6
Facebook Page. *See also* tabs
  accessing from Ads Manager, 190
  activities on, 15
  administrators, 68–69, 153
  ads on, 32
  applications, adding, 55, 66, 83, 87–88
  blogs, adding, 236
  categories, 57–58
  components, 16
  connections on, 53
  content, adding, 104
  converting Profile to, 54
  cost, 47
  creating, 34, 56–58, 103–104, 153
  custom applications, adding, 55
  customizing, 16, 58–64, 83
  Delicious bookmarks, adding, 236
  described, 9, 14, 15, 51–52, 215
  description of business, 60
  Fan Page Owners, 88, 216
  finding, 63
  Groups compared, 55–56, 216–217
  importance to business, 15
  launching, 101–102
  Likes, content revealed by, 87, 183–184
  Likes, effect of, 53–54
  Likes, monitoring, 153
  Likes, types of, 147
  limitations, lack of, 53
  limiting access, 61, 63
  making easy to find, 107–108
  monitoring activities on, 29, 41–45
  monitoring links to, 44
  optimizing, 243–244
  overview report, 123
  permission settings, 61, 63
  Places compared, 205
  post report, 150–151
  posting as, 129–132
  Profiles compared, 53
  releasing to public, 101–102
  removal by Facebook, 53, 70, 206, 281–282
  RSS feeds, adding, 16, 236
  searching, 16, 53, 107
  tagging, 122
  Twitter, adding, 236
  types, 56–57
  Unpublish option, 61
  updates via e-mail, 142–143
  uses, 34, 51
  videos, adding, 106
  views, tracking, 156
  visibility, 16
  visitors viewing your, 72
  Visits to Your Page report, 156
Facebook Page, promoting
  blogs, 114
  effect of user activity, 124
  e-mail, 110–111, 113–114, 236–237
  friend networks, 35, 108–109, 122
  importance, 101
  outside Facebook, 35, 233–234, 236,
    240–242
  photo tagging, 111–113
  preparing for, 103–104
  printed material, 114
  profile, 109–110
  Sponsored Story Ads, 117–118
  stages, 102
  starting, 34–35
  in store, 116–117, 213
  Tell Your Fans feature, 110–111, 113–114
  user activity, 124
  webinars, 114–115
  on websites, 236
  YouTube, 115–116

Facebook Page examples
  Brain Aneurysm Foundation, 80, 102–103
  Hyundai, 84
  Inbound Zombie, 86, 183, 286
  Marketing Solutions, 69
  National Wildlife Federation, 130
Facebook Places
  accessing, 196–197
  appropriateness for business, 198–199
  check-in activity, 148, 158–159
  claiming, 204–205
  creating, 200, 205–206
  deals, approval process for, 210
  deals, creating, 208–211
  deals, described, 207–209
  deals, maximizing benefit, 211–212
  deals, notification of, 208
  deals, promoting, 212–214
  deals, uses, 206
  described, 14, 195–196
  other location-based services compared,
    200–201, 203
  Pages compared, 205
  reasons for using, 199–200
  tagging, 197
  uses, 197–198
  word-of-mouth marketing, 208
Facebook Profile
  commercial use, 53, 275–277
  converting to Page, 54
  described, 9, 52
  fan actions on, 17
  friending, 53–54, 282
  liking a page from, 153
  limitations, 53
  Pages compared, 53, 129–131
  posting as, 129–131
  subscribe feature, 53, 143–144
Facebook Wall
  allowing fans to post, 124–125
  described, 9, 16
  determining which posts appear, 63
  inappropriate posts, 282–283
  liking stories on, 147
  monitoring, 39
  overuse, 282–283

promoting deals on, 212–213
settings, 286–287
updates on, 16–17, 72, 146
Facepile plug-in, 252–253, 269–270
Fan Appz promotional app, 226
fan gating, 184
Fan of the Month promotions, 80
Fan Page Owners, 88, 216
FanPageEngine custom tab services, 90, 286
fans
  angry, dealing with, 135–136, 283
  appreciation for, 80, 287
  attracting, strategies for, 245–246
  attracting from outside Facebook,
    233–234, 236, 240–242
  communicating with, 40
  engaging, 81–82, 102–104, 134, 137,
    139–140
  gathering information on, 118, 146, 237,
    239, 246
  increasing number, JVC example, 43
  information about, 148, 152–153
  inviting during startup, 60, 102
  inviting in physical location, 116–117, 213
  inviting via blog, 114
  inviting via e-mail, 110–111, 113–114,
    236–237
  inviting via friend networks,
    35, 108–109, 122
  inviting via printed material, 114
  inviting via Sponsored Story ads, 117–118
  inviting via Tell Your Fans feature,
    110–111, 113–114
  inviting via webinars, 114–115
  inviting via website, 236
  inviting via YouTube, 115–116
  listening to, importance, 45
  motivations for, 113
  on News Feeds, 16–17
  polls, 81–82, 127, 134
  Profile, actions on, 17
  promoting to friends of, 149
  quizzes, 81–82, 134
  recognizing, 287
  responding to, importance, 283, 286–287
  tests of knowledge, 81–82, 134

thanking, 80
tracking acquisition, 146, 237, 239, 246
updates by, 124–125
Wall posts, allowing, 124–125
feedback from Facebook members
  asking for, 80
  critical, 135–136, 283
  listening to, 38–39, 45
  responding to, 283, 286–287
fictional characters, use to understand
    target audience, 23–24, 168
Flash specials, Foursquare, 201
forums, marketing on, 28
Fotolia, 231
Foursquare, 28, 201–203
Frequency (advertising metric), 188
friend deals, 208–209
friending a Profile, 53, 54, 282
Friends list, 229
Friends of Fans, 149
Friends specials, Foursquare, 201
Fuddruckers, 51–52, 83–84
FundRazr e-commerce app, 91–92
funnel, marketing, 20–21

 • G •

Garman, Tim, 12
gender factor in target audience selection,
    22, 25
Get Fans feature, 60
giveaways
  adapting for Facebook, 46
  Ads, integrating with, 226
  advertising, 242
  applications for, 16, 85, 224, 226–227,
    236, 246
  best practices, 225–226
  call to action, translating into, 77, 79,
    172, 276
  described, 223, 225
  to develop content strategy, 39–40
  environment for, 224
  Facebook rules, 223–224
  Fan of the Month, 80
  to obtain photos, 112

promoting, 225–226
requiring user to Like, 32, 43, 54, 86, 184
in-store example, 116–117
goals, marketing
  choosing applications to meet, 87
  defining, 29, 30, 33–34
  met by companies using Facebook, 9–10, 13
  for posts, 78–79
  setting, 43
goals factor in target audience selection, 26
going viral, 248
Google, Facebook activity compared, 166
Google Analytics, tracking user behavior,
    44–45
GOSO's Sweepstakes applet, 86
Gowalla, 203
Graham, Karen, 12
group deals, 13
Groups
  accessing, 219–220
  closed, 217, 222
  commercial use, 55
  common interests, 37
  creating, 217, 220–222
  deleting, 223
  described, 14, 37, 52, 215–217
  e-mail settings, 222
  finding, 218, 221
  frequency of contact, 37
  hierarchy, lack of, 56
  inviting friends to join, 217
  joining, 219
  landing page, 218
  limitations, 217
  for marketers, 88–89
  for marketing, 276
  member feedback, 38
  membership requirement, 217
  naming, 221
  open, 217, 222
  Pages compared, 55–56, 216–217
  participation, 220–221
  precautions when using, 220
  privacy options, 222
  searching discussions, unavailability, 38
  secret, 217, 222

Groups *(continued)*
  sharing activities on Wall, lack of, 56
  social cause-related, 37–38
  user behavior, 55
guidelines, Facebook, 70, 206, 213, 276

• H •

Hallmark Channel, Mother's Day
    promotion, 32–33
Happiness Index, 133
Haydon, John, 1, 6, 70
helping others, value of, 286
home page (News Feed)
  content ranking, 75–76, 124, 139, 279
  described, 71–72
  fan actions on, 16–17
  features, 73
  filtering, 73–75
  grouping posts, 75
  posting information on fan Feeds, 16
  sharing on, 73
  spreading stories via, 39
  viewing, 130
  visitors viewing content on, 72
HootSuite analytics, 160
hosted custom tabs, 95–98
How People Check In at Your Place report,
    158–159
HTML, creating custom tabs with, 94–95
human side, sharing, 79
Hyundai Page with Shopping Tools app, 84

• I •

IBM Coremetrics analytics, 160–161
icons in book, 5
iLike app, 31
image file, exporting Insights data as, 159
images, advertising. *See also* videos
  adding, 105
  albums, 105, 126
  applications for adding, 102–103
  applications for tagging, 138

  avatar, selecting, 174
  choosing, 171–172
  comments on, 137–139
  contests, 55
  creating for tagging, 112
  engagement, 137
  Events, 222, 227, 231–232
  Likes, 137–139
  organizing, 105
  posting guidelines, 139
  profile, 58–61
  promotions to obtain, 112
  questions about, 134
  sharing, 137–139
  tagging, 105, 111–113, 138
  updates, 126, 127
  uploading, 102–103, 105, 126–127, 143
  user interaction with, 137–139
  viewing details about views, 122
In A Pickle, use of photo tagging, 138
Inbound Zombie Page, 86, 183, 286
incentive offers, Ann Taylor example, 32
inconsistent participation, 287
individual deals, 208–209
Info Tab
  customizing, 60, 62–63
  as default tab, 276
  described, 16
  keywords in, 107–108, 244
  privacy considerations, 284
Inside Facebook (website), 70, 174
Insights, Facebook
  accessing, 122, 147–148
  Advertising Performance, 191
  availability, 53
  Check Ins, 148, 158–159
  Conversions by Impression Time, 191
  Dashboard, 42, 148–150
  data available to third-party analytics,
      160–161
  described, 145
  e-mail updates, 159–160
  engagement, measuring, 104, 121–122
  exporting data, 159

fan acquisition information, 118, 146, 237, 239, 246
How People Check In at Your Place, 158–159
information available, 30, 41–42, 44, 146–148
integrating social plug-ins, 255–258
Likes, 148, 152–153
overview, 130–131
Page overview report, 123
Page Posts, 150–151
post-level report, 123–124
Reach, 148, 150, 154–156
Responder Demographics, 191
Sponsored Stories, fans acquired through, 118
Talking About This, 104, 121–125, 148–149, 151, 157–158
tracking by time period, 124
using to create relevant content, 76
Viral Reach graph, 104, 122–123, 157–158
insights, sharing, 80
Institution Page type, 56
in-store promotion, 116–117, 213
interests factor in target audience selection, 22, 26, 169
Invite Friends feature, 35, 108–109, 153
Involver
  applications, 85
  use of Facebook analytics, 160
iParty promotion example, 116–117

• J •

JVC, contest, 43

• K •

Kent, Peter, 108
key performance indicators, monitoring, 41–42
keywords, using to improve findability, 107–108, 244
Klondike, 40

• L •

landing page
  advertisement, 173, 179, 182–183, 245
  Group, 218
  reveal tabs on, 87, 183–184
Landing Tab, default, 63–64
Lands' End customer service, 80–81
language factor in target audience selection, 25
launching Page, 101–102
launching products, 9, 13
lead-generation applications, 85
Lee Jeans, social cause promotion, 37–38
length of visit, monitoring, 44
Like Box plug-in
  adding to website, 239–240, 267–268
  attracting viewers with, 245
  badges compared, 237
  blog updates using, 236
  described, 146, 251–252
  Like button compared, 249
Like button
  adding to website, 258–259
  described, 16, 248–249, 258
  Like Box plug-in compared, 249
  membership requirement, 109
like-gates, 87
Likes
  effect of, 17, 234
  photo, 137–139
  requiring of user, 32, 43, 54, 86, 184
  responding to, importance, 135–136
  sources of, 153
  tracking, 149
  types, 147
  viewing details, 148, 152–153
likes factor in target audience selection, 22, 26, 169
Likes Report, 148, 152–153
liking a Page
  content revealed by, 87
  described, 53, 147
  methods for, 153
  required for Page access, 54

liking a post, 21, 147
link updates, 126, 127
links to Facebook Pages, monitoring, 44
links to relevant information, providing, 81, 107
listening to fans, importance, 45
Live Stream plug-in, 246–247, 253–254, 270–272
Local business Page type, 56
location factor in target audience selection, 22, 25, 168
location-based services, 195. *See also* Places
Login button plug-in, 252–253, 262–263
loyalty deals, 208–209
loyalty programs, as sales strategy, 13
Loyalty specials, Foursquare, 202
loyalty stage of customer behavior, 20

• M •

marketing, Facebook. *See also* Ads Manager; budget, marketing
  accessing, 185
  adding users, 192–193
  advantages, 27
  budget changes, 189–190
  campaign information, 186–189
  creative library management, 193–194
  evaluating, 43
  factors for success, 285–288
  integrating with other, 29, 45–46
  learning resources, 194
  monitoring, 46, 104, 122–123, 148, 150, 154–158, 186–189
  objectives, 13
  payments, tracking, 193
  performance data, 185–186
  planning, 29–30, 198–199
  power of, 15
  reports, 191–192
  as research tool, 24–25
  resources for learning, 69–70, 165, 194
  scheduling changes, 190
  tools, 14–15

  traditional, compared, 27–28, 46
  traditional marketing, adapting for, 46
marketing, integrating online and offline, 29, 45–46
marketing, traditional, 27–28, 46–47
marketing funnel, 20–21
marketing on Internet, 28
marketing plan, 29–30, 198–199
Marketing Solutions Page, 69
Marketplace, 46
Mashable's tip sharing, 80–81
Mayor specials, Foursquare, 202
media, Facebook coverage, 11
mentions, viewing details about, 122
Mentos polls, 82
metrics, monitoring Facebook, 29, 41–45. *See also* Facebook Insights
mistakes, marketing
  applications, overuse, 282
  appropriateness, violations of, 282–283
  birthdays, ignoring, 284
  comments, ignoring, 279
  drinking, 281
  failure to plan, 277
  ineffective default tab, 276
  lengthy updates, 278–279
  privacy options, not using, 284
  responding to every message, 283
  selling too much/too little, 278
  shortened URLs, 277
  timing posts, 277–278
  using Groups for marketing, 276
  using Profile for marketing, 275–277
  Wall, inappropriate posts on, 282–283
mobile browser URL, 140
mobile devices
  Facebook site, 196
  liking a page from, 153
  monitoring use information, 158–159
  using Facebook via, 140–142
mobile site, Facebook, 196
monitoring. *See also* Facebook Insights
  branding, 38–39, 45
  campaigns, advertising, 104, 122–123, 148, 150, 154–158, 186–189

clicks, 44
comments, 44
conversions, 45, 161, 191
downloads, 44
Facebook results, 288
key performance indicators, 41–42
length of visit, 44
links to Facebook Pages, 44
marketing, 46, 104, 122–123, 148, 150,
    154–158, 186–189
metrics, 29, 41–45
mobile device use, 158–159
Page activity, 29, 41–45
sharing, 44
views, 44
visitors, 44–45
Wall, 39

• N •

National Wildlife Federation Page, 130
Nature Conservancy, word-of-mouth
    marketing, 14
NetworkedBlogs app, 83, 85–86
networking, offline, 241–242
Newbie specials, Foursquare, 202
News Feeds
    content ranking, 75–76, 124, 139, 279
    described, 71–72
    fan actions on, 16–17
    features, 73
    filtering, 73–75
    grouping posts, 75
    posting information on fan Feeds, 16
    sharing on, 73
    spreading stories via, 39
    viewing, 130
    visitors viewing content on, 72
The Nonprofit Facebook Guy (website), 70
notifications, viewing, 130–131

• O •

obtain photos, promotions to, 112
offensive language, 125

1-800-Flowers, 36
OneRiot, 45
Open Graph protocol, 160
open groups, 217, 222
Organization Page type, 56

• P •

Page. *See also* tabs
    accessing from Ads Manager, 190
    activities on, 15
    administrators, 68–69, 153
    ads on, 32
    applications, adding, 55, 66, 83, 87–88
    blogs, adding, 236
    categories, 57–58
    components, 16
    connections on, 53
    content, adding, 104
    converting Profile to, 54
    cost, 47
    creating, 34, 56–58, 103–104, 153
    custom applications, adding, 55
    customizing, 16, 58–64, 83
    Delicious bookmarks, adding, 236
    described, 9, 14, 15, 51–52, 215
    description of business, 60
    Fan Page Owners, 88, 216
    finding, 63
    Groups compared, 55–56, 216–217
    importance to business, 15
    launching, 101–102
    Likes, content revealed by, 87, 183–184
    Likes, effect of, 53–54
    Likes, monitoring, 153
    Likes, types of, 147
    limitations, lack of, 53
    limiting access, 61, 63
    making easy to find, 107–108
    monitoring activities on, 29, 41–45
    monitoring links to, 44
    optimizing, 243–244
    overview report, 123
    permission settings, 61, 63
    Places compared, 205

Page (continued)
  post report, 150–151
  posting as, 129–132
  Profiles compared, 53
  releasing to public, 101–102
  removal by Facebook, 53, 70, 206, 281–282
  RSS feeds, adding, 16, 236
  searching, 16, 53, 107
  tagging, 122
  Twitter, adding, 236
  types, 56–57
  Unpublish option, 61
  updates via e-mail, 142–143
  uses, 34, 51
  videos, adding, 106
  views, tracking, 156
  visibility, 16
  visitors viewing your, 72
  Visits to Your Page report, 156
Page, promoting
  blogs, 114
  effect of user activity, 124
  e-mail, 110–111, 113–114, 236–237
  friend networks, 35, 108–109, 122
  importance, 101
  outside Facebook, 35, 233–234, 236,
    240–242
  photo tagging, 111–113
  preparing for, 103–104
  printed material, 114
  profile, 109–110
  Sponsored Story Ads, 117–118
  stages, 102
  starting, 34–35
  in store, 116–117, 213
  Tell Your Fans feature, 110–111, 113–114
  user activity, 124
  webinars, 114–115
  on websites, 236
  YouTube, 115–116
Page examples
  Brain Aneurysm Foundation, 80, 102–103
  Hyundai, 84
  Inbound Zombie, 86, 183, 286
  Marketing Solutions, 69
  National Wildlife Federation, 130

Page Likes ads, 117
Page overview report, 123
Page post ads, 117
Page post Likes ads, 117
Page Posts Report, 150–151
Pagemodo custom tab services, 90
Parature customer-service applications, 85
Payvment marketplace app, 91
People Talking About This, 149
permission settings, Page, 61, 63
personal experience with Facebook,
    value, 285
personas, use to understand target
    audience, 23–24, 168
petitions, applications, 83
photos. *See also* videos
  adding, 105
  albums, 105, 126
  applications for adding, 102–103
  applications for tagging, 138
  comments on, 137–139
  contests, 55
  creating for tagging, 112
  engagement, 137
  Events, 222, 227, 231–232
  Likes, 137–139
  organizing, 105
  posting guidelines, 139
  profile, 58–61
  promotions to obtain, 112
  questions about, 134
  sharing, 137–139
  tagging, 105, 111–113, 138
  updates, 126, 127
  uploading, 102–103, 105, 126–127, 143
  user interaction with, 137–139
  views, monitoring, 122
Places
  accessing, 196–197
  appropriateness for business, 198–199
  check-in activity, 148, 158–159
  claiming, 204–205
  creating, 200, 205–206
  deals, approval process for, 210
  deals, creating, 208–211
  deals, described, 207–209

deals, maximizing benefit, 211–212
deals, notification of, 208
deals, promoting, 212–214
deals, uses, 206
described, 14, 195–196
other location-based services compared, 200–201, 203
Pages compared, 205
reasons for using, 199–200
tagging, 197
uses, 197–198
word-of-mouth marketing, 208
plug-ins. *See also* Like Box plug-in; social plug-ins
Activity Feed, 246–247, 250–251, 263, 265–267
Comments, 247, 249–250, 253, 263–265
Facepile, 252, 253, 269–270
Live Stream, 246–247, 253–254, 270–272
Login button, 252–253, 262–263
Recommendations, 246, 250–251, 260–262
Registration, 247, 252, 269
Send button, 247, 249
podcasts, costs, 47
poking, 282
Poll Daddy Polls app, 82, 135
polls, fan, 81–82, 127, 134
Porterfield, Amy, 69
Post Planner, 277
posting. *See also* content
as Page, 129–132
planning, 78
as Profile, 129–131
strategy, 29, 39–41, 71
timing, 133, 246, 277–278
via e-mail, 142–143
via mobile phone, 140–141
Posting Ability, customizing, 64
posting calendar, 78
post-level report, 123–124
posts. *See also* content
information on, 150–151
liking, 147
privacy options, Facebook, 284
prizes, promotional, 223, 225
product differential, 29

Product Page type, 56
profanity, dealing with, 125
Profile
commercial use, 53, 275–277
converting to Page, 54
described, 9, 52
fan actions on, 17
friending, 53–54, 282
liking a page from, 153
limitations, 53
Pages compared, 53
posting as, 129–131
subscribe feature, 53, 143–144
profile photos, 58–61
promoting deals, 212–213
promoting Events, 46, 228, 230
promoting other businesses, value, 286
promoting Page
blogs, 114
effect of user activity, 124
e-mail, 110–111, 113–114, 236–237
friend networks, 35, 108–109, 122
importance, 101
outside Facebook, 35, 233–234, 236, 240–242
photo tagging, 111–113
preparing for, 103–104
printed material, 114
profile, 109–110
Sponsored Story Ads, 117–118
stages, 102
starting, 34–35
in store, 116–117, 213
Tell Your Fans feature, 110–111, 113–114
user activity, 124
webinars, 114–115
on websites, 236
YouTube, 115–116
Promotion Builder app, 246
promotional applications, 85
promotions
adapting for Facebook, 46
Ads, integrating with, 226
advertising, 242
applications for, 16, 85, 224, 226–227, 236, 246

promotions *(continued)*
  best practices, 225–226
  call to action, translating into, 77, 79,
    172, 276
  described, 223, 225
  to develop content strategy, 39–40
  environment for, 224
  Facebook rules, 223–224
  Fan of the Month, 80
  to obtain photos, 112
  promoting, 225–226
  requiring user to Like, 32, 43, 54, 86, 184
  in-store example, 116–117
psychographic variables, 31
Public Figure Page type, 56

• Q •

QualityHealth advertisements, 183–184
question updates, 127
questionnaires, uses, 31
questions, engagement via, 134
Questions, Facebook, 245
quizzes, fan, 81–82, 134

• R •

reach of marketing campaign, measuring,
    104, 122–123, 148, 150, 154–158, 186–189
Reach Report, 148, 150, 154–156
really simple syndication (RSS) feeds,
    customizing Page with, 16, 236
reciprocity, 286
recognition, fan, 287
recommendations, personal
  on Facebook, 13–14
  on Facebook Places, 208
  importance to business, 13
  liking a page from, 153
  plug-in for, 246, 250–251, 260–262
  power, 13–14
Recommendations plug-in, 246, 250–251,
    260–262

referrers, external, 156
Registration plug-in, 247, 252, 269
registration wizard, 153
relationship status factor in target
    audience selection, 26
releasing Page to public, 101–102
Remember icon, 5
reordering tabs, 68, 94
reports
  Advertising Performance, 191
  Check Ins, 148, 158–159
  Conversions by Impression Time, 191
  Dashboard, 42, 148–150
  How People Check In at Your Place,
    158–159
  Likes, 148, 152–153
  Page overview, 123
  Page Posts, 150–151
  post-level, 123–124
  Reach, 148, 150, 154–156
  Responder Demographics, 191
  Talking About This, 104, 121–125, 148–149,
    151, 157–158
Responder Demographics report, 191
Response graph, 187–188
reveal tab, 87, 183–184
ROI metrics for advertising results, 188
Rose, Kevin, 144
RSS (really simple syndication) feeds,
    customizing Page with, 16, 236

• S •

sales, linking to website, 36
Sandberg, Sheryl, 143–144
satisfaction surveys, uses, 31
search, liking a page from Facebook, 153
search engine optimization (SEO), 53, 107,
    108, 233
Search Engine Optimization For Dummies
    (Kent), 108
search engines, improving rankings, 53,
    107–108, 233

searching
  for applications, 87–89
  for discussions about brand, 38–39
  Facebook content, 16
  Group discussions, unavailability, 38
  for Groups, 218, 221
  helping users to find your page, 63
  improving visibility using social plug-ins,
      236, 244–245
  liking a Page from results, 153
  optimizing Page for, 243–244
  for Page, methods, 16, 53, 107
  with search engines, 53, 107–108, 233
  for terms, 38–39
secret groups, 217, 222
selling products
  applications, 9, 90–92
  Facebook tools, 9
  strategies, 13, 278
Send button plug-in, 247, 249, 258–260
SEO (search engine optimization),
      53, 107–108, 233
Share link, 108–110
sharing
  monitoring, 44
  motivations for, 286
  photos, 137–139
shopping cart applications, 91
ShopTab e-commerce app, 91
shortened URLs, 277
ShortStack custom tab services, 90
sidebar, Facebook, 9
signature, promoting Page via e-mail, 113
slide presentation applications, 83
SlideShare app, 83
Smart List, 229
Smith, Mari, 69
SMS (text messaging), using Facebook via,
      141–142
social causes, promotion example, 37–38
social connections, 11–12
social graph, Facebook, 1, 101
social media, as cultural shift, 195
Social Media Examiner (website), 69

social media-management platforms using
      Facebook analytics, 160
social mention, 45
social plug-ins. *See also* Like Box plug-in
  adding, 254–255
  attracting fans, 245
  checking, 271
  described, 247–248
  examples, 248–254
  Facebook resources, 248
  improving search visibility using, 236,
      244–245
  integrating Insights, 255–258
  limitations, 254
Social Reach (advertising metric), 188
spam, posts viewed as, 131–132, 220
special offers
  adapting for Facebook, 46
  Ads, integrating with, 226
  advertising, 242
  applications for, 16, 85, 224, 226–227,
      236, 246
  best practices, 225–226
  call to action, translating into, 77, 79,
      172, 276
  described, 223, 225
  to develop content strategy, 39–40
  environment for, 224
  Facebook rules, 223–224
  Fan of the Month, 80
  to obtain photos, 112
  promoting, 225–226
  requiring user to Like, 32, 43, 54, 86, 184
  in-store example, 116–117
Spent (advertising metric), 188
Sponsored Story ads. *See also* advertising
  Audience graph, 187
  described, 117–118, 167–168
  Facebook ads compared, 174
  liking a page from, 153
  promoting Page, 117–118
  restrictions, 173
  showing fans acquired via, 118
  targeting, 178

spreadsheets, exporting Insights data as, 159

stakeholders, 30

Static HTML: iframes tab app, 95

Status Update Field, 16

status updates, 16, 125, 127, 133

stories, 16–17, 72, 146

"Strategies for Effective Facebook Wall Posts: A Statistical Review" (Buddy Media), 133

strong ties, 14

subscribe feature, 53, 143–144

success, factors for marketing, 285–288

success, sharing stories of, 80

Swarm specials, Foursquare, 201

sweepstakes. *See also* promotions

  applications, 16, 83, 86

  example, 43

  motivators for, 46

  photo, 55

Sweepstakes applet, 86

symbols in book, 5

• T •

T3, poll use, 135

tabs

  adding to Page, 64–66

  applications, 84, 87, 95

  custom, creating, 94–98

  custom tab services, 90, 286

  default, 276

  described, 64

  editing, 66–68

  getting view statistics, 43

  landing, 63–64

  preset, 64

  removing, 65, 67–68

  renaming, 67, 93

  reordering, 68, 94

  reveal, 87, 183–184

  Static HTML: iframes tab app, 95

  third-party custom, 89–90, 93

  views, tracking, 156

  welcome, 276

TabSite custom tab services, 90

TabSite user participation applications, 85

tagging

  Facebook Places page, 197

  Page, 122

  photos, 105, 111–113, 138

  removing tags, 113

take your child/dog to work day example, 79

Talking About This Report

  described, 104, 123, 148–149

  uses, 121–122, 157–158

  in Virality calculation, 123, 151

target audience

  defining, 19, 21–22

  described, 19

  factors for, 22, 25–26, 168–169

  personas to understand, 23–24, 168

  researching, 24–25

  understanding, 22–24

Technical Stuff icon, 5

Teesey Tees advertisement, 183–184

television, marketing on, 12

Tell Your Fans feature, 110–111, 113–114

Terms and Conditions, Facebook, 70, 206, 213, 276

tests of knowledge, fan, 81–82, 134

text messaging (SMS), using Facebook via, 141–142

thanking fans, 80

Thefacebook, 10–11

third-party analytics, Facebook metrics for, 160–161

thumbnail profile picture, 59–61

Tip icon, 5

Tips, sharing, 80, 134

Tom's of Maine, 31

Total Likes, 149

traditional marketing, 27–28, 46–47

trending topics, 75

trust, building, 131–132, 287

Twitter

  marketing on, 28

  plugging into Page, 236

• *U* •

Unique Selling Proposition (USP), 29–30
Unique Users by Frequency, 155
Unpublish Page option, 61
updates
  allowing fans to post, 124–125
  blog using Like Box plug-in, 236
  importance, 125
  of Insights information, 159–160
  limiting access, 127–129
  link, 126–127
  of Page via e-mail, 142–143
  photo, 126–127
  question, 127
  size, 278–279
  status, 16, 125, 127, 133
  subscribing to public, 53, 143–144
  types, 125–127
  via e-mail, 142–143
  via mobile device, 140–142
  video, 126–127
  on Wall, 16–17, 72, 146
URLs
  custom, 114, 116, 234–235, 244
  linking from advertisements, 183
user participation applications, 85
username, custom
  advantages, 114
  choosing, 234, 244
  creating, 116, 234–235
  described, 234
users. *See also* Talking About This Report
  customers as, 22
  demographic information on, 148, 150,
    154–156
  information provided by, 15
  number of Facebook, 9
  types, 154–155
USP (Unique Selling Proposition), 29–30

• *V* •

value proposition, 29–30
vanity username
  advantages, 114
  choosing, 234, 244
  creating, 116, 234–235
  described, 234
VendorShop e-commerce app, 91
videos
  adding to Page, 106
  costs, 47
  fan engagement, 137
  limitations, 106
  promoting Page, 115–116
  recording, 106–107
  tagging, 107
  updates, 126–127
  uploading, 126–127, 143
  viewing details about plays, 122
  YouTube app, 85
views, monitoring, 44
viral reach, 122
Viral Reach graph, 104, 122–123, 157–158
Virality, 123, 151
visitors, monitoring, 44–45
Visits to Your Page report, 156
Vitrue promotional app, 226

• *W* •

Wall
  allowing fans to post, 124–125
  described, 9, 16
  determining which posts appear, 63
  inappropriate posts, 282–283
  liking stories on, 147
  monitoring, 39
  overuse, 282–283
  promoting deals on, 212–213
  settings, 286–287
  updates on, 16–17, 72, 146

Warning icon, 5
weak ties, 14
web addresses
  custom, 114, 116, 234–235, 244
  linking from advertisements, 183
webinars, 114–115, 139–140
websites
  addresses, 114, 116, 183, 234–235, 244
  integrating Facebook software, 257–258
  Like Box plug-in, adding, 239–240, 267–268
  Like button, adding, 258–259
  linking from advertisements, 183
  linking to, 36
  marketing on, 28
  marketing resources, 69–70, 174
  promoting Page, 236
  sharing content with Like button, 16, 109,
    248–249, 258–259
  sharing content with Send Button, 247,
    249, 258–260
Webtrends analytics, 160–161
Weekly Total Reach, 149
What's On Your Mind? box, 16
wikis, costs, 47

Wildfire Interactive promotional
  applications, 85, 226–227, 246
WiseStamp add-in, 113, 237
Woobox Coupons app, 86
Woobox Group Deals app, 86
wording, careful, 283
word-of-mouth marketing. *See also*
  recommendations, personal
  on Facebook, 13–14
  on Facebook Places, 208
  importance to business, 13
work factor in target audience selection, 26
writers of online content, 47

YouTube, promoting Page with, 115–116
YouTube Video app, 85

Zarrella, Dan, 286
Zuckerberg, Mark, 1, 10

Notes

Notes

Notes

Notes

ple & Mac

ad 2 For Dummies,
d Edition
8-1-118-17679-5

hone 4S For Dummies,
h Edition
8-1-118-03671-6

od touch For Dummies,
d Edition
8-1-118-12960-9

ac OS X Lion
r Dummies
8-1-118-02205-4

ogging & Social Media

yVille For Dummies
8-1-118-08337-6

cebook For Dummies,
Edition
8-1-118-09562-1

m Blogging
Dummies
8-1-118-03843-7

tter For Dummies,
Edition
-0-470-76879-2

rdPress For Dummies,
Edition
-1-118-07342-1

iness

h Flow For Dummies
-1-118-01850-7

sting For Dummies,
Edition
-0-470-90545-6

Job Searching with Social
Media For Dummies
978-0-470-93072-4

QuickBooks 2012
For Dummies
978-1-118-09120-3

Resumes For Dummies,
6th Edition
978-0-470-87361-8

Starting an Etsy Business
For Dummies
978-0-470-93067-0

Cooking & Entertaining

Cooking Basics
For Dummies, 4th Edition
978-0-470-91388-8

Wine For Dummies,
4th Edition
978-0-470-04579-4

Diet & Nutrition

Kettlebells For Dummies
978-0-470-59929-7

Nutrition For Dummies,
5th Edition
978-0-470-93231-5

Restaurant Calorie Counter
For Dummies,
2nd Edition
978-0-470-64405-8

Digital Photography

Digital SLR Cameras &
Photography For Dummies,
4th Edition
978-1-118-14489-3

Digital SLR Settings
& Shortcuts
For Dummies
978-0-470-91763-3

Photoshop Elements 10
For Dummies
978-1-118-10742-3

Gardening

Gardening Basics
For Dummies
978-0-470-03749-2

Vegetable Gardening
For Dummies,
2nd Edition
978-0-470-49870-5

Green/Sustainable

Raising Chickens
For Dummies
978-0-470-46544-8

Green Cleaning
For Dummies
978-0-470-39106-8

Health

Diabetes For Dummies,
3rd Edition
978-0-470-27086-8

Food Allergies
For Dummies
978-0-470-09584-3

Living Gluten-Free
For Dummies,
2nd Edition
978-0-470-58589-4

Hobbies

Beekeeping
For Dummies,
2nd Edition
978-0-470-43065-1

Chess For Dummies,
3rd Edition
978-1-118-01695-4

Drawing For Dummies,
2nd Edition
978-0-470-61842-4

eBay For Dummies,
7th Edition
978-1-118-09806-6

Knitting For Dummies,
2nd Edition
978-0-470-28747-7

Language &
Foreign Language

English Grammar
For Dummies,
2nd Edition
978-0-470-54664-2

French For Dummies,
2nd Edition
978-1-118-00464-7

German For Dummies,
2nd Edition
978-0-470-90101-4

Spanish Essentials
For Dummies
978-0-470-63751-7

Spanish For Dummies,
2nd Edition
978-0-470-87855-2

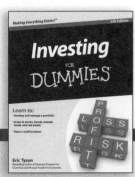

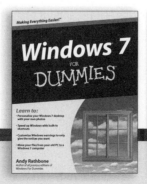

able wherever books are sold. For more information or to order direct: U.S. customers visit www.dummies.com or call 1-877-762-2974.
U.K. customers visit www.wileyeurope.com or call (0) 1243 843291. Canadian customers visit www.wiley.ca or call 1-800-567-4797.

Connect with us online at www.facebook.com/fordummies or @fordummies

Math & Science

Algebra I For Dummies,
2nd Edition
978-0-470-55964-2

Biology For Dummies,
2nd Edition
978-0-470-59875-7

Chemistry For Dummies,
2nd Edition
978-1-1180-0730-3

Geometry For Dummies,
2nd Edition
978-0-470-08946-0

Pre-Algebra Essentials
For Dummies
978-0-470-61838-7

Microsoft Office

Excel 2010 For Dummies
978-0-470-48953-6

Office 2010 All-in-One
For Dummies
978-0-470-49748-7

Office 2011 for Mac
For Dummies
978-0-470-87869-9

Word 2010
For Dummies
978-0-470-48772-3

Music

Guitar For Dummies,
2nd Edition
978-0-7645-9904-0

Clarinet For Dummies
978-0-470-58477-4

iPod & iTunes
For Dummies,
9th Edition
978-1-118-13060-5

Pets

Cats For Dummies,
2nd Edition
978-0-7645-5275-5

Dogs All-in One
For Dummies
978-0470-52978-2

Saltwater Aquariums
For Dummies
978-0-470-06805-2

Religion & Inspiration

The Bible For Dummies
978-0-7645-5296-0

Catholicism For Dummies,
2nd Edition
978-1-118-07778-8

Spirituality For Dummies,
2nd Edition
978-0-470-19142-2

Self-Help & Relationships

Happiness For Dummies
978-0-470-28171-0

Overcoming Anxiety
For Dummies,
2nd Edition
978-0-470-57441-6

Seniors

Crosswords For Seniors
For Dummies
978-0-470-49157-7

iPad 2 For Seniors
For Dummies, 3rd Edition
978-1-118-17678-8

Laptops & Tablets
For Seniors For Dummies,
2nd Edition
978-1-118-09596-6

Smartphones & Tablets

BlackBerry For Dummies,
5th Edition
978-1-118-10035-6

Droid X2 For Dummies
978-1-118-14864-8

HTC ThunderBolt
For Dummies
978-1-118-07601-9

MOTOROLA XOOM
For Dummies
978-1-118-08835-7

Sports

Basketball For Dummies,
3rd Edition
978-1-118-07374-2

Football For Dummies,
2nd Edition
978-1-118-01261-1

Golf For Dummies,
4th Edition
978-0-470-88279-5

Test Prep

ACT For Dummies,
5th Edition
978-1-118-01259-8

ASVAB For Dummies,
3rd Edition
978-0-470-63760-9

The GRE Test For
Dummies, 7th Edition
978-0-470-00919-2

Police Officer Exam
For Dummies
978-0-470-88724-0

Series 7 Exam
For Dummies
978-0-470-09932-2

Web Development

HTML, CSS, & XHTML
For Dummies, 7th Edition
978-0-470-91659-9

Drupal For Dummies,
2nd Edition
978-1-118-08348-2

Windows 7

Windows 7
For Dummies
978-0-470-49743-2

Windows 7
For Dummies,
Book + DVD Bundle
978-0-470-52398-8

Windows 7 All-in-One
For Dummies
978-0-470-48763-1

Available wherever books are sold. For more information or to order direct: U.S. customers visit www.dummies.com or call 1-877-762-
U.K. customers visit www.wileyeurope.com or call (0) 1243 843291. Canadian customers visit www.wiley.ca or call 1-800-567-4797

Connect with us online at www.facebook.com/fordummies or @fordummies